The
Illustrated Gift Book
1880-1930

COLOUR PLATE 1. Arthur Rackham
Arthur Rackham's Book of Pictures, Heinemann, 1913

The Illustrated Gift Book 1880-1930

with a checklist of 2500 titles

MICHAEL FELMINGHAM

WILDWOOD HOUSE

First published in hardback 1988
by Scolar Press

This paperback edition published 1989 by
Wildwood House Limited
Gower House,
Croft Road,
Aldershot,
Hampshire GU11 3HR,
England.

British Library Cataloguing in Publication Data
Felmingham, Michael
    The illustrated gift book 1880-1930:
    with a checklist of 2,500 titles.
    I. Illustration of books
    I. Title
    741.64   NC9600
    ISBN 0-7045-0627-0

Printed in Great Britain at
The Bath Press, Avon.

Errata
The plates on pp.134 - 5 should be transposed.
The captions are correct as they stand.

Contents

Acknowledgements

In writing this book I have incurred a debt of gratitude to many people. In particular I would like to thank John Lewis, John Commander and Rowland Hilder for their generous advice and encouragement, Robin de Beaumont and John Russell Taylor for so freely sharing their knowledge and libraries, and Susan Stokes for her hard work and patience in compiling the Checklist of Illustrators.

For help in many ways including loan of books and manuscripts, answering endless questions and the correction of errors my thanks are due to Mary Barnard, Geoffrey Beard, Brian Baumfield, Barry Burman, Alice Coats, David Cuppleditch, Malcolm Easton, Ian Gilchrist, Gaby Goldscheider, Marie Gracey, Rigby Graham, Simon Houfe, C. M. Kelley, Niki Rathbone, Gordon N. Ray, William Ridler, Bay Robinson, Brian Robb, Una Rota, Graham Sutherland, Merle Taylor, Geoffrey Wakeman, John Webb, Peggy Wickham and Tim Wilkinson. The staffs of a number of institutions have patiently endured my demands and enquiries, notably the St Bride's Institute, The Fine Art Society, The Bank of England, Sotheby & Co., and the Victoria and Albert Museum. The staffs of the Birmingham Reference Library and the Coventry (Lanchester) Polytechnic Library have been unfailingly helpful. I am also very grateful to the innumerable booksellers whose shelves I have examined and whose advice has been so valuable; David Temperley, Jan Weddup and Denis Hall in particular have pointed to much that I might have missed.

I would also like to thank the following publishers who gave permission for the use of copyright material: Associated Book Publishers, B. T. Batsford Ltd., Constable & Co. Ltd., William Heinemann Ltd., Kingsmead Reprints, MacDonald and Jane's, Seeley Service and Cooper, the Horn Book Inc., and Wordens of Cornwall. Finally I would like to express my thanks to my wife Brenda for all her help and support.   M.F.

The publishers thank the following for permission to reproduce copyright illustrations: Lucie Attwell Ltd 58; Blackie & Son Ltd 59, 64, 69, 70; The Bodley Head Ltd III, 1, 23, 38, 41, 42, 43, 46, 63, 65; Brewer 24; Jonathan Cape Ltd 6; Chatto & Windus Ltd 72; Doubleday & Company, Inc. 25; Alison Greenwood 76; William Heinemann Ltd 1, 55, 56; Hodder & Stoughton Ltd II, IV, 9, 51, 57; Macdonald & Co. (Publishers) Ltd 60, 62; Macmillan Publishers Ltd 7; Methuen & Co. Ltd VII, Fig. 4, 45; Thomas Nelson and Sons Ltd 75; Oxford University Press 77; C. Arthur Pearson Ltd 16, 74; The estate of J. C. Robinson 47, 48, tailpiece; The Rockwell Kent Legacies 24; Routledge & Kegan Paul Ltd 36; Charles Scribner's Sons 29, 30.

List of Illustrations

Colour

Figures in the text

Plates

Tailpiece

Introduction

Towards the end of the nineteenth century the appearance of illustrated books and magazines changed dramatically. The old craft of wood-engraving was superseded by the new photo-mechanical methods of reproduction, and the harnessing of the camera to the production of blocks for illustrations brought faster, cheaper and more colourful results. The number of new publishers of books and periodicals increased rapidly, for the public appetite for illustrated material of all kinds seemed insatiable. The artists who worked for these publishers found themselves addressing a new and vast market and enjoyed a public following and a degree of influence far surpassing that enjoyed by artists of former years. Phil May, John Hassall, Arthur Rackham, Heath Robinson, and in America Howard Pyle, N. C. Wyeth, Maxfield Parrish, Charles Dana Gibson and many more became popular heroes with their own following. The boom in illustrated gift books which followed the development of these new photographic processes of reproduction forms the subject of the present book.

Even today, in this age of film, television and video, there are still gift books of a kind. The development of photo-lithography over the last twenty years has led to a spate of cheap colour-plate 'coffee table' books which have gained enormous popularity and sales on the strength of their illustrations. The book tables of our larger department stores bear witness to this contemporary taste. Seventy or eighty years ago those same tables would undoubtedly have carried the illustrated books dealt with here, particularly at Christmastime. Today it is the photo-litho book; yesterday it was the letter-press process book.

Given the impetus provided by a new process and the availability of new markets, publishers have been quick to provide for the public's mood, at least for as long as it has lasted. The early decades of the nineteenth century, for example, saw a growing demand for literary annuals and gift books[1] illustrated with etchings and engravings made on the newly patented (1819) steel printing plates. From 1823 until about 1850 there issued a stream of elegant volumes such as *The Forget-me-not* (1823), *Friendship's Offering* (1824), *The Bijou* (1828), *The Keepsake* (1828) and *Fisher's Drawing Room Scrapbook* (1832). Great attention was paid to their appearance. Bindings were ornately embossed and heavily gilt; some had slip-cases and ribbon ties. They contained short stories, essays and poetry of a lightly entertaining nature although the text was always subsidiary to the engraved pictures. Their very titles suggested their purpose as gifts, tokens, souvenirs, mementoes or keepsakes.

By mid-century these largely monochromatic offerings had been superseded by a new kind of book profusely illustrated in full (some might think garish) colour by chromolithography with illustrations by such artists as Owen Jones and Henry Noel Humphreys.[2] A particularly popular, if relatively useless, example of this type was

1. Frederick W. Faxon, *Literary Annuals and Gift Books*, 1912, reprinted by the Private Libraries Association, 1973.
2. Ruari McLean, *Victorian Book Design and Colour Printing* (Faber, 1963), p. 60.

the illuminated gift book in which the text was almost suffocated with a profusion of neo-medieval ornament. It was the development of a new process of picture reproduction which provided the stimulus to creativity; the emergence of the artists followed. Because this aspect is sometimes ignored I have dealt with the origins and development of the photographic processes, line and half-tone, which lay behind the production of the illustrated books considered here. This then is a book about the ordinary trade book aimed at the mass market and employing the cheapest and most up-to-date processes of reproduction then available. Consequently the private press books of those years, which usually employed the older, hand processes of etching and engraving, have been omitted.

Perhaps the greatest achievement of these illustrators in the early decades of the twentieth century has been to provide, particularly for children's books, the images of setting and character which succeeding generations have so closely identified with the texts. It is scarcely possible to imagine any other Thames river bank than that of Ernest Shepard, or a Kensington Gardens without Arthur Rackham's pools and twilight, or any Lake District other than that of Beatrix Potter. It is W. Heath Robinson's bald-headed professors, Edmund Dulac's sheikhs and caliphs, Mabel Lucie Attwell's babies, Arthur Rackham's gnomes and Cecil Aldin's puppy dogs which populate our memories and come so easily to mind. Not all of their books had so close and ideal a fusion of text and illustration. Many books, being reissues of long-familiar texts, were only produced as a vehicle for the illustrator's talents. In others the texts were relegated to a subsidiary role and the artist's name alone used to sell the books, as with *Arthur Rackham's Book of Pictures* (1913), *Edmund Dulac's Fairy Book* (1916), *The Cecil Aldin Book* (1932), and *Howard Pyle's Book of Pirates* (1921).

The term 'gift book' is difficult to define with precision as it is not an exclusive category, although most children's books should be included. It is easier to say what gift books were not. They were not, for example, produced for the student or scholar but were intended for the drawing-room coffee table or nursery shelf. Commenting on the gift books of the early nineteenth century Iain Bain has remarked that they 'were not intended for serious reading but for intermittent perusal . . .';[3] this is true of later gift books as well, but perusal was frequently of the illustrations alone. The appearance and format of the gift books considered here are more easily described:

They were well made, well bound in fine cloth often with a coloured illustration plate – sunk on the front cover surrounded by richly blocked designs in gold and colours. Sometimes they had ornamental headbands and coloured or decorated endpapers. Inside, apart from the many black-and-white illustrations, the coloured plates would be tipped on to cartridge paper or boards, often printed with wash lines round the pictures and covered with tissue.[4]

The expense of all this could be considerable and, not surprisingly, such books often appeared in more economical dress. Although the years immediately preceding the First World War saw perhaps the best of these books, their production scarcely abated during the war, as my checklist will show. The decade that followed, however, was one of decline, and the type was finally extinguished by the financial slump of 1929–30 which brought both increased costs of new materials and greatly diminished markets.

To attempt a complete catalogue of the illustrated book of this period is an almost impossible task. It was attempted by R. E. D. Sketchley in his invaluable *English Book Illustration of Today* (1903), but his lists closed in September 1901, when the market had scarcely begun. I have attempted to carry the catalogue forward until 1930, when the golden years were past.

3. Frederick W. Faxon, *Literary Annuals and Gift Books*, (1912, reprinted by the Private Libraries Association, 1973), p. 15.
4. John Lewis, *Heath Robinson* (Constable, 1973), p. 91.

CHAPTER 1

The Golden Age

Wood-engraving, which had been used for the bulk of illustrated material throughout the nineteenth century, had been a slow business. The box tree itself, whose wood proved most suitable for the process, grows only slowly and is small in girth. Consequently for large pictures, such as those used in *The Illustrated London News*, the drawing had to be done on a composite block made from many small ones cramped tightly together. Moreover, boxwood grain is hard and tight and requires great expertise to cut with sharp burins. Craftsmen working in teams and under considerable pressure had to chip away those parts of the surface not required to print, leaving the printing surface standing in relief. Not surprisingly publishers quickly saw the advantages the new photographic processes offered.

'Process' reproduction, as it was called, provides basically two sorts of illustration from two types of block: the simple photographic line block for reproducing pen-and-ink drawings, and the screened illustration in monochrome or colour known as half-tone. Both are printed letterpress – that is to say, from the relief surface of the block.

The British genius has often best displayed itself in a linear and decorative art, employing muted and tender colours, and the artists who exploited this new process were no exception. During what we may think of as the golden period of the process, from 1880 to 1930, there were active in Britain alone just under a hundred illustrators, and in America many more. Their art was largely uninfluenced by the successive convolutions and revolutions of the larger world of art in the early twentieth century. Certainly Aubrey Beardsley is popularly regarded as being something of an *enfant terrible* of the Art Nouveau movement, but the *fleurs du mal* of his particular genius were home grown in the London literary hot-house of the early 1890s. Of his love for early German etchings, Burne-Jones and Japanese prints we are constantly reminded, but of Impressionism, Post-Impressionism, Cubists or Nabis there is not a hint, and it is hard to realise that Vuillard, Bonnard and Lautrec were his seniors by ten years. For Beardsley line was enough: he was, in contemporary parlance, a 'black and white' man. He worked, as did most artists of that time, for publishers who employed the line block where they had once used wood-engravings, and who were concerned with the unity of letterpress printing, for the sympathy of block and type printed together. The professional illustrator, who understood these problems, was therefore essential to their plans.

To get some idea of the wealth of illustrative talent available in those seemingly golden pre-First World War years one can do no better than glance through a typical fat Christmas number of *The Bookman*. With its coloured supplements of plates by Nielsen, Dulac or Rackham, and its columns packed with reproductions from children's books available for the Christmas market, it lays the period vividly before us. The 1912 issue contains a special feature on the gift book market and was able to announce a quite staggering list for that season, including Heath Robinson's *Bill the Minder*, Arthur Rackham's

Aesop and *Peter Pan*, Edmund Dulac's *The Bells*, Edward Detmold's *Aesop*, Charles Robinson's *Bee* and *Big Book of Fables*, Eleanor Fortescue-Brickdale's *Saint Elizabeth of Hungary*, Honor Appleton's *Nursery Rhyme Book*, Hugh Thomson's *She Stoops to Conquer*, Willy Pogány's *Parsifal*, Beatrix Potter's *Tale of Mr. Tod*, Anne Anderson's *Chaucer*, Florence Harrison's *Elfin Song* and many additional books from Russell Flint, Warwick Goble, the Brocks, Mabel Lucie Attwell, Charles Folkard, Noel Pocock, Chloë Preston and Paul Woodroffe. Here are the story books for younger children, full of fairies, goblins and witches, myths and legends and tales of many lands, illustrated by Anne Anderson, Henry Ford, Katherine Cameron, Margaret Tarrant or Honor Appleton. Poetry, too, sold well. An example of the best in this field was M. G. Edgar's *Treasury of Verse for Little Children*, from Harrap, illustrated in colour and black and white by Willy Pogány, its handsome cover resplendent in gold and three colours, and all for five shillings.

Some firms specialised in 'improving' works, often of a religious flavour; typical of these books was *Our Island Saints* (1912) by Amy Steedman, published by Jacks of Edinburgh and illustrated with very pretty watercolours of the nursery wall or Sunday School variety by M. Dibdin Spooner. They were well served by their illustrators who sometimes, as in the case of Katherine Cameron, drew their inspiration from the contemporary taste for Art Nouveau. Their cloth bindings were gay and varied but the proselytism of their authors sometimes undid all this and made for dull presents.

Then there were the annuals to which most illustrators contributed from time to time, especially in their early days when they were glad to sell a drawing wherever they could. These annuals were often well produced on good paper, usually with a dozen colour plates and strongly bound within attractive glazed pictorial boards. They often carried an advertisement or two exhorting the nippers to drink Eno's Fruit Salts every morning or Ovaltine at night. Such books were the indispensable comforts of bedridden minors.

Of all the children's annuals that poured from the presses in Edwardian England few could compare with *Blackie's Children's Annual* – the brain child of John Alexander Blackie. The first issue in 1904 was something new to booksellers and they were reluctant to order copies. Its enormous popularity, however, soon changed that and future issues ran to very large printings. Blackie's quickly followed up with annuals for *Little Ones*, *Girls* and *Boys*, and faced strong competition from Partridges, Raphael Tuck (*Father Tuck's Annual*) and other publishers. Walter W. Blackie had, it seems, 'a penchant for civilisation's frontiers'[1] (a legacy of his time lumberjacking in Canada), and patronised such authors as Robert and Alexander Macdonald, Captain Brereton, Strang and Henty for 'reward' books. Aimed at older boys, they were stirring tales of daring, discovery and Empire adventure and were issued in what the press called 'handsome' bindings with 'splendid' or 'striking' illustrations. These sepia half-tone plates show youthful protagonists in violent action, repelling all manner of savages with accurate fists and a casual heroism that helped to develop the 'pluck' and 'grit' dissipated in the waste of the First World War. They carried such captions as 'Touch and Go' – Jack fending off sixteen irate Chinamen with one hand and launching a sampan with the other. The cloth bindings of such books are a joy to the collector, blocked, as they usually were, in several colours and gold and often with dazzling gilt edges. Illustration, however, was sparse and usually amounted to several full-page half-tone reproductions of wash drawings by Sidney Paget, Will Owen, Stanley Wood, Edward Hodgson, Cyrus Cuneo and others who merit a book to themselves. These 'reward' books were produced cheaply at prices ranging from sixpence to six shillings for *de luxe* volumes. In this latter category Blackie's were supreme. Charles Robinson produced some of his most beautiful books for Blackie. *The Story of the Weathercock* (1907) and

1. Agnes Blackie, *Blackie and Son 1809–1959* (Blackie and Son, Glasgow, 1959), p. 49.

The Child's Christmas (1906), both by Evelyn Sharp, are luxurious by any standards, with red or green buckram heavily blocked in gold, all edges gilt enclosing elaborate compilations of line and three-colour illustrations. They must have been dazzling presents when new: my copy of *The Child's Christmas* is inscribed 'Kitty from Uncle Jack and Aunt Florry, Christmas 1906' – lucky Kitty, for it is hard to find copies in good condition today. In the same style and grander if anything is Blackie's *Big Book of Fairy Tales*, also illustrated by Charles Robinson, and edited by Walter Jerrold; it is difficult to imagine that such luxury once cost only seven and sixpence. Carton Moore Park's *Alphabet of Animals* with twenty-six full-page plates for five shillings was a similar bargain. 'The price of five shillings is exceedingly low for this beautiful book', said *The Westminster Budget*. 'The Camel is capital', said *The Athenaeum*.

Prices were indeed low, but not as low as they had been prior to the Net Book Agreement concluded by publishers in 1900 in an attempt to stop the disastrous situation in the retail trade where price-cutting was the order of the day. The public could purchase a book marked at six shillings for as little as two thirds of that price, but this state of affairs was ruinous for booksellers and many bookshops had closed as a result. According to Percy Muir, the Net Book Agreement was not properly observed until 'the rigours of wartime enforced it after 1914'.[2] Price-cutting was certainly a feature of the Edwardian gift book market and resulted in some cheap and nasty productions. Often a book that came out in a respectable trade edition, bound in gold-blocked buckram with gilt edges on good paper, would be followed by a series of ever cheaper editions, although this did not infringe the Net Book Agreement. Popular fairy stories were good candidates for this treatment, and both Edmund Dulac's and Heath Robinson's editions of *Hans Andersen* went through a variety of cheap editions. Mabel Lucie Attwell's *Peter Pan* (1921) and *Water Babies* (1915) are still in print today, if in a watered-down paperback fashion. The drawings of Margaret Tarrant, Beatrix Potter, Ernest Shepard, Arthur Rackham, Walter Crane, Cecily Barker and many others are also still to be found amongst the children's books on sale today, and seem likely to remain so.

The most luxurious illustrated books, however, were reserved for the adult market, as it cannot really be supposed that, whatever their titles, strictly limited signed editions, bound in gold-blocked leather or vellum, sometimes with extra plates tucked in, could be intended for children. Like the opulent gift books of the nineteenth century they were designed for the drawing-room rather than the nursery. Together with a Lutyens house, a Jekyll garden or a Daimler car, they were tokens of Edwardian 'refinement' – though this was no fault of the artists, and should not hinder an objective view of their merits.

2. Percy Muir, *Victorian Illustrated Books* (Batsford, 1971), p. 202.

CHAPTER 2

The Photomechanical Revolution

Because these artists intended their illustrations for photomechanical reproduction, it is only right that their work should be judged by the printed result. The original art-work was only a means to an end and was often an unlovely collage of different scraps of paper heavily touched with process white, although Arthur Rackham and other well-known artists sometimes sold clean originals through the London galleries as pictures for hanging. To understand their problems it is necessary to know something about the new processes and their effect upon artists' working methods.

From about 1870 onwards the popularity of the wood-engraving began to decline, but it took thirty years to approach vanishing point: thirty years in which a new generation of artists grew up with the steadily improving process line block quickly followed by the half-tone process. The importance of the new line block as the first effective photomechanical method of reproduction cannot be overstated. Although the process engraver now lay between the artist and his public very much as the professional wood-engraver had done previously, there was no doubt that sympathetic drawing and good blockmaking brought the printed result very close to the original. According to Thomas Balston, 'The new process required a new art, or a new branch of art for its sustenance. And Hugh Thomson was its pioneer.'[1] However, it should be borne in mind that the inventors of the process line block were not interested in creating a 'new art' but merely in lowering the costs of reproduction and speeding up the printing itself.

For the illustrator, the new blockmakers were at first no less tyrannical than their predecessors. Artists were asked to produce drawings with the blackest of Indian ink on smooth white Bristol board. It was impressed upon the draughtsman that his lines should be of even thickness, firm and wide apart and enlarged half a size. In 1901 Charles Harper described the process in biblical prose:

And so by reason of these things, the pen-work of that time [twenty years earlier] is become dreadful to look upon at this day. The man who drew with a view to reproduction squirmed on the very edge of his chair, and with compressed lips, and his heart in his mouth, drew upon his Bristol board slowly and carefully, and with so heavy a hand that presently his wrist ached consumedly, and his drawing became stilted in the extreme. Not yet was pen-drawing a profession, for few men had learned these formulae; and the zincography of that time made miserable all them that were translated by it.[2]

A line block is a letterpress printing block in which the lines to be printed stand out in relief, the non-printing areas being etched or bitten away. They are usually made of zinc (hence the popular term 'zinco'), and used for the reproduction of black-and-white drawings. The drawing is photographed in reverse onto a zinc plate. The lines of the drawing being protected against the action of the acid the block is

1. John Carter, *New Paths in Book Collecting* (Constable, 1934), p. 167.
2. Charles Harper, *A Practical Handbook of Drawing for Modern Methods of Reproduction* (Chapman and Hall, 1901), p. 11.

then etched and the image to be printed remains in relief. At best a good line block is almost indistinguishable from the original drawing. Firmin Gillot of Paris is credited with the invention of the process in 1850, but his method did not use the camera and was basically a method of transferring drawings from lithographic stones to zinc plates which were then etched. He called this method 'paniconography' but it is better known as 'gillotage'. The adaptation of this process by his son and by others followed fast upon developments in photography, and by the late 1880s photographic line blocks were in common use. It seems that they were first introduced into book work during the 1870s, following their use in magazines; the first line block in commercial use may have been a map printed in *The Graphic* in 1876. However, no clear temporal dividing line can easily be drawn between the use of wood-engraved and photo-engraved blocks, owing to the common practice of printing wood-engravings from indistinguishable electrotypes.

Despite Charles Harper's misgivings the comparative ease, cheapness[3] and reproductive faithfulness of the new processes led to a passion for pen and ink which rivalled the earlier Victorian enthusiasm for photography. Its 'popular' arrival is sometimes credited to that issue of Macmillan's *English Illustrated Magazine* which appeared in April 1886 with Hugh Thomson's illustrations to the second instalment of *Sir Roger de Coverley*, but it was the 1890s which saw its common acceptance: *Punch* used it first on 3 December 1892.

Artists faced with the difficulties of the new process were not short of advice. Joseph Pennell's monumental *Pen Drawing and Pen Draughtsmen* of 1899 and *Modern Illustration* of 1895 set the tone. Critics used to discussing the finer points of the earlier autographic processes of wood-engraving and etching turned their attentions to the new photographic processes with considerable pedantry. They felt themselves to be the guardians of the sanctity of 'good illustration' and were careful to give precise instructions on technique, errors to be avoided and the wise choice of models to emulate. Hence Henry Blackburn in *The Art of Illustration* (1894) lamented that in drawing for the new processes there was no past to refer to and so cautiously recommended contemporary artists worth studying, Daniel Vierge or Herbert Railton for example, but not 'Aubrey Beardsley and others of the dense black, reckless school of modern illustrators'. Daniel Vierge, who was born in 1851 and spent his early years in Madrid before moving to Paris in 1869, was in fact a considerable influence at this time.[4] After a period drawing for *La Vie Moderne* and *Le Monde Illustré*, he achieved fame with his line drawings for *Pablo de Segovie* by Francisco Quevedo-Villegas (perhaps the first major use of process in book work) – published in England in 1892 with comments on the artist by Joseph Pennell. Pennell also recommended Fortuny and Rico as models and joined with Blackburn in admiring the almost forgotten Herbert Railton – 'In facility, I suppose there is no-one to equal Herbert Railton, unless it be Hugh Thomson.'[5] Railton's talent was for closely hatched drawings of cathedrals and historic houses; he is now best remembered for illustrating, with Hugh Thomson, W. O. Tristram's *Coaching Days and Coaching Ways* (1898). Also influential at this time were *The Studio* articles contributed by 'G. W.' (almost certainly Gleeson White), who examined the problems of black-and-white drawing, photographic reduction and photo-engraving and dived headlong into the arguments surrounding them. He came out strongly for 'same-size' drawing when working for process reproduction as 'the feeling of a woodcut is more easily imitated in this way'. There is no doubt that he and Pennell were largely responsible for the seriousness with which the new art came to be taken. There was no mistaking, either, the genius of Beardsley or Phil May, and as they

3. In 1894 the cost of a process line block was 6d per square inch.
4. Percy Bradshaw owned Vierge's *Tavern of the Three Virtues* and a monograph on Fortuny which he liked to lend to students.
5. Joseph Pennell, *Modern Illustration* (Bell, 1895), p. 105.

both worked almost exclusively in pen and ink for process it was impossible to avoid the conclusion that a major new medium capable of transmitting genius had appeared.

Pennell too was an etcher and a disciple of the great Whistler, and it is not surprising that something of Whistler's etching technique – the light dancing line and areas of close hatching – can be seen in the pen drawings of the artists Pennell so admired, Vierge and Rico. Indeed it seems likely that the high prestige of etching at this time and the respectability of its ancestry from Rembrandt onwards were largely responsible for paving the way to the acceptance of the new art. It is significant that in his *Pen Drawing and Pen Draughtsmen* (1899) Pennell gave a number of line illustrations the *de luxe* treatment by printing them in sepia by photogravure within artificial plate lines on Dickinson's deckle-edged hand-made paper, to give them the appearance of etchings. It may be objected that in so encumbering a purely commercial process with the rather precious trappings of spurious rarity he was defeating his own object, but as Ruskin had always shown, enthusiasm was far more telling than consistency. 'Consistency', Oscar Wilde once remarked, 'is the last refuge of the unimaginative' – not a fault of Pennell's. And although Pennell once claimed that the fixed English idea of a drawing or sketch being a somewhat lowly art form had inhibited the spread of process in England, it may also be true that the tedious quality of much contemporary academic art acted as a spur to the younger generation to discover the exciting freedom of the pure line, whether drawn or etched. Certainly the lively contents of the early volumes of *The Studio* magazine are in marked contrast to, say, the *Magazine of Art*, and the air of excitement in the former has much to do with the discovery of the new processes. For 'line' was linked with discussions of line and form, the theories of Crane and Dresser, or the work of Mackmurdo, Voysey, the Glasgow School and others; line was the vehicle of Art Nouveau expression[6] and was to lead on to the heady delights of twentieth-century design. In a word,

it was 'modern'. *The Studio* responded to this enthusiasm not only with informative articles but with prize competitions for its readers, offering monetary prizes for the winners and 'honourable mentions' and 'commendations' for innumerable runners-up; they were lavish in illustrating the submissions and kind in their brief comments – 'pleasing', 'a pretty fancy', 'good detail', 'full of charm', 'all good, especially the doggie', and so on.

Blackburn spoke of 'a revolution in illustration at the present time', and Charles Holme, editor of *The Studio*, of

a renaissance which has come forth with such richness, that it is difficult for the keenest observer to keep mere count of the new draughtsmen in the field of line-work. You publish a handbook to the illustrations of this year, and by the end of next it is hopelessly out of date. And we are only on the threshold of the new school, with its bewildering ingenuity and its beautiful technique, for the army is being recruited from the ranks of the creators who, twenty years ago, would have found their dreams attainable only in many shades of the canvas or the water-colour.[7]

Nevertheless Holme made an attempt at such a handbook with his *Modern Pen Drawings: European and American* (1901), in which he provided an opportunity to compare the native English product with the best from abroad. The British section occupied the major part of the book, but even allowing for the patriotism of the times it was perhaps a not unfair reflection of the importance of the British contribution to line illustration in book work. Holme may not have been aware of the Americans' dominance in magazine illustration, or, being English, may have preferred to consider only books. The exclusion of Aubrey Beardsley from his handbook is more difficult to account for, unless the author belonged to the considerable faction which detested his work. Nevertheless Beardsley's influence was strongly felt and is apparent in

6. Almost a celebration of this is the single branching line of Beardsley's cover for Dowson's *Verses* of 1896. It recalls Hogarth's 'line of beauty'.
7. *Modern Pen Drawings* (*The Studio*, 1901), p. 14.

COLOUR PLATE II. Edmund Dulac
Princess Badoura retold by Laurence Housman, Hodder and Stoughton, 1913

COLOUR PLATE III. Alastair (Hans Henning Voight)
Forty-three Drawings, Lane, 1914

many of the examples shown here. It is odd too that Arthur Rackham and both Charles and William Heath Robinson are also omitted, although all three were then becoming well known. Writing in *The Studio* in 1904, Gleeson White noted that

there can be little doubt that the decorative school is to foreign eyes the most conspicuous to-day. Especially in this time of black and white illustration . . . Hardly a single example of the modern use of the Dürer line is to be found among American illustrators. Howard Pyle and George Wharton Edwards stand almost alone. In France until very recently, Grasset, Schwabe and a few others served to emphasise the indifference of the majority.

Many artists who turned almost exclusively to line for their livelihood found that magazine editors were often their best customers. Throughout the 1890s there was scarcely a year in which a major monthly magazine was not started. Some of the most important for the illustrator were *The Strand Magazine* (1891), *The Idler* (1892), *Pall Mall Magazine* (1893), *Windsor Magazine* (1895) and *Pearson's Magazine* (1896). In America *Harper's Magazine*, *Scribner's Magazine* and the *Century Magazine* had many imitators. These together with the weeklies, of which *Black and White* was quite outstanding for the wealth of illustrative talent it employed, and the quarterlies which followed the example of Beardsley's *Yellow Book*, provided enormous scope for artists capable of working for the new process. *Once a Week*, famous with an earlier generation for the wood-engraved illustration after Millais and other Sixties artists, gave the young William Heath Robinson his first commission and is representative of the strong links that held together this long tradition of black-and-white from wood-engraving to photo-engraving.

Many magazines throughout this period had a strangely unsettled transitional look about them, with dashing line drawings and chalky half-tones rubbing shoulders with staid wood-engravings. All had a funereal black aspect which it is perhaps not too fanciful to regard as a mark of their Victorianism – black ink, soot and

Sabbath clothes. By 1910 many artists of the younger generation had become well known for their use of the new process, and as the twentieth century dawned the books of the old school began to look very old-fashioned indeed with their small dark engraved vignettes and their heavily embossed bindings.

The success of process reproduction largely depended upon the skill of the photo-engravers, in which the Americans and the French had a considerable lead. Even as late as 1899 many British blocks were being sent to Paris for reproduction – perhaps for this reason *Punch* was still using wood-engravings. That same year Joseph Pennell remarked:

In England, until French and American magazines proved the artistic value, and not merely pecuniary advantage, of pen drawing for process reproduction, comparatively little attention was paid to it by artists. Even yet but few publishers have discovered anything but the cheapness of the medium.[8]

In the 1890s Beardsley and Phil May were almost exclusively black-and-white artists. After 1900 there was no technical reason why anyone else should be so specialised. Half-tone and three-colour (or four-colour) half-tone were common and the younger artists, of whom Arthur Rackham is perhaps today the best known, are usually remembered for their colour work. Three-colour (or trichromatic) half-tone printing was a development of the half-tone process – a method of reproducing the delicate half-tones of photography through letterpress printing. Its history goes back to mid-century, for that early pioneer of photography Henry Fox Talbot had suggested methods of breaking up the tones of a photograph by means of a screen of ruled lines on glass as early as 1852. His experiments were followed by others, particularly those of the Frenchman M. Berchtold, who took out a patent five years later for a glass coated with a substance impermeable to light and covered with a multitude of very fine parallel lines set close

8. Joseph Pennell, *Pen Drawing and Pen Draughtsmen* (Macmillan, 1899), p. 183.

FIGURE I. Daniel Vierge
Pablo de Segovie, Francisco Queredo-Villegas, 1882

together, made by a pointed steel tool which removed the coating substance without cutting the glass. In this process, however, the screen was not present in the camera, being impressed onto the sensitised zinc plate after the photographic image was printed. Berchtold also suggested the idea of turning a single line screen through ninety degrees so as to cross the lines, an idea later patented by J. W. Swan, the renowned electrician, in 1879. It appears to have been left to the firm of E. and J. Bullock of Royal Leamington Spa to suggest the idea of placing the screen in front of the sensitive plate in the camera. This had obvious advantages and led to the experiments of J. W. Swan, Georg Meisenbach of Munich and Frederick Ives of Philadelphia.

Meisenbach took out a patent in 1882 for a method which embodied these ideas. To translate the image into dots of varying sizes he used a glass screen ruled with fine parallel lines placed between the lens of the process camera and the negative plate; halfway through the exposure this was turned through ninety degrees. Frederick Ives improved on this by placing two ruled screens together at right angles but as he failed to take out a patent in England his work was confined to America, where he specialised in half-tone work for the growing number of magazines, starting with *Harper's Magazine* in 1884. Meisenbach soon moved to London with his advanced process and adapted Ives's improvement. Commercial success followed, but these were still early days and Meisenbach was always dependent upon skilful handwork with graver, burnisher and roulette by the blockmakers. This was necessary because his pictures were still chopped into small dots of the same size, and in this chopping half of the picture disappeared. The credit for the term 'half-tone' goes to Frederick Ives, who discovered and applied a most important principle still missing in Meisenbach's work – that in order to achieve dots of varying size it is necessary to have an appreciable distance between the screen and the plate. It was soon realised that a critical relationship existed between the extension of the camera, the size of the lens aperture and the size of openings in the screen. If the plate and the screen openings were close together a chopped-up effect resulted, owing to the lines masking part of the plate; removing the screen to the critical distance allowed for a perfect graduation of dot. These screens were subsequently developed and supplied to the trade by the firm of L. and M. Levy of Philadelphia.

The major problems attending photomechanical reproduction were thus resolved, and the adoption of the process sounded the death-knell for the wood-engravers. Yet in their attempts to keep pace with the vast demands for illustration in tone the wood-engravers continued to battle against the encroachments of half-tone process. By the late 1880s the wood-engraving industry was well organised, blocks being produced to order in large quantities by such firms as Swain and Dalziel through the technique of employing several skilled engravers on one illustration. And indeed the vast amount of illustration turned out for periodicals at this time is evidence of phenomenal business efficiency on the part of the wood-engravers. For some years they managed to delay the introduction of the process half-tone by learning from it. The multiple-tint tool, which could engrave several fine parallel lines at once, was employed in transverse directions to produce dots of varying size – a result that vied with the early half-tones. In this way wash drawings could be reproduced in facsimile. Initially the engraver undoubtedly had the upper hand, as the engraved line, cut by sharp steel, produced a much sharper result for letterpress printing than the rather blotchy early half-tones. Even as late as 1901 Charles Harper could declare: 'No tint or halftone process can ever render sufficiently well the wash drawings that the best engravers render so admirably . . . He and his delightful art will survive because they preserve the personal note of the wash drawings they render while lending to them the sweetness of the engraved line.' In addition the early half-tones were poor in quality, leading the process engraver to try and remedy their deficiencies by working over the blocks by hand.

The results of such efforts are often recognisable by the rather chewed look of the final print. Some printers too did not easily discern the basic differences between the half-tone and line blocks; they became so anxious about their half-tones that they allowed line blocks to take their chance and often printed them with bright inks on the same coated art papers with unhappy results.

A quick look at any run of periodicals of the time will reveal the enormous advances made by the half-tone process. The *Art Journal* of 1884 has no half-tones at all although it employed virtually every other process then current; half-tone first appeared in the magazine early in 1885 and within ten years became the major process used. In America *Harper's Magazine* came out with a fine half-tone reproduction of a drawing by Fred Remington in the issue for 2 February 1889. *The Studio* (which first appeared in April 1893) contained in its first issue only one wood-engraving, and that may well have been reproduced by an electrotype line block. As early as August 1896 this periodical started to feature the occasional three-colour half-tone. The first issue contained Joseph Pennell's article 'A new illustrator', which introduced the twenty-one-year-old Mr Beardsley to a startled but receptive world through that other new photomechanical medium, the line block. Seldom has a new sense of energy and direction in the arts been so closely accompanied by revolutionary changes in technology.

The use of the half-tone block to produce colour prints followed naturally upon these developments, for the principle of three-colour separation was by then well known. Frederick Ives is credited with originating the three-colour half-tone. Although by 1890 it was possible to produce colour reproductions in this way, much remained to be perfected and throughout the 1890s experiments continued in search of suitable plates and filters. In addition correct blocks and inks, suitable paper and fine registers were all necessary. Messrs Waterlow set a high standard in the Nineties, especially with their three-colour supplement 'A Twelfth Night Belle', produced for *The Lady's Pictorial* (8 January 1898). Other good work at this time was being undertaken by Carl Hentschel, John Swain, Hare & Sons, The Typographic Etching Co. of West Norwood, The Art Reproduction Company, D. C. Dallas, Vincent & Hahn and many others. It was for a while the custom of these blockmakers to sign their line blocks in the manner of the old wood-engravers, but this was seldom so in the case of half-tone reproduction and most colour plates are anonymous. Henry Stone & Co. of Banbury, who worked extensively for Hodder and Stoughton, were usually credited at the back of their books for their fine colour reproductions of such artists as Kay Nielsen, Hugh Thomson, Mabel Lucie Attwell and Heath Robinson, but this takes us well into the twentieth century.

During the 1890s three-colour process work was making slow but steady inroads upon all other colour printing methods. An examination of the early volumes of *Penrose's Pictorial Annual*, significantly subtitled *The process year book*, shows that a high proportion of the articles were devoted to the three-colour process. In its early days the half-tone process suffered significant limitations such as the coarseness of the screens and a want of texture which provided ready targets for those wedded to the older colour printing methods.

Much heated argument revolved around the problem of whether to use the three primary colours alone or to support them with a fourth printing in black. The absence of a fourth printing coupled with a poor choice of tints for the colours meant that many early blocks had a washed-out look. Put simply, the procedure is as follows. The coloured drawing is photographed through three separate filters. A blue/violet filter picks out all yellow in the original, a green filter removes the magenta and a red filter the cyan. If a half-tone screen is placed in the camera the result will be three separate negatives with the image broken into dots as in the monochrome process. If each screen is set at a slightly different angle the dots of one screen will not fit exactly over the others. Half-tone

FIGURE 2. A photographic studio for the production of process blocks by
Hare & Co. in 1897

blocks are then made from all three, each block being linked in its correct colour, and the resulting print will reproduce all the colours of the original; great care needs to be taken with the final register.

Throughout the Eighties and Nineties interest in colour theory ran high. In passing it is interesting to note that only slightly earlier an argument had developed amongst French painters along similar lines. At the Café Guerbois in Paris, where the Impressionists gathered around Manet, discussion sometimes turned towards the vexed question of the use of black. Degas always maintained that he was not an Impressionist, on the grounds that he, like Mary Cassatt, used black in his palette. Their friend Edmond Duranty was in touch with Chevreul, whose colour theories were by then well established; in 1879 the American physicist N. O. Rood had published his work in colour theory. The Impres-

sionists and Neo-Impressionists adopted these theories and experimented with arranging their palettes according to the chromatic tables available to them. Duranty complained that this was too slavish an approach as it led, in his view, to an absence of depth. 'This comes', he wrote, 'from their denial of black, from the absence of this colour in their palettes', a criticism which, as we have seen, could be well applied to the early three-colour printers.[9]

The publication in 1901 of Beatrix Potter's *Tale of Peter Rabbit*, with a coloured frontispiece reproduced by the trichromatic process on art paper, suitably marked the triumph of the new technique and the start of a new century. From this time on quality colour reproduction was a commercial possibility. In 1905 Heinemann published Arthur Rackham's *Rip Van*

9. L. E. E. Duranty, *La Nouvelle Peinture* (Paris, 1946).

Winkle with fifty-one colour illustrations, the enormous success of which led other publishers and artists to follow the same path. Despite its popularity with the public, however, the rise of the colour process was not altogether approved of in bookish quarters. In 1906, in *English Coloured Books*, Martin Hardie wrote: 'It can be understood that a collector may treasure an aquatint, a chromolithograph, a coloured wood-engraving, but a process plate never. Moreover it is extremely unlikely that the clay surfaced paper, essential to the finest printing from half-tone blocks, will survive for a hundred years.'[10] On the first count he could not have been more wrong, as the current collecting of the colour plate books attests. In recent years some Philistines have even found it profitable to remove the colour plates from books by Rackham, Dulac, the Robinsons and others and sell them to the gullible as 'prints', a term which nowadays can mean anything. On the other point he may very likely be proved right. Charles Harper noted in his *Practical Handbook of Drawing for Modern Methods of Reproduction* (1901): 'It seems unlikely that any mechanical processes, save the strictly autographic which reproduce line, will be of permanent artistic value.' This disapproval was perhaps due to a feeling that had grown strongly in the last decade of the nineteenth century that the ideal book – and therefore good book design and illustration – consisted of a perfect marriage of paper, type and illustration.

In *Penrose's Pictorial Annual* for 1912–13 the editor, William Gamble, announced that

the three-colour process was welcomed as an agreeable change [from the half-tone monochrome], and it has certainly led to a renaissance of colour work, but the quantity of it and the indifferent quality of so much of it has palled on the public taste. Moreover, the necessity of printing on glazed paper, as in the case of the half-tone monochrome, is offensive to cultured eyes.

He held out no hopes for its future and predicted the survival of the wood-engraving. Certainly the wood-engraved block lived on until very recent years as illustration for small advertise-

ments or in catalogues for tools and hardware, for its clarity of line was well suited to the reproduction of detail on poor quality apper. The reluctance of the wood-engraver to leave the field can be seen in the fact that in 1901 there were still eighty professional engravers in London, although the number had dropped sharply from the 162 of 1884. But the growth of process was not to be denied: in 1876 London had one firm, in 1906 fifty-six. In 1883 there were four sixpenny weeklies using a total of eighty process blocks; by 1901 one thousand blocks were being used each week by fourteen weekly papers.

Undoubtedly process in its infancy had been disappointing and inevitably comparisons were drawn between contemporary smudgy half-tones and the engraved illustrations of, say, the books from Edmund Evans. To those brought up with the ideals of the Arts and Crafts movement the new developments must have seemed almost a betrayal of their birthright. Morris's clarity of line, colour and thought and his delight in handicraft and love of materials had been abandoned. J. H. Mason, a trusty servant of this school who had worked on the Doves Press Bible, expressed this distaste in *The Imprint* of 17 March 1913, where he wrote of

the destruction of the real art of book illustration which the halftone process has brought about. I think, too, that now there is a vast crowd caught in another unattractive industry, and of the warping and narrowing of their natures which must follow from such an occupation and from the limited ideals of their work: and I think by contrast of the delight – the just delight – that comes through a true handicraft or trade.

Despairing of the turn things had taken, Mason and many others found consolation in the private press movement that flourished until the Second World War and produced precious and beautiful books without the camera's aid. Some of the grandeur of the best private press productions comes in part from a timeless quality they

10. Martin Hardie, *English Coloured Books* (Kingsmead Reprints, Bath, 1973), p. 294.

possess as a result of their divorce from the trade; the whole movement had too something of the pervasive melancholy which attends grandeur in exile.

Returning to the commercial world we find that Art Nouveau illustrators such as Beardsley, Bradley or Anning Bell, whilst using the revolutionary medium of the line block, had at least this in common with the earlier generation: they produced illustrations which could be set up and printed letterpress together with type on the same paper. One of the great disadvantages of the trichromatic half-tone was the necessity to print on special glossy 'art' paper which was at odds with the text paper of the books. One way round this (and the method usually adopted) was to mount the art paper plates on blank text pages, often within ruled borders, and protected with a tissue leaf. A slightly cheaper method frequently employed was to tip in single sheets of art paper at appropriate points in the text, but these had a tendency to come loose and fray at the edges. Attempts to print both text and illustration on art paper were, in this field, fortunately rare. Most collectors can remember pouncing on some long-desired item in a book-shop only to discover that exposure to damp or water had dissolved the china clay coating and welded the volume into a creaking lump. For periodicals of a popular nature – for instance *The Strand*, *Windsor Magazine*, *English Illustrated Magazine* – which required a complete integration of type and illustration of all kinds at a bearable cost, the use of art paper throughout became the rule. In addition to the illustrated classics and children's gift books the trichromatic process proved ideally suited for books on travel and art. Adam and Charles Black were the first in the field to recognise its potential for travel literature, and produced a whole series entitled 'Black's Beautiful Books'. *Japan* by Mortimer Mempes (1901) is perhaps the most attractively designed of these volumes; it carries numerous colour plates made for Blacks by Carl Hentschel and was well printed by R. & R. Clark. Blacks used a variety of printers and blockmakers and the results, particularly in the later volumes, are somewhat uneven. Nevertheless the results are often very attractive and as gift books they proved popular. 'The new process restored to many watercolour artists the prosperous conditions under which Turner and the topographers had flourished a century before. The modern printer, like his predecessors, but without the intervention of the aquatint engraver, could produce watercolours, mainly of topographical views, which could be sold as pictures and which could be used for the plates of a published volume.'[11]

Despite many justified criticisms the three- and four-colour half-tone had come to stay and, fortunately or not, it is the only form in which we may judge the work of many artists, for it was the printed result that artists, publishers and printers aimed for and not the production of exhibition pictures.

11. Martin Hardie, *Watercolour Painting in Britain* (Batsford, 1968), vol. 3, p. 146.

CHAPTER 3

The World of the Illustrator

In a letter written in 1909 to an aspiring illustrator, Arthur Rackham remarked:

As a profession it is one to which no parent would be justified in putting a son without being able to give him a permanent income as well. Then, of course, if he fails, he will have something to live upon: I know several such, and believe me their bitter disappointment at their professional failure is only just prevented from being misery by the possession of an independent income . . . So this is my advice: stick to your business: go as regularly as you can with enthusiasm to a school of art (at New Cross, or Camberwell the schools are excellent) – among other things you will be associating yourself with the men who will be your professional companions . . . Don't waste your time attempting to earn money at it now, it's not worth it. Wait till you can go into the arena properly trained. Carry a sketch book – at least I did and have never regretted the assiduous thoughtful sketching I did.[1]

The need for some other form of income was paramount and meant that without private means the budding illustrator needed to live a double life, in his own and others' employ, and that free time was a luxury he could ill afford. Both Arthur Rackham and Aubrey Beardsley worked during the day for insurance companies and attended art classes in the evenings, Rackham at Lambeth School of Art and Beardsley at the Westminster School of Art.

For many, teaching in such schools helped to supplement their slim incomes. Charles Robinson taught black-and-white drawing at Heatherley's Art School (the original for Thackeray's 'Gandishes' in *The Newcomes*); Edmund Sullivan

taught at Goldsmith's, E. A. Abbey at the Royal Academy Schools, R. Anning Bell at Liverpool and Glasgow, and Jessie King and Maurice Greiffenhagen at Glasgow, whilst J. Byam Shaw and, in America, Howard Pyle, ran their own schools.

Illustration demanded qualities of persistence and resilience, good health and strength, in addition to artistic ability of a high order. Even those who were to reach the greatest heights were not immune from early struggles. The Australian Harry Rountree arrived in London in 1901 armed only with a bundle of sketches, a small sum of money, and an introduction to an art editor who promptly suggested he use the money to buy a return ticket. Phil May recalled in later years how he took a single ticket to London at the age of sixteen determined to make his living by his pencil: 'It was a hard fight. I had no friends and no introductions worth speaking of. There were comparatively few illustrated papers in those days [the early 1880s] and prices ranged very low. Once I remember I was in such a desperate mood that I seriously contemplated burgling a coffee stall.'[2] During this time, he recalled, he begged broken biscuits from public houses, drank from public fountains and slept rough on the Embankment. His situation was so miserable at one point that he was reduced to persuading a small child to take his walking

1. Derek Hudson, *Arthur Rackham* (Heinemann, 1960), p. 36.
2. Conversation with Percy Bradshaw, mentioned in his *Advanced Course of Instruction*, 1919.

FIGURE 3. Jessie M. King

stick in exchange for a bacon sandwich. Tom Browne left school at eleven and after working for a few years as an errand boy in a Nottingham millinery firm was apprenticed to a firm of lithographers. 'It was arranged that I should work for a year for nothing, and afterwards receive a shilling a week, this salary to be raised by eighteen pence each succeeding year. I didn't live during that period, I existed. I suppose I was tough so I stayed alive. But I used to make extra money after business hours by designing cigar labels.'[3] At twenty-three he went to London and started the slow climb upwards. Writing in *The Bookman* for October 1925, Arthur Rackham commented on his own struggles: 'I think I may say that at the beginning of my career I had far from an easy time. I was working mainly as a freelance for various illustrated journals and magazines. Work was hard to get and not well paid, and such efforts as I made along the lines I have since followed received little encouragement. And then came the Boer War. That really was a very thin time indeed for me . . .'.

The art schools of that day were dry, dirty and dispiriting places, but any training was perhaps better than none and for those newly arrived in town the schools provided at least a common meeting ground, congenial friends and, for the lucky ones, some inspired teaching. The nineteenth century had seen the proliferation of private art schools, the better ones rivalling the Royal Academy Schools on which they were modelled, the function of which was to train students for entry to the Royal Academy itself. One of the oldest and best known was the St John's Wood School of Art. Rex Vicat Cole, who joined 'The Wood' in 1887 with J. Byam Shaw and Lewis Baumer, recalled: 'Our task was to draw from the antique for five and a half days a week.'

The atmosphere of such schools was indeed far from encouraging. In darkish rooms peopled in silence by tidy youngsters and frigid casts of Hermes, Illysus, Theseus and Discobolus, talking was strictly forbidden except during 'rest' periods, and the only sounds were the gentle scrubbing of 'stumps' on paper and the whispered comments of the master. 'Stumping', then in vogue, and practised in all art schools, was the art of drawing in tone by pushing powdered chalk about with the end of a 'stump' of tightly rolled paper. Highlights could be improved with India rubber. Those studying for the entrance examination to the Royal Academy Schools worked their way through a carefully graded programme: 'First a fortnight was spent in imitating the light and shade of a cup and ball; followed by a cast of ornament in high relief. Next came six outline and one finished drawing, of each of the features. After these, drawings of hands and feet, a mask, the head and bust and finally a cast of the whole figure.'[4] Heath Robinson, then at the Islington Art School, had a similar experience: 'We became so accustomed to drawing fragments that we were inclined to prefer figures in a state of mutilation to the commonplace examples with the normal number of limbs.'[5] Success at 'The Wood' was crowned by permission to stretch up a sheet of double elephant Whatman paper to make a painting in preparation for the Royal Academy Schools. The long studio hours were only relieved by often dry lectures on anatomy and perspective, or, more happily, by the short rest periods when the boys could rush out into the yard and play football. There were more cheerful interludes, however. Sometimes, for the students' enjoyment during rest periods, the principal, A. A. Calderon, would fold up his frock coat and perform astonishing feats on a horizontal bar, and when the silence and tedium became too much to bear they could always be overcome by the furtive rolling of a cannon ball the length of the studio, or broken by rapturous whistling in imitation of bird song.[6] Speaking to girl students was forbidden, and strict segregation of the

3. Ibid.
4. Rex Vicat Cole, *The Art and Life of Byam Shaw* (Lippincott, Philadelphia, 1932), p. 24.
5. W. Heath Robinson, *My Line of Life* (Blackie, Glasgow, 1938), p. 72.
6. Rex Vicat Cole, *The Art and Life of Byam Shaw* (Lippincott, Philadelphia, 1932), p. 24.

FIGURE 4. Ernest Shepard
John Crompton teaching at the Royal Academy. From *Drawn from Life*, Methuen, 1961

sexes was common to many schools. Laurence Housman and his sister Clemence enrolled together at Miller's Lane School, South Lambeth: 'While my sister learned wood-engraving Ricketts and Shannon were doing the same thing in an adjoining room; but though there were communicating doors, the men's and the women's classes were kept respectably separate.'[7]

Byam Shaw and Cole went on to found their own School of Art in Kensington in 1910. Shaw, who died early in 1919, and Cole, who carried on the School until 1926, ran a drawing and painting course with the emphasis firmly on life drawing supplemented with classes in illustration, perspective and anatomy.

The teaching staffs of such schools were regarded with an awe difficult to imagine today. It was the age of 'Great Men', and many of them lived up to the part. Ernest Shepard, who started at Heatherley's Art School in 1896, remembered the principal, John Compton, as

an imposing presence. He wore a beige frock coat and a flowering salmon-pink tie. He was a small man, but his carriage lent him height so that he seemed to tower above me. To be addressed as Mister Shepard was startling. His criticisms were conducted in the plural. Standing before my drawing he would say: 'If we look at our legs, Mister Shepard, I think we shall find them a trifle on the heavy side.' Nothing seemed to put him out and he never forgot his dignity. It was a rare thing to see him smile.[8]

Graham Sutherland remembers Edmund Sullivan at Goldsmith's as a grand figure of 'extreme elegance, always beautifully dressed and with a

7. Laurence Housman, *The Unexpected Years* (Cape, 1937), p. 107.
8. Ernest Shepard, *Drawn from Life* (Methuen, 1961), p. 93.

FIGURE 5. Edmund Sullivan
A photograph of c. 1918 and an unfinished self-portrait (pen and ink over pencil)

monocle which added to the picture.'[9] A fellow student, Rowland Hilder, recalled that 'in appearance he so closely resembled Asquith that as he walked through the park people very naturally doffed their hats to him.'[10] His students enjoyed his velvet suits and his grand manner enormously and looked upon him with respect. A great draughtsman, he was perhaps an even better teacher, and encouraged his students to believe with Blake that the more distinct, sharp and wiry the bounding line, the more perfect the work of art. In his view the drawn line should have the vitality of a bow drawn across a violin, producing a sympathetic effect as it moved.[11] To help his students achieve rapidity and sureness of execution he made up sketch-pads for them from cheap litho paper and took them on sketching forays on rattling suburban trains. 'Technically', remembered Sutherland, 'he taught one a great deal and naturally,

bearing in mind the nature of his own work, a great deal about pens and what they would do. "One sun, one horizon" was a particular maxim of his.' Something of his style, wit and scholarship is preserved in his writings, notably *The Art of Illustration* (1921).

These full-time schools however were concerned with 'art' and not 'illustration', the two being seen as distinctly separate. There were then no specific 'graphic design' courses (indeed the term had not been coined) but 'commercial art' was understood, if not admired.

In the introduction to his Press Art School's

9. Letter to the author, April 1975.
10. Conversation with the author, 1974.
11. A musical simile that was frequently used. Joseph Pennell, in *Pen Drawing and Pen Draughtsmen* (1899) advised the pen artist to have the same amount of preparation as a great violinist, remarking that 'there are not more great pen draughtsmen today than there are great violinists.'

Advanced Course of Instruction (1919), Percy Bradshaw pointed out that 'the career of the average professional painter is nowadays almost a hopeless one for the man who has no private means.' In support of this view he quoted some recent Christie's auction prices, noting a Tissot which had fetched only four guineas. It was undoubtedly extremely difficult for artists turned out by the art schools to survive and many turned to book work, magazine illustration and advertising for their living. In Bradshaw's view they were then destined for a shock, for 'editors and the public want clever, original up-to-date sketches and drawings with life and character in them – not art school studies and stodgy paintings of such classical subjects as the Government Board of Education encourage.' In his autobiography he commented that the job of the art schools 'was to train *Artists* – not mere Black and White men; and they were emphatically not concerned with finding a market for their students' work. These students were very familiar with gipsy girls, Italian peasants, Greek maidens, and other stock models of the Life Class. Editors wanted artists who could draw policemen, and Pullman cars, pretty girls and smart men.'[12]

It is to Bradshaw's credit that in devising a correspondence course to meet this need he was in direct contact with these editors and in many cases even persuaded them into the role of part-time tutors. If ever anyone saw an opportunity and took it with both hands it was Bradshaw. At that time the successful illustrator was something of a popular hero. He moved in an aura of romance in the manner of present-day film stars, actors and popular novelists; his autograph was coveted, his activities fit material for gossip columnists; his fan mail was enormous, the mannerisms of his style were mimicked by countless schoolboys, and his drawings were cut from magazines and carefully pasted into scrap albums with society beauties from *Country Life*, war heroes, Christmas cards and coloured scraps. Bradshaw was an impresario with a sharp eye for talent and a gift for organisation. His course offered the prospect of success to any

that cared to follow his detailed instructions. His advertisements could hardly be missed for his photograph appeared as often in the popular press as the Player's sailor or Johnnie Walker and looked just as dependable.

During his early days contributing drawings to the *Boys' Own Paper*, Bradshaw was inundated with letters from aspiring young people sending sketches for criticism and seeking advice. His correspondence grew at such a rate that the problem it presented could not be ignored. With a capital of £100, a desk in his dining-room and an Accrington bank clerk as a first pupil, Bradshaw founded the Press Art School. Within a few years it had so expanded that he was forced to take larger premises at Tudor House, Forest Hill. His first lessons included, predictably, 'the neglect of black and white drawing by art schools', and more usefully 'Advice to students by famous pen draughtsmen', 'Black and white mediums and materials', 'The formation of a Reference Library', 'Dealing with Editors', 'Story Illustration', and 'Line Reproduction'. The down-to-earth approach proved popular and gaps in his own knowledge were filled by pressing into service the art editors of *The Tatler, Bystander, Illustrated London News, Sketch* and *Strand* magazines and also the art directors of such leading publishers of illustrated books as Blackie's and Hodder and Stoughton. With the outbreak of the First World War, Bradshaw's school seemed in danger of collapse, but with the skill of an accomplished entrepreneur he turned the war to his advantage and through clever advertising swelled the ranks of his students at the rate of several thousands per year – including twelve generals. Sketching was then in vogue; many a lonely Tommy thumbing his way through *Pearson's* or *The Strand* during a lull in the fighting felt the urge to draw and whiled away quiet moments making perky drawings in the style of Bruce Bairnsfather or Phil May. Add the importance of the postman to the soldier and

12. Percy Bradshaw, *Drawn from Memory* (Chapman and Hall, 1943), p. 40.

Bradshaw's success was assured: by 1918 he employed twenty-two full-time assistants and the GPO needed a special van to deliver his mail. His advertisements carried the encouraging legend 'sketching is really the jolliest thing possible'. Referring to this period in later life Bradshaw once remarked: 'The only difficulty I had was keeping going *between* wars.'[13] One pupil of these years was Fougasse (C. K. Bird) whose calligraphic satire was to become well known in the next war. Ralph Steadman too has confessed to owing his first instruction to Bradshaw's course.

One of Bradshaw's great talents was his ability to encourage established artists to give freely of their time and advice. He not only persuaded well-known illustrators to contribute to his books, but also assembled the work of some illustrators in a series of large portfolios published as *The Art of the Illustrator* in 1916. Each consisted of a photograph of the artist, ten pages of descriptive text and a series of reproductions showing one work, usually through six stages. Detailed information on paper sizes, pen nibs, inks and drawing boards used, together with a step by step exposé of method, left few tricks of the trade undisclosed. His *Advanced Course of Instruction* omitted nothing. Correspondents were advised to use John Mitchell's no. 0299 nib, costing one shilling for half a gross, and Gillot's Lithographic Crow Quill no. 659 for fine work (also used and recommended by Pennell) and to buy Goodall's Bristol Board and a bottle of Chinese white for repairing mistakes. The portfolios highlighted the work of C. E. Brock, Harry Rountree, W. Heath Robinson, Lawson Wood, W. Russell Flint, Cyrus Cuneo, Frank Reynolds, Bert Thomas, E. J. Sullivan and Dudley Hardy. One can envy Bradshaw the trips he made to interview contributors; to the aesthetic red brick of Bedford Park to find Russell Flint; to Cambridge, where he found C. E. Brock 'in a large old world studio, working with his three artist brothers in a Jane Austen atmosphere';[14] and to Glasgow to find Warwick Reynolds patiently rendering animals and fish in soft conté crayon at the top of a grim tenement. Some of

FIGURE 6. Phil May
Guttersnipes, Leadenhall Press, 1896

these artists later joined what he called his Advisory Board. Their written criticisms of students' drawings were often trenchant. Thus Fred Pegram: 'Men and women are not scarce – get 'em to sit for you'; or 'I notice that your child has no nose. There may, of course, be some special reason for the omission.' Leo Cheney advised one student: 'Don't keep on drawing pirates or ruffians biting the dust. This melodramatic death-grip stuff doesn't suit you.' For those who could take it such criticism proved extremely valuable. It was at least straight from the horse's mouth and the illustrators of that time won enormous respect from their pupils.

If Bradshaw's school was the best known, it had many rivals. Typical of these was 'Mr

13. To Rowland Hilder.
14. Percy Bradshaw, *Drawn from Memory* (Chapman and Hall, 1943), p. 76.

FIGURE 7. Lawson Wood in his studio

Charles E. Dawson's Art Course' obtainable from the Practical Correspondence College in the Strand. The single sheets sent to students, printed on one side only, were devoted to black-and-white work and were primarily aimed at training competent hacks for the advertising agencies, although the techniques discussed were common to all fields of illustration and give a good idea of the seriousness of the whole business. Each sheet was crammed with a variety of line drawings by Mr Dawson himself, and gave advice on materials and such techniques as line drawing, cross hatching, brush work, splatter work, bleach-out drawing, shadow drawings, silhouette drawing and tint work. Splatter work, in his description, consisted of covering the drawing with tracing paper in which holes had been cut corresponding to those parts of the drawing to which 'splatter' was to be added. A toothbrush brushed with Indian ink was held over the drawing and the bristles scraped with a pen-knife to cause a fine spray to cover the drawing (or, if held wrongly, the artist). It was more usual to strike the brush with a ruler, which gave greater control. Bleach-out work was extensively used for newspapers and magazines, where haste and descriptive accuracy were vital and costs had to be kept low. A matt-surfaced bromide paper was used and the photographic print made rather pale; over this the artist could work rapidly in ink. The photo was then bleached out using iodine bleach leaving the pen drawing ready for the blockmaker. Tint work involved the application of mechanical tints then available. Stock tints, as they were called, were supplied by such firms as the Swain Engraving Company, who transferred them to the metal plate before etching. Parts of the plate, where tints were not wanted, were protected with a 'resist'. The tints themselves were patterns finely engraved upon metal, inked with a special thick ink and printed on a gelatine sheet which was then pressed onto the waiting block. All the artist had to do was to mark his drawing in blue pencil with the number of the required tint and an indication of where it was wanted. Like the bleach-out technique this process was used primarily for commercial purposes, but it can sometimes be detected in book illustration.

Dawson was less helpful when he turned from practicalities to general advice: 'when drawing masonry try to make it look like stonework' and 'the secret of success in pen dot work is to ink a dot at a time, a big pen for big dots and a smaller pen for smaller dots' were typical, and it was undoubtedly the detailed practical advice on materials which accounted for the popularity of these courses.

Artists' magazines such as *The Artist* were full of advertisements for such courses, some of them run by practising artists themselves. There was the A.B.C. School of Drawing founded in 1912 in Pilgrim Street, which advertised that students wishing to specialize in story illustration would receive a practical training from an experienced book illustrator. Adrian Hill ran a postal tuition course, and Arthur Ferrier supplemented his income by taking a few pupils and writing articles on illustration full of 'tips'. His advice on finding models, for example, was to go to the film studios: finding them in the street was possible, but presented difficulties – 'The thought of being taken for a cheap masher is a painful one.' He also advised the budding illustrator to invest in useful 'props' and to keep a stock of bowler hats, toppers, golfing clothes and evening wear.

Getting started was not easy. Novice illustrators had to do battle with publishers' art editors in a world where good illustrators were not hard to come by and in which competition was consequently fierce. Armed with portfolios of their best drawings they trudged the concentration of streets around Covent Garden which included Grant Richards in Leicester Square, Heinemann and J. M. Dent in Bedford Street, George Bell, Pearson's in Henrietta Street and

Newnes in Southampton Street. John Hassall admitted to being 'metaphorically kicked out of every editorial office in London'. Many publishers employed a guard dog in an outer office to deal with the stream of aspirants. Frank Swinnerton performed this service at J. M. Dent's; he was paid to sit in an office whose walls were covered with drawings by Beardsley, Heath Robinson and Leslie Brooke and deal with all callers, 'and with the lady art students in long cloaks and eccentric witch like hats who brought so many hopeless children's books for consideration. Every hour of every day some new person pushed open the door which was light and looked heavy so that the nervous smashed it back against its stopper and very nearly burst into hysterical tears.'[15]

Publishers of magazines usually proved more amenable, for their demand for illustrations at this time was virtually limitless, and many artists were very glad of the work they provided. Heath Robinson's earliest sale was a drawing for *Little Folks* published by Cassell; John Hassall and Cecil Aldin first appeared in *The Graphic* in 1891 and Arthur Rackham's earliest sale was to the 4 October 1884 issue of *Scraps*, which had earlier taken the first published drawing by Edmund Sullivan. When H. M. Bateman was fourteen his mother anxiously wrote to Phil May for advice and received the sensible reply: 'Your son shows a strong comic bent, but the proper thing would be for him to learn to draw seriously.' This he did, and after a spell at Westminster Art School and Goldsmith's Institution successfully sold his first efforts to *Scraps* in 1903; he was then sixteen.[16] For many artists whose first opportunities had come from magazines the demise of the gift book market, caused by the First World War, meant a return to magazine illustration. Charles Robinson was particularly badly hit by the war. His daughter recalled that in 1915 her father 'had no money, and no books to illustrate, but with six children,

15. Frank Swinnerton, *Autobiography* (Hutchinson, 1937), p. 80.
16. Michael Bateman, *The Man Who Drew the Twentieth Century* (Macdonald, 1972).

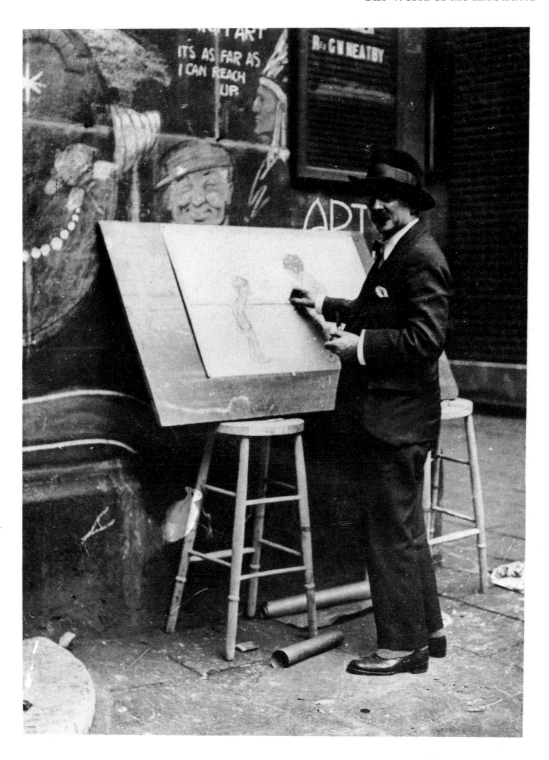

FIGURE 8. Charles Robinson drawing for charity, c. 1920

FIGURE 9. Mabel Lucie Attwell in her studio, c. 1923

five at school, he was very glad to get odd magazine jobs to do.'[17]

Other outlets were not to be scorned, and there was plenty of commercial work to be done; some even found this work congenial and profitable. Mabel Lucie Attwell's output was enormous; posters, postcards, advertisements, fabric designs of all kinds flowed from her pen, together with patterns for a range of pottery and china figures for Shelley Potteries and elaborate biscuit tin houses, trees and fairy cottages for Crawfords. By the early 1920s her dimpled children were everywhere, as common and as popular as the cherubic and ridiculously solemn bald-headed old men drawn by Heath Robinson, who were soon to be found clambering around the pages of *The Bystander*, *Pearson's*, *The Sketch* or *The Graphic*, or engrossed in absurd activities on behalf of a variety of commercial firms. Charles Robinson, John Hassall and Harry Rountree

were typical of many who in the post-war years turned increasingly to advertising. At the smart end of the market commercial giants such as Lever Brothers, Selfridge's and Dewar's employed the masters of line to give distinction to their publicity. Edmund Sullivan, Garth Jones and Byam Shaw were in demand. Sullivan did a splendid series of drawings for Selfridge's with such stirring titles as 'The Spirit of Empire' and 'The Romance of Trade'. In America the opportunities were even greater, which only helped to siphon the best talent away from purely book work. Remuneration for this kind of work could be extremely good, though the rewards for book illustration could vary widely, success depending largely upon popularity and a good agent. With the help of the latter an artist could expect to keep his originals and perhaps sell them. Many

17. Conversation with the author, May 1974.

artists, notably Rackham, Dulac and Kay Nielsen, regularly exhibited their drawings and sold them for respectable sums at such places as the Dowdeswell and Leicester galleries.

Very often publishers only waited for a book to go out of copyright before quickly issuing a new, illustrated version. In 1842 the period of copyright had been extended to forty-two years, or the life of the author plus seven years, and this obtained until 1911 when the term was extended to the life of the author plus fifty years. Thus the gift book era coincided with the release from copyright of a number of Victorian classics. The expiry in 1907 of the British copyright of *Alice's Adventures in Wonderland* was celebrated before the end of the year by the publication of no fewer than eight illustrated versions.[18] *The Water Babies* was freed from copyright restrictions in 1905 and Stevenson's *Treasure Island* (1883) and *Kidnapped* (1886) became available in 1925 and 1928, causing a rush of new, illustrated editions. Where this happened the illustrator had a chance to secure royalties, which could accumulate over the years and become a useful supplementary income. Arthur Rackham relied heavily, in his later life, on royalties and the sale of originals.[19] In one marvellous year, 1920, he earned £7000, equivalent to £67,555 today (1984),[20] but generally his income in the 1920s fluctuated between £1500 and £3500, at a time when the professional classes were doing quite nicely on £500 and farm workers less happily on £75 a year.[21] Few illustrators were in this class, however, and most made do with a good deal less. In 1898 the almost unknown Heath Robinson had been paid £187 (or £5339 today – a quite respectable sum) for an edition of the *Arabian Nights* containing not fewer than 250 drawings, many full-page, that is about fifteen shillings (£21 today) per drawing. This was considerably less than the £3 per drawing that Hugh Thomson was accustomed to.[22] In 1909 he received only £250 from Hodder & Stoughton for thirty colour plates and cover designs, and £1.11.6d each for the black-and-white illustrations, to Kipling's *Song of the English*. By 1913 he had advanced to £200

(£4825 today) for his illustrations to *The Water Babies*, 110 drawings including eight colour plates and fifty-two full-page line – a little less than £2 per drawing.[23]

This contrasts poorly with the £500 Arthur Rackham received in 1909 from J. M. Dent for fourteen illustrations to *Gulliver's Travels* plus fifteen for an edition of Lamb's *Tales*, that is, almost twice what Heath Robinson received for his Kipling. By this time Rackham and Dulac were in a class of their own and could charge accordingly. In 1912 Hodder & Stoughton paid Dulac £700 (£16,889) for his thirty colour plates to *Hans Andersen*, and in the same year another £700 for twenty-eight colour plates and other decorations to Poe's *Bells and other poems*: this is about £582 per drawing at present rates – riches indeed. In that same year Charles Robinson had been content with an outright payment of only £70 (£1688) for his illustrations to *Bee*, i.e. exactly one tenth of Dulac's fee for *Hans Anderson*. The First World War badly affected many artists and some reputations did not survive the end of the great period of the illustrated gift book. Dulac and Rackham were favoured in that their popularity never seemed to wane; others were much less fortunate.

In times of fluctuating prosperity, artists naturally relied upon one another for help, and also upon the clubs which they formed and joined and which performed a variety of functions. Liveliest of the meeting grounds was undoubtedly the London Sketch Club, founded in 1898 by Phil May, John Hassall, Dudley Hardy and Tom Browne as a place to meet, eat, draw and drink in congenial company. Meetings were held every Friday evening in an old studio

18. For an account of them see *The Illustrators of Alice* by Graham Ovenden (Academy Editions, 1972).
19. He once admitted that his technique of colour-tinted line drawing was prompted by the need to turn line illustrations into saleable watercolours.
20. Derek Hudson, *Arthur Rackham* (Heinemann, 1960), p. 70.
21. Monetary equivalents supplied by The Bank of England, March 1984.
22. Percy Muir, *Victorian Illustrated Books* (Batsford, 1971), p. 198.
23. John Lewis, *Heath Robinson* (Constable, 1973), p. 149.

FIGURE 10. The London Sketch Club, Wells Street Studio, c. 1914.
Harry Rountree pulling Homer's nose and Harold Earnshaw on the far right

next to a brewery in the Marylebone Road, the premises being cosy rather than elegant. Membership quickly increased, and it was not long before W. Heath Robinson, Cecil Aldin, Edmund Dulac, Lawson Wood, Frank Reynolds, H. M. Bateman, Harold Earnshaw and Harry Rountree joined the growing company of illustrators and cartoonists. Their Friday evenings began with two hours of drawing from a model or illustrating a subject chosen in advance, after which chairs and easels were moved aside to allow for the setting of a long trestle table and a plain but nourishing meal (steak pudding and potatoes was a common dish). Supper was followed by home-made entertainments of the light-hearted variety then fashionable in arty circles – funny turns, dressing up, impersonations, recitations, comic songs, practical jokes and perhaps a sing-song to conclude. Such hearty pleasures provided a welcome relief after

a week spent in lonely concentration over a drawing board.

Diversions of this kind were not to be found at gatherings of more august societies, such as the Art Workers' Guild. The Guild went in for formal proceedings, lectures and intellectual debates with great wits scoring points – G. B. Shaw used to attend. Its declared aim was to bring together practitioners in all the arts for their mutual benefit, although its meetings were sometimes regarded by 'mere illustrators' as rather upstage and decidedly highbrow. Founded in 1884 by five young architectural disciples of Norman Shaw, it was from the first inspired by William Morris's vision of an earthly paradise, and served as a platform for the Arts and Crafts movement and the ideas of its progenitors: Ruskin, Webb, Morris, Lethaby, Emery Walker, Walter Crane and others. Selwyn Image in his frequent addresses to the Guild spoke the authentic Arts and Crafts neo-gothic dialect. 'Look you,' he said to the assembled Brethren in 1906, 'it has done a great work; it has been a great influence for good up and down the land!' The fortnightly meetings discussed such topics as 'Things Amiss with Art and Industry', 'Leadwork', 'The Blacksmith's Art', 'Dyeing of Textiles' and 'Memorial Brasses.' Something of the flavour of these meetings was recorded by the Secretary, H. J. L. Massé:

A frequent speaker was F. Hamilton Jackson. He was sometimes a trifle too dogmatic and a little longwinded, but he was always interesting. His collection of tinted lantern slides to illustrate *Romanesque Architecture in Southern France* was the finest ever shown at a Guild meeting . . . Joseph Pennell irritated his audience by beginning each sentence with 'And I do think . . .' and then leaving them unfinished.

The ensuing discussions were not always good-natured; on one occasion at least the Secretary recorded a bout of 'fisticuffs' though tact forbad him to record the names of those involved. 'Illustrators readily make friends', he noted, but 'Architects seem more conscious of a feeling of rivalry.' Arguments too could become heated; the keen discussion of Impressionism in January 1908 led to the consumption of one gallon of whisky in the interval.[24] The business of the Guild was, and is, conducted as a slightly elaborate ritual which owes something to masonic precepts, but despite the formalities many illustrators of those days found it a useful body to belong to; it has always had close connections with the arts and education, and initiated various charitable and benevolent activities which were especially valuable before the advent of the welfare state.

Both the Royal Watercolour Society and the Royal Institute of Painters in Watercolours could prove useful, through the social life they supplied, in finding wealthy clients, for it must be remembered that many illustrators were also successful watercolourists in an age when the medium was taken seriously and could even lead to a knighthood, as it did for Sir William Russell Flint. Quite different from the London Sketch Club with its knockabout humourists and irreverent fun was the Chelsea Arts Club, said at one time to be almost an extension of the Royal Academy itself. It was even unkindly suggested that one could not hope to be an RA unless one graduated through membership of the Club. Though untrue, this gives some idea of the importance attached to membership: the chief occupations seem to have been billiards, eating, drinking and talking shop at Academy level.

24. H. J. L. Massé, *The Art Workers' Guild* (Oxford, 1935), p. 162.

CHAPTER 4

Decorative Illustration

Whilst the convention of grouping like artists together for the purposes of ordering a narrative has its attractions for the historian, the practice may often mislead the reader into the assumption of a 'school' where none existed. Nevertheless it is possible to discern at the turn of the century a number of artists whose concern lay more with the decorative possibilities of the book as a whole than with any close interpretation of the text. In this they reflected the contemporary passion for the arts of decoration, an enthusiasm which was fuelled by the Arts and Crafts movement. It is significant that a number of the artists discussed in this chapter were leading figures in the movement and furthered its ideals with contributions in a wide variety of media. Some, like Crane and Bell, were prominent in the fine art world and moved in academic and artistic circles to which mere illustrators could not aspire, a world of well-upholstered studios and Academy banquets rather than art editors' offices and Sketch Club dinners. The distinctive grouping of these artists at the time was more real than we can easily imagine today.[1] The illustrated books of the 'decorative' artists reflect this distinction: they were gift books *par excellence* and sometimes supremely useless; they were art for art's sake. They were also, on occasions, extremely beautiful. Their artists showed a predilection for an 'architectural' framework and often balanced text and illustrations in panels of equal weight – a practice which owes much to the example set by Walter Crane (1845–1915).

There is a curious lack of warmth about Crane's impeccable graphic style. But his influence was such that he should not be ignored, for it cannot be maintained that he was primarily concerned with the expressive use of the new processes, or with new themes or markets. His style harked back variously to a Pre-Raphaelite past,[2] or to a prim and decorous 'golden age' of Greece. His Toy Books of the 1870s, which contain his best work for Evans, are amongst the earliest examples of the taste for Japanese art that was to become a hallmark of the Aestheticism of the Beardsley period; yet he will always be associated with William Morris and the Arts and Crafts movement, of which he was such a sturdy pillar. Crane spent his energies prodigally: he was at various times lecturer, writer, teacher, painter and illustrator, as well as designer of murals, ceramics, textiles, wallpapers, and decorations in plasterwork, glass and faience. It is therefore not surprising that what was spread so widely was sometimes spread rather thinly.

His nursery favourites *The Baby's Opera* (1877), *The Baby's Bouquet* (1879) and *The Baby's Own Aesop* (1887) are wonderful examples of the colour printer's art, but today their chief interest is the insight they give into that strangely exquisite mixture of styles now known as the Aesthetic movement. Aesthetes there certainly were, but it is less easy to see in the period,

1. The 'high art' prejudice against illustrators had also been levelled at Victorian engravers, who were not admitted on an equal footing to the Royal Academy until 1928. Cf. Hilary Beck, *Victorian Engravings* (HMSO, 1973).
2. In *An Artist's Reminiscences* he tells of saving his pocket money to buy Moxon's *Tennyson*.

the late Seventies and Eighties, a 'movement'. Crane's rather flat and demure figures gesticulate elegantly against a 'greenery yallery' background of sunflower gardens, lily borders and tall red-brick Queen Anne houses. As in so much of his work it is rather as if the population of Botticelli's paintings, having taken lessons in deportment from Burne-Jones, were to be found promenading in Bedford Park or Kensington. It was perhaps to his disadvantage to be living at a time of rapid technical change, from wood-engraving to photo-engraving, for he had, inevitably, a foot in each camp. His wood-engraved illustrations appeared together with Kate Greenaway's in *The Quiver of Love* (Marcus Ward, 1876), at which time it would have been hard to foresee his later appearance with Jessie King in Mantegazza's *Legend of the Flowers* (Foulis, 1908), in which his four-colour halftones look very ill at ease with her line-block decorations. There was always something ponderous about his approach and a lifelessness about his figures that make them seem much less human than those of Kate Greenaway. In her books it is the figures, expressionless though they often are, that dominate; in Crane's it is the decorative layout as a whole and the backgrounds in particular. His strongly architectural style was to stamp its mark on a younger generation, some of whom, Harold Nelson and A. Garth Jones for example, are now all but forgotten.

There is something, too, of Crane's architectural Arts and Crafts approach in the production of the Birmingham School, in the work of Arthur Gaskin, E. H. New, Bernard Sleigh, Henry Payne and C. M. Gere. The rather colourless books of the Birmingham Guild of Handicraft followed the precepts of Arthur Mackmurdo's Century Guild and were well within the tradition of Morris's Kelmscott Press. Morris had visited the School in 1894 and addressed it on the subject of book-making. In 1893 he published at the Kelmscott Press *News From Nowhere* with a frontispiece by Gere, and in 1896 an edition of Spenser's *Shepheard's Calendar* with illustrations by A. J. Gaskin: in all it produced the Birmingham School met with his approbation. Arthur

Gaskin (1862–1928) was perhaps the most accomplished of these artists and his *Hans Andersen* of 1893 shows the clear influence of both Crane (The Angels and the Child) and Burne-Jones. On its appearance the *Studio* critic noted:

Andersen is everybody's favourite and this Winter it is particularly noticeable that the opposite ideals of bookmaking should each choose the same classic for a typical instance of their separate taste. Indeed by noticing which edition is on the drawing room table – for no-one of taste can afford to be without at least one – callers at a strange house may safely deduce therefrom the tendencies of their hostess and risk opinion on current art with confidence.

He went on to explain that the difference lay in Mr Gaskin's fulfilling 'the expectation aroused by William Morris . . . as opposed to those whose sympathies and styles are drawn from Paris, either directly or by way of America.' This presumably refers to *The Little Mermaid and other stories*, illustrated by T. R. Weguelin with wash drawings reproduced by a rather coarse halftone, published at the same time. Such remarks only corroborate the assumption that these books were not meant for the nursery. There is no doubt that illustration was taken very seriously at this time in cultured circles, and nowhere more than in Birmingham, where the newly built Art School was the focus of much industry.[3] In this ornate enclave of tile and terracotta, in the shadow of an art gallery filled by local generosity with the best examples of Pre-Raphaelite art, heady enthusiasm for the arts and crafts was generated. Morris and Crane, Selwyn Image, Mackmurdo and Horne were the heroes, and the woodcuts of the fifteenth century, particularly those in Aldus's *Hypnerotomachia Poliphili*, their models. Mrs Arthur Gaskin was to make a considerable reputation for herself as author and illustrator of children's books in a clear, slightly wooden style. The work of Edmund H. New (1871–1931) followed this

---

3. Witness the disproportionate number of entries for *Studio* Prize Competitions from Edgbaston, Handsworth and Moseley.

pattern. His architectural drawings are also reminiscent of the work of F. L. Griggs (1876–1938) – who was not a member of the group. New is best known for his line drawings to Mackail's *Life of William Morris* and for the topographical drawings he provided for such books as Bertram Windle's *Malvern Country* (1901) and *Shakespeare Country* (1899). If Griggs had something of New's approach he also showed a more lively imagination which was given full rein in his etchings of architectural fantasies – not so grand as those of Piranesi, but then his subject was typically the Cotswolds of the Tudors rather than the Rome of the Caesars. His best-known drawings were done for Macmillan's Highways and Byways series, but they are not well reproduced. This deservedly popular guide to the English counties brought together the talents of Griggs and Hugh Thomson, each of whom made drawings for several volumes. It is to Thomson's credit that his drawings do not compare unfavourably with those of Griggs, for the latter had had an architectural training which invested his line with authority and feeling.

Associated with the Birmingham Group through his membership of the Tempera Society, Frederick Cayley Robinson (1862–1927) produced work of a highly distinctive nature which showed few of the School's mannerisms. Instead he turned to the work of Puvis de Chavannes and the Renaissance painters for inspiration. In his illustrations, notably to Maeterlinck's *Blue Bird* (1911), and *Genesis* from the Riccardi Press (1914), the figures are placed and grouped so precisely and dressed in such cool colours as to have the appearance of statuary. Robinson indeed had a fondness for the almost empty picture frame from which his figures are sometimes in danger of slipping altogether. He did not illustrate many books, which is a pity, for the *Genesis* must have claims to being one of the finest English illustrated books ever produced, and the lightly coloured pencil drawings achieve a sense of mystery and majesty particularly appropriate to the subject.

Whilst not a member of the Birmingham Group, Maxwell Armfield (1881–1972) was closely linked with them. The list of his illustrated books is not long, and contains few titles with illustrations to equal his ones to William Morris's *Life and Death of Jason* (1915). These are surprisingly austere drawings for someone who had so obviously fallen in step with the earlier fashion of artistic aestheticism. A self-portrait of 1901 shows Armfield with a Beardsley coiffure, sporting a cravat in the form of an enormous bow and a daisy in his buttonhole, with volumes by Rossetti and Maeterlinck on a shelf and carnations in a vase beside him. In contrast, the drawings for the *Jason*, whilst illustrating a Grecian tale by the great medievalist, speak more of the Viennese Secession. Feeling perhaps that some justification was needed, the artist wrote a prefatory note to the book, stating that it had been his intention to provide a 'sense of unity, not so much with the ideas of the text as with the book as book . . . to consider the embellishments not so much as illustration proceeding *from* the text as a continuation of the binding and page purposing to present the text to the eye.' This describes well the decorative artist's approach. It is indeed a fine book, if only of ordinary trade materials, with an elegant mauve cloth binding and adequate straightforward typography. More typical of his art perhaps was the earlier *Færy Tales from Hans Andersen* (Dent, 1910), where the twenty-four colour plates are in the messy Byam Shawish watercolour tradition which demanded the finest half-tone work. Armfield is perhaps better known for his tempera paintings, his books about his travels in America and Italy and his stage decorations.

Excellent, if limited, work was produced by Birmingham students such as Sidney Heath, Winifred Smith, G. C. France and Florence Rudland, but the road they travelled was a cul-de-sac, and Morris was surely wrong when he announced: 'The only thing that is new strictly speaking is the rise of the Birmingham School of book decorators. These young men – Mr Gaskin, Mr New and Mr Gere – have given a new start to the art of book decorating.' By 1894, as Joseph Pennell foresaw, the direction lay elsewhere.

However, Morris's idea of the 'decorated' book based on a respect for the unity of its elements (paper, type, and illustration) was fortunately shared by the more adventurous artists of the Art Nouveau book, although they might not have agreed with him on the choice of those elements. Indeed, from Beardsley to Housman it was the respect for the printed page that was the hallmark of the school – a distinctly British and bookish concern that over-rode all fluctuations of taste.

With this concern for the page went an architectural sense of design. Both traits are shown to perfection in the work of Robert Anning Bell (1863–1933). Trained in an architect's office and sympathetic to Florentine art (a sympathy he expressed in his own mosaics, murals, and painted bas-reliefs), he became, like Crane, a teacher of design,[4] and his book illustrations offered practical examples to others. Early examples of his style were two tiny volumes contributed to Dent's Banbury Cross series: *Jack the Giant Killer and Beauty and the Beast* and *The Sleeping Beauty and Dick Whittington*, both published in 1894. There were twelve volumes in all; copies were bound in a variety of cloths, gold, apple green, maroon and white vellum. Each artist contributed thirty-five small line drawings, and these books must have been something of a bargain at one shilling each. Other artists included Alice Woodward, Isabel Adams, H. Granville Fell, Violet Holden and Charles Robinson. In the following year Dent brought out Bell's most successful book, *A Midsummer Night's Dream*. Here the almost square format has been used to good effect: there are many double-page spreads, each neatly or elaborately framed so that it does not run into the gutter. On other pages there are a variety of drawings – head- and tail-pieces, roundels and pictorial borders all drawn with lightness and vivacity. There is more than a hint of the influence of Charles Ricketts in his drawing of the cool classic rooms and courts that form the background to his figures. If fault can be found with them it is that his maidens are often a trifle insipid – not as cold as Crane's perhaps, but

definitely chaste. They are also much in evidence in his next major book, *Poems by John Keats* in Bell's Endymion series of 1897. Here are only too apparent the weaknesses of the decorative approach: a certain coldness and dullness which might please the typographical purist but which add little to the pleasure of the text. His Naiads in 'Endymion' and his Madeline in 'The Eve of Saint Agnes' have the pert good looks of Angela Brazil's pictured heroines. But there are surprises, and the plate 'I saw pale Kings and Princes too . . .', with its elongated figures and bold use of space, anticipates the designs of Edward Gordon Craig. Two other titles in the Endymion series came his way, *English Lyrics* (1898) and Shelley's *Poems* (1902). Nor can any survey of his work ignore *The Tempest* (1901), which might be regarded as one of the best produced books of the period if the printing, especially of the ordinary trade editions, were not so poor. The blockmaking, too, is not of the best; writing to his friend George Frampton in November 1901, Bell remarked:

I send you a copy of what I think is the best book I have done yet: it is also about the best in get up although they have treated me badly with the title page. Both those pages I had back to work on again after the first blocks were made and I strengthened them & did new little drawings for the swan and dolphin – but they made a new block of one so the difference of detail is not my fault.

The printing of most of the blocks is blotchy, which must have caused the artist considerable distress. The type chosen by Freemantle for this book was similar to those used by the Vale and Eragny presses, which, with the Ricketts style of illustration, gives the book an imitative air. Bell was less happy with colour, and his version of Palgrave's *Golden Treasury* (1907), though beautifully dressed in conventional gift book style, is disappointing as an example of his art. The smudgy colour plates are not helped by being tipped onto a dark-green Ingres paper.

4. In 1894 he was appointed Instructor in Painting and Design at Liverpool Municipal Craft School and went on to posts at Glasgow and the Royal College of Art.

No doubt these gift books put a strain on their illustrators, for their publishers, with an eye to sales, insisted on bulk, and fifty colour plates and twice as many line drawings were common.

Also engaged in illustrating books in a decorative vein were two artists whose careers were closely linked – J. Byam Shaw (1872–1919) and Eleanor Fortescue-Brickdale (1872–1945). Both were of that late Pre-Raphaelite persuasion which followed Lord Leighton and turned heretically to Titian, Veronese and other Venetian Post-Raphaelite painters for inspiration rather than to the Pre-Raphaelite art advocated by Ruskin and Rossetti. Byam Shaw had trained at the St John's Wood School and at the Royal Academy Schools in the Nineties with Heath Robinson and Lewis Baumer. Like many other students he turned to illustration to supplement his income, and, as with Heath Robinson, it was Bell's Endymion series which helped to put his drawings before a wider public – his title being an edition of Browning's poems. It is a young man's work, full of enthusiasm and inconsistency. Even allowing for the blockmaker's reduction the drawings are over-fine and the shading and cross-hatching he employed show how little he understood printers' requirements. The results compare badly with the illustrations by Bell or Heath Robinson in the same series. In 1899 Byam Shaw enjoyed success at the Royal Academy and a near sell out at his one-man show, as well as the publication of three illustrated books. One of these, a *Boccaccio* from George Allen in a florid Art Nouveau binding, contains some of his best illustrative work. Unfortunately, he seldom improved on these beginnings. His *Pilgrim's Progress* (Jack, 1904) is typical of the poorer sort of gift book that abounded at that time: a smart buckram exterior hides a collection of thirty poor colour plates and some worse printing. In 1914 the votary of Lord Leighton became the publicist of Gordon Selfridge, and Byam Shaw produced a number of drawings on such themes as 'The Romance of Trade' and 'The Spirit of Empire' to advertise the Oxford Street emporium. In these he returned to his old *Boccaccio* style and the

illustrations were none the worse for that. But it was an inauspicious year for publishing and his illustrated version of Laurence Hope's *Garden of Karma*, while showing evidence of a happier and looser style, came too late to be repeated. By the time the war ended his career was all but over too.

To some extent Byam Shaw's style was carried on in the work of Eleanor Fortescue-Brickdale (1872–1945). Her ambitions and inclinations, like his, were those of a painter, and she was a frequent exhibitor at the Royal Academy, showing watercolours for the most part.[5] Her talents as an illustrator were first remarked upon in *The Studio*; in March 1898, it reproduced some of her early line drawings made in a distinctly Pre-Raphaelite manner. By 1905, when Bell commissioned seventy line drawings for an edition of Tennyson's *Poems*, her style was well formed. During 1908 and 1909 she was busy on the watercolour illustrations for an ambitious series of poems and ballads for Chatto and Windus, a series including two volumes by her and two by Byam Shaw. Although clearly under his influence, her drawings look the more accomplished. The series comprises: Byam Shaw's *Legendary Ballads* and *Ballads and Lyrics* (1908), and her *Pippa Passes* (1908) and *Dramatis Personae* (1909) by Browning. Each volume has ten colour plates and was issued in a variety of editions, from the numbered *de luxe* to the rather ordinary. A better opportunity to study Fortescue-Brickdale's mature style was provided by her *Idylls of the King*, published by Hodder & Stoughton in 1911. There are in the quarto version twenty-one colour plates, full of Pre-Raphaelite imagery which must have seemed rather outmoded by then, but which nevertheless sorts well with Tennyson's poetry. Those familiar with Pre-Raphaelite painting will find much to remind them here of Collins and Holman Hunt, although her inclusion of fritillaries and a horse chestnut or two displays more botanical enthusiasm than historical accuracy. This is

5. G. L. Taylor, Introduction to *The Centenary Exhibition of Works by Eleanor Fortescue-Brickdale* (Ashmolean Museum, 1972), p. 4.

essentially a Victorian vision, such stuff as the dreams of Ruskin and Morris were made of, a world of fainting Rossetti heroines, glowing colours, brilliant fields and prancing steeds. Brickdale's contribution to the Autumn of the gift book after its golden Summer appeared in 1915 – *Old English Songs and Ballads* from Hodder & Stoughton. This and the Tennyson are easily the most attractive of her books. By contrast, *Fleur and Blanchefleur*, published by Daniel O'Connor in 1922, is hardly recognisable as her work. The illustrations are drawn in a stiff Lovat Fraserish style as though made with a reed pen. Inevitably change had to come in a changed world and this may partly account for the appearance of these works. Perhaps also the artist's work for stained glass had its effect. A third reason for the new simplicity of these drawings must have been her deteriorating eyesight. Her last illustrated book appeared in 1928 and thereafter she increasingly concentrated her efforts on designs for stained glass.

It must be admitted that the Pre-Raphaelitism of these two artists was at best of the late sentimental variety, mixing the hot hues of Rossetti's final chloral-tinted vision with the colour of the Venetians. One artist who managed to unite successfully bright early Pre-Raphaelite fervour with end-of-century Aestheticism was Laurence Housman (1865–1959), brother of the poet A. E. Housman. In the 1890s his fairy stories and book illustrations created a great stir. Due to failing eyesight his career as an illustrator was shortlived, and was all but over by 1900 when he commenced an unceasing flow of poems, plays and essays on pacifism, socialism, women's suffrage, censorship and other causes dear to him. In his earliest years he was grateful to Whistler's old enemy Harry Quilter ('Mr. 'Arry') for the commission to produce a series of drawings for George Meredith's poem *Jump to Glory Jane* (1892). Far from his best work, it nevertheless contained enough of his particular magic to catapult his own name into prominence. His celebrity was confirmed the following year with the publication of *Goblin Market* by Christina Rossetti. From then until the end of

the decade Housman produced some striking books: Jane Barlow's *End of Elfin Town* (1894), his own *Farm in Fairyland* (1894), *Green Arras* (1896) and *Field of Clover* (1898). In these volumes his fastidious and original ideas on the unity of subject, typography, illustration, format and binding were given full rein, and he achieved for his publishers, Kegan Paul, John Lane and Macmillan, a distinction in ordinary trade books which was seldom equalled by the more esoteric world of private printing. Writing in 1937 he recalled:

John Lane had what he called his 'nest of singing birds' . . . [;] in 1895 I became one of the ruck and he published my *Green Arras* . . . I was just then designing book covers for John Lane, so I naturally did what I thought an extra good one for myself: it was at all events rich and elaborate.[6]

The title-page and frontispiece are enclosed in borders of rolling scrolls of vine in his beloved knotwork style – a device he used for a number of other titles, in which the feeling is altogether different, despite more than a touch of Arts and Crafts influence. In Jane Barlow's *End of Elfin Town*, for example, the shadow of Beardsley can be felt in the bold use of black and white on the title-page, and the influence of Rossetti in the Afro-haired fairy folk who populate the eight crowded full plates. *Goblin Market* (1893), Housman's masterpiece, has the slim format that Lane was to adopt, notably for John Gray's *Silverpoints* of the same year with a binding by Charles Ricketts.[7] Lane's productions are so often thought of as epitomising the Nineties book that it is sometimes forgotten that it was the enterprising Macmillan who brought out *Goblin Market* and *Elfin Town*, as they had also earlier promoted Hugh Thomson. *Goblin Market* can lay claim to being the most beautiful book of the time. Certainly it is hard to fault, for

6. *The Unexpected Years* (Cape, 1937), p. 162.
7. A. J. A. Symons suggested (*The Fleuron*, vol. VII (1930), p. 111) that the model for the *Green Arras* binding of 1896 was Rickett's *Silverpoints* of 1893, but overlooked the fact that Housman had also designed the very similar *Goblin Market* of 1893.

binding, format and decoration are all wonderfully sympathetic to Christina Rossetti's poem. The poet herself was not impressed: 'I don't think my goblins were so ugly,' she wrote to the artist. Fortunately he received more cheering correspondence from Lord Leighton, and from Aubrey Beardsley an invitation to draw for *The Yellow Book*.

Laurence's sister Clemence, who had come to London with him in 1883, trained as a wood-engraver and was employed by *The Graphic* until the advance of process reproduction put her employer out of business. She turned to engraving for her brother, commencing with *The Field of Clover* (1898), although she had re-touched some of the process blocks of his earlier books, including *The House of Joy* (1895). Housman's work is thus a curious reversal of the usual course of events, his earliest work being reproduced by the process line block and later work by facsimile wood-engraving.

Any list of artists covering decorative illustrators of the classics at this time must include the names of A. Garth Jones, Harold Nelson, Percy Bullock, Paul Woodroffe, Herbert Cole, Henry Ospovat, Philip Connard and H. Granville Fell, and also to some extent those enormously popular artists Frank Brangwyn and Sir William Russell Flint. In most cases the quality of their work is very mixed, and nearly all of them are capable of giving as much disappointment as delight. Whilst working for the line block many of them show the distinct ancestry of the wood-engravers of the Sixties. Like Housman, Philip Connard (1875–1958) strongly reflects Arthur Boyd Houghton, but is perhaps more poetical. His two little books for Lane's Flowers of Parnassus series, particularly *Marpessa* by Stephen Phillips, run Housman very close. Garth Jones (1872–1930) produced few books of his own but his decorative line drawings are often to be found in company with colour plates by Byam Shaw. In these he showed a predilection for heroic figures, winged cherubs and the vaguely classical masonry that was popular with the architects of Edwardian banks. Jones was among the artists who contributed to

Bell's Endymion series and was nearly always employed for the small-format series of reprints which were then so popular with gift book publishers. Harold Nelson (1871–1946), too, did a considerable amount of this sort of work, of which Newnes's Caxton Series in limp leather is typical, and he provided numerous decorations for the popular series of art books issued by Bell. A major commission for him was *Early English Prose Romances* (1904), a period piece in the Kelmscott manner in which the many full-page and other decorations struggle to do justice to such archaic lines as 'Robert gate a murderer or bodkin, and thrast his mayster in the bely that his guttes fell at his fete.' Not surprisingly Nelson was happier working on a smaller scale and his *Book of Bookplates* (1904) contains the best of his work. Although it must be conceded that both Jones and Nelson were minor artists, their line drawings show remarkable sensitivity to the printed page.

Finally, we should not forget those artists whose illustrations usually consisted of colour reproductions of their own paintings, the best known of whom are Russell Flint (1880–1969), and Frank Brangwyn (1867–1956), whose decorous maidens and muscled sailors are to be found in a number of luxurious productions. Flint was the more prolific illustrator of the two. His *Song of Songs* (1909) is typical, and, as so often with his work, it is overdressed and given the deckle-edged treatment. Both Flint and Brangwyn were most at home when treating Oriental subjects which gave full scope to their delight in grouping colourful figures. Of all the colour-plate versions of *Omar Khayyám* (and there were many), few could excel in atmosphere Brangwyn's work of 1910. Born in Bruges in 1867, Brangwyn soon crossed the Channel, and at the age of fifteen was helping William Morris design textiles. After some while he went to sea as a ship's boy, sketching constantly, and saw Africa and Asia at first hand. His early illustrated books reflect this adventurous seafaring life: *Collingwood* (1891), *Wreck of the Golden Fleece* (1893) and *Tales of Our Coast* (1896) are full of windy pictures of ships and sea based on accurate observation. He was the ideal illustrator for *The Last Fight of the Revenge* (1908), and his colour plates of heaving galleons and battling sailors do justice to the subject even if some of them look as though they were painted in plasticine – a mannerism that sometimes detracts from his merits. The brush-drawn head- and tail-pieces on every page show his versatility. Brangwyn was an inveterate sketcher at a time when the practice was taken seriously, and seemed always at his best with rapid slashing strokes executed with considerable aplomb. This is seen to perfection in his *Windmills* (1923) and *Book of Bridges* (1915). Also worthy of note are his topographical works *Belgium* (1916) and *The Pageant of Venice* (1922), the latter confirming his affinity with ships and the sea: his canals and tottering palaces are seen through a jumble of masts and spars, even when his foregrounds have the inevitable picturesque vegetable markets. Brangwyn, like Flint, was eventually knighted, becoming a great man in an age of 'Great Men'. His energy and industry were legendary: he designed houses, furniture, pottery, carpets, tapestries, bookplates, books and much else besides, and was famous for his murals, etchings and woodcuts. Such versatility and the reaction it can provoke may account for his comparative obscurity today, for his once enormous reputation has vanished with the Empire that was so often the subject of his colourful canvases.

CHAPTER 5

The Wig and Powder School

The phrase 'the Nineties' instantly brings to mind the coterie that revolved around the Bodley Head bookshop, the world of Oscar Wilde, Beardsley, Max Beerbohm, John Lane and his poets. Yet there were at that time many vigorous developments in the arts which were left untouched (or unscathed) by this taper-lit world of conscious decadence: the work of Hugh Thomson and Macmillan's other 'Cranford' illustrators; the topographical and architectural draughtsmen; William Morris and the Arts and Crafts movement; the graphic work of the Beggarstaff brothers; the Florentine style of Charles Ricketts and Anning Bell; and the colour printing of Edmund Evans and his popular triumvirate of pre-Nineties artists, Kate Greenaway, Walter Crane and Randolph Caldecott.

Hugh Thomson (1860–1920) and the other 'wig and powder' artists reflected an aspect of contemporary taste that is hard to account for and harder still to label. It is sometimes called the 'Queen Anne' revival, and thought to be a late reaction to the predominantly Gothic revivalism of the nineteenth century. The Queen Anne style was certainly popular enough for a time and inevitably left its mark. Its physical aspect is plentifully displayed in the rows of seventeenth- and eighteenth-century style houses with high-pitched roofs, Flemish gables and white or green painted sash windows that were built in the 1870s and 1880s in the suburbs of English towns and cities following the lead of Bedford Park, Hampstead and Chelsea. It was a style for the new 'artistic' middle classes – a

Kate Greenaway world of comfort and refinement that revolved around the home. The perfect celebration of such homes can be found in the children's books that graced the nursery tables, particularly those engraved by Edmund Evans or chromolithographed by Marcus Ward. Ward's *At Home* (1881), illustrated by Thomas Crane, is perhaps the perfect example of the latter variety. 'Home' is a Queen Anne style house packed with the paraphernalia of Aesthetic taste – painted screens, Whistlerian colour schemes, Japanese fans and Morris furniture – and inhabited by doll-like infants in eighteenth-century Kate Greenaway costumes. Here are displayed all the elements that fused to make the style.

The 'wig and powder' artists were a part of this and reflected in their way the taste for the English vernacular and the wearing of powdered hair, which survived from the Stuarts until the early nineteenth century. For the works of the great novelists and prose writers of this period they provided delicate pen drawings and watercolours which were reproduced by the new photomechanical processes – line block and halftone. In this way process reproduction became identified with a certain style of illustration, and itself became an expression of period sensitivity. This becomes apparent in any comparison of the wood-engraved books of Edmund Evans and the process illustrations of Hugh Thomson. Evans's work, however skilful and dainty the cutting, has something ponderously nineteenth-century about it compared with the breezy informality of the process-reproduced pen line in, say,

Thomson's illustrations to Dobson's *Ballad of Beau Brocade* (1892). Though purists might object to the over-reduction of the drawings, the pen-drawn title-pages, the old-fashioned typography and the excessive air of rococo prettiness in such volumes, they wonderfully express their time, and the best of them represent a perfect fusion of the work of author, artist and book designer.

Thomson was familiar with Edmund Evans's work for Marcus Ward and Co., the Belfast chromolithographers to whom he was at first apprenticed and who had printed the work of both Crane and Greenaway. Thomson arrived in London in December 1883 with a few pounds, several letters of introduction and high hopes for a career in illustration, to be met at first with disappointment. There was no shortage of illustrative talent in the capital at that time and competition was intense. A fortunate letter to Joseph Comyns Carr, editor of *The English Illustrated Magazine*, produced results. Amongst others drawing for the magazine at that time were Randolph Caldecott, Walter Crane, Harry Furniss and George du Maurier, and under their genial influence Thomson's style developed rapidly. Carr introduced him into the charmed circles of late Pre-Raphaelite society:

on Sunday I am invited up to Mr Carr's and he will take me to Mr E. Burne-Jones's studio. They seem to be great chums. I was up to dinner one night two weeks ago and there saw a painting and many sketches of Mr Jones's, the painting being a beautiful portrait of Mr Carr's boy, not unlike Fra Angelico, only with long aesthetic hair.[1]

Unlike Beardsley, who was also to visit Burne-Jones's studio, Thomson shows in his work little sign of Pre-Raphaelite influence. Falling into step with the tastes of Carr and Caldecott, it was not long before he was illustrating the *Spectator* papers for *The English Illustrated Magazine*. So began his long association with the rural England of Jane Austen, Mrs Gaskell, Joseph Addison and Oliver Goldsmith. Although theirs was perhaps a somewhat rose-tinted vision, Thomson was nevertheless at great pains to find its visible manifestations. For a model

for the Vicar of Wakefield's cottage he purposefully stalked round Dorking and as far afield as the Antrim coast. Published in time for the Christmas market in 1890, *The Vicar of Wakefield* was at once an enormous success. Thomson wrote excitedly to his father: 'They predict at Macmillan's that in half a dozen years a copy of the first edition, published at six shillings will sell to book collectors at thirty-five shillings or maybe three pounds.' In these drawings, as in his search for local colour, the influence of the American E. A. Abbey is to be felt. Present, too, is the influence of his admired mentor Caldecott, who had illustrated the first two titles in the Cranford series, Washington Irving's *Old Christmas* (1876) and *Bracebridge Hall* (1877). The fourth title, in the following year, was again illustrated by Thomson and set the pattern for the years to come. These books, in elaborately blocked green cloth bindings with all edges cut and gilt, became an attractive feature of the Christmas market and quickly accustomed the public to the new line medium.

Not surprisingly, this series had rivals in almost identical shape and form. Chief among these were those of Kegan Paul with Austin Dobson's *Ballad of Beau Brocade* (1892), illustrated by Thomson, and *Proverbs in Porcelain*, with even better illustrations by Bernard Partridge, and George Allen, who published *Pride and Prejudice* and not only secured Thomson to illustrate it but emulated the Cranford series in format. To further this successful series Macmillan's engaged other artists to relieve the hard-pressed Thomson. They included C. E. Brock, George Boughton, Herbert Railton, W. Frank Calderon and Edmund Sullivan. For their Illustrated Standard Novels series begun in 1895 they extensively employed Charles and Henry Brock, both steeped in the Caldecott–Thomson tradition. To explain this late Victorian mania for the good old days and rural ways is not easy but Percy Muir suggested that

Thomson arrived on the scene just when the consciousness of the squalor and shoddiness of the

1. Letter to his father, 14 March 1884.

mechanical age awakened a nostalgia for 'the good old days' when life was simpler, more decorative; when the countryside was peopled by benevolent squires, served by a loyal retinue of loyal and picturesque rustics, and when such rural retreats were reached by horse-drawn transport, rather than stinking locomotives; when male costume was not confined to stove-pipe hats and drain-pipe trousers, and all England was a pastoral paradise.[2]

The Brock brothers continued this tradition in a world which saw the motor car become the established method of transport, and in which the coaching inn gave way to the roadhouse and garage, rustics ceased to bob in the villages, the churches emptied, benevolence disappeared and the countryside was invaded by suburbia. From their Cambridge homes (C. E. Brock called his 'Cranford') there issued a constant stream of illustrations for books and magazines. Their work for children, too, was considerable, including classics, gift books, novels, annuals and school text-books, and in all this work they remained faithful to the Caldecott–Thomson tradition. Charles's first commission from Macmillan's was for Hood's *Humorous Poems* (1893), issued in the Cranford series: its success led the following year to an edition of *Gulliver's Travels*, thought by many to be his finest work.

Of the brothers, H. M. Brock (1875–1960) had the stronger line and at his best, as in *Treasure Island* (1928), possessed great gifts of conveying atmosphere and capturing vigorous action. His late attempts to enter the world of the large colour-plate gift book are less happy, as can be seen in *A Book of Old Ballads* (1934), where the large scale quickly exposed his weaknesses – a line that becomes mannered and undescriptive and a certain doll-like similarity of drawn features. His early and enduring enthusiasm for the work of Caldecott is obvious, and he shared that artist's enthusiasm for the good old days and ways. Not surprisingly he is best known for illustrations to the popular classics – Thackeray, Jane Austen and Goldsmith, though not the Brontës. With his brother he created a world of delicate china, Georgian silver and afternoon tea, reflecting perhaps something of the serenity of their own lives, for they appear to have had few struggles and to have been always in demand.

Macmillan's success with the 'Cranford school' was later emulated to some extent by Hodder & Stoughton, who produced larger, handsome technicolour versions of the old black-and-white tradition of illustration. In particular Lewis Baumer and Frank Reynolds were recruited to illustrate many old novels. One of Baumer's most successful books was *Vanity Fair* (1913), a large quarto volume handsomely bound in gold-blocked buckram with tipped-in colour plates. It is competent enough, although with the handicaps of a famous text and the obligatory period costumes it must have been difficult for the artist to avoid dullness. In similar vein Frank Reynolds illustrated *David Copperfield* in 1911 and *The Posthumous Papers of the Pickwick Club* the following year with twenty-one colour plates in each. These are clever and detailed watercolours, full of character, and clear evidence of the artist's enjoyment of the stories. They are also very much in the rollicking Dickensian tradition of 'Phiz' and Fred Barnard. In 1911 Hodder commissioned Hugh Thomson to re-illustrate in colour *The School for Scandal* and *Quality Street*. Covered in fine mauve, blue or white buckram and blocked with an overall pattern in an exquisite rococo style, these are some of the most elegant books of the period. The plates are tipped in within decorative mounts and harmonise well with the text. The prevailing atmosphere of these books, in contrast to those of Baumer and Reynolds, is of lightness and grace. Thomson's watercolours were well printed by Henry Stone and Company of Banbury, who undertook most of Hodder's gift books, including work by Dulac and Heath Robinson. Much criticism has been levelled at the trichromatic process but these cannot be faulted, and it is refreshing to see Thomson for once not over-reduced.

Perhaps the greatest of the artists contributing to Macmillan's Cranford series was Edmund

2. Percy Muir, *Victorian Illustrated Books* (Batsford, 1971), p. 199.

COLOUR PLATE IV. Kay Nielsen
In Powder and Crinoline by Sir Arthur Quiller-Couch, Hodder and Stoughton, 1913

COLOUR PLATE V. Harry Clarke
Fairy Tales by Charles Perrault, Harrap, 1922

Sullivan (1869–1933), now unjustly neglected. He was, in his way, a philosopher and thinker who expressed himself pictorially. For this reason, perhaps, there is an element of sketchiness about his work – as though, in the act of setting down one idea, his mind was busy investigating others. His illustrations are often not mere depictions of events outlined by an author but contributions to our understanding by means of allegory or symbol. With the slight tools of pen and ink he was able, like Bewick with burin and block, to give expression to profound thought and human sympathy. His teaching, as we have noted, was remembered with gratitude by his students and there is no doubt that he was largely responsible for the great respect which pen draughtsmen finally achieved. His illustrations to *The Kaiser's Garland* (1915), a book of satirical cartoons, show how closely Rackham followed him. These are some of his finest drawings; he appeared most at ease dealing with large themes which allowed scope for his philosophical bent.

The publication of the *Daily Graphic* in January 1890 ushered in a decade of prosperity for process reproduction. Sullivan's work first appeared in this journal. After three years he was sacked for pursuing too independent a line and he turned to John Latey, editor of the *Penny Illustrated* paper. Latey, a benevolent figure to struggling artists, offered him small jobs. Sullivan went on to illustrate all the best magazines of the time – *The Pall Mall Budget, Pearson's Magazine, Black and White* and *The Windsor Magazine* – which with teaching left little time for book illustration. Nevertheless he produced illustrations for some seventeen books – novels, classics and poetry. His first, *Lavengro* (1896), appeared in Macmillan's Illustrated Standard Novels series. This ran to forty titles in all – there were two others illustrated by Sullivan in the following year, *The Pirate* and *Newton Forster*, both by Captain Marryat. His illustrations for these are not outstanding, and the loose sketchy style was not helped by over-reduction by the blockmaker. There is more than a touch of Millais and Pinwell about some of the draw-

ings, notably 'Now Jenny, lay down the towel and pump for your life', but in other, less densely hatched drawings a new freedom of approach is apparent. Always careful in preparation, for *Newton Forster* Sullivan made studies of gypsies. Macmillan's also employed him for their Cranford series, to which he contributed *The School for Scandal and The Rivals* and *Tom Brown's Schooldays*. These drawings do not compare favourably with Hugh Thomson's illustrations. In many of them the drawing, particularly of architecture, is weak and unconvincing – the *Tom Brown* vignettes, for example, show difficulties of composition. By 1898, however, his mature style had developed and was matched by a text to his liking in Carlyle's *Sartor Resartus*. These illustrations are extremely varied in style, some strong and simple in outline, others densely hatched and all showing his complete mastery of the pen. Thereafter the appearance of a Sullivan book was something of a sensation and *A Dream of Fair Women* by Lord Tennyson in 1900 and *Pilgrim's Progress* of 1901 sealed his reputation. In the preface to *A Dream of Fair Women* he wrote:

Between the extremes of an art entirely ephemeral and journalistic on the one hand and a cold aestheticism on the other there is a large field; and an artist is justified if he can find a subject which will at the same time afford scope for the exercise of his art and a wider channel to the public sympathy.

Here the illustrations are strongly constructed with the vital musical line he was to commend to his students. Sullivan's method of working was to some extent similar to that of Beardsley and Phil May, for their apparent ease of execution with the pen was built on the foundation of a detailed pencil drawing which was later erased. It was his practice to work on parts of the pencilled under-drawing whilst also working on the inking-in. Faces, figures and details of all kinds would be brought to a high pitch in pencil before being touched with the pen.

Sullivan's two books *The Art of Illustration* (1921) and *Line* (1922) set forth with style and energy his views on everything touching his art. From them we can see why he did not turn to the half-tone and trichromatic half-tone: for him line was enough, and who can say that his reputation is not the better for it? Like Bewick, Keene, Beardsley and Phil May, his fame rests firmly on black and white alone. 'Any medium that compels selection rather than offers facility of inclusiveness is likely to squeeze the best out of any artist. The severer the limitations and the more fully they are accepted the better will be the result.'[3]

In his last book, Tennyson's *Maud* (1922), Sullivan's style reached new heights. Of the twenty full-page line drawings eight are lightly tinted with colour wash, a rarity for him. The white buckram binding is also a surprise, being blocked in silver rather than gold, with stars, dewdrops and rococo scrolls in an eighteenth-century manner.

In 1903 R. E. D. Sketchley observed that there were very broadly two schools of 'wig and powder' illustrators, 'adherents of Mr Abbey and the American school or of Mr Hugh Thomson and the Caldecott–Greenaway tradition.'[4] Artists he named as being influenced by Abbey included Fred Pegram, F. H. Townsend, Claude Shepperson, Sidney Paget and Stephen Reid. Abbey's disciples were an unexciting lot. Fred Pegram and F. H. Townsend, for instance, whose work is most commonly found in the small reprints of the classics that followed the success of Macmillan's Cranford series, both employed the Abbey technique of wiry, bounding lines and rather sketchy cross-hatching and both illustrated very much the same sort of book – the novels of Peacock, Scott, Jane Austen and Captain Marryat. It is hard to tell the difference between their illustrations. There is the same grasp of story and action, the same light humour and ability to catch the author's mood which makes them adequate companions for texts that were printed to be read. Today, when illustrated books of all kinds are eagerly sought

by collectors, they are not much in demand.

Over the years Macmillan's reprinted the Illustrated Standard Novels series in a cheaper format as Illustrated Pocket Classics in limp leather bindings. More elegant and easier to read than the Everyman series, these pocket-sized classics assured the Abbey–Thomson style of a kind of immortality. Townsend and Pegram also worked for the Cranford rivals, such as Service and Paton's Illustrated English Library in company with the Brocks, Lancelot Speed and Chris Hammond. Unfortunately their style of drawing is no longer fashionable, nor has it yet seen a revival, and it is now difficult to picture the time when these 'black-and-white' men were regarded with a respect bordering upon awe.

Any complete list of artists working or sometimes working in the eighteenth-century style would be a long one. For some it was only a part of their output. Sir Bernard Partridge, for instance, was primarily a cartoonist well known for his political caricatures in *Punch*, though he made occasional forays into pastiche, as with his *Proverbs in Porcelain*. Cecil Aldin's love of the eighteenth century went much deeper and is often evident in his illustrations to children's books. It was given full play in his equestrian books with their racy huntsmen and jovial coachmen, very much in the Caldecott manner. Beatrix Potter and Beardsley were not immune; thus we have the embroidered waistcoats and eighteenth-century costumes of *The Tailor of Gloucester* (1903) and Beardsley's rococo fashions in his *Rape of the Lock* (1896).

Despite the continued survival of eighteenth-century pastiche into later times, with for example Lovat Fraser's chap-book-style illustrations of the 1920s or Rex Whistler's elegant line drawings of the 1930s, this particular 'Queen Anne' 'wig and powder' variety seems to have been extinguished entirely by the First World War.

3. *The Art of Illustration* (Chapman and Hall, 1921), p. 196.
4. R. E. D. Sketchley, *English Book Illustration of Today* (Kegan Paul, 1903), p. 68.

CHAPTER 6

In America

Although in 1899 the indefatigable Joseph Pennell was of the opinion that America led the world in adopting the process line block, that superiority was soon to be questioned by the rising stars of British illustration. There is certainly some truth in his assumption that the American pioneers were inspired by the Europeans Daniel Vierge, Mariano Fortuny, and Alfred Menzel, but it is possible to overestimate their importance, and Pennell tended to do this, for reasons apparent on considering his own drawings and etchings, which reflect his enthusiasm for European work. A much stronger platform for American expansion was undoubtedly that school of British illustrators known, somewhat inaccurately, as the 'illustrators of the Sixties'. The work of Charles Keene, Arthur Boyd Houghton, Birket Foster and the Pre-Raphaelites had been flooding into America over the previous thirty years, together with the various English illustrated magazines, and all were avidly sought by young American artists. The impact of this continual, inexpensive, and readily accessible display of illustrative talent is not yet fully appreciated. Van Gogh, we know, excitedly collected his own sets of *The Illustrated London News* and *The Graphic*.

In America Howard Pyle (1853–1911), the father of the American school, also studied them to good effect. So did his contemporary Winslow Homer, and these two artists were perhaps more responsible than any others for American painting and illustration breaking new ground. With them came a largeness of vision and a fresh out-of-doors approach based on solid drawing which put life into the emerging magazines and narrowed the gap between painting and illustration.

Homer's direct contribution to illustration was admittedly rather small. There is only one book entirely by him – J. R. Lowell's poem *The Courtin'* – and his magazine illustrations were made more for livelihood than love. Nevertheless his paintings, particularly the watercolours of later years of sea-swept coasts and pine-clad mountains populated by sturdy youths and bearded backwoodsmen, with their eyes fixed upon far horizons, helped Americans to recognise the value of their own recent pioneering past. It is strange then to realise both artists' reliance upon the British school of the Sixties. Homer particularly admired the work of Millais, whose illustrations appeared in *Good Words* and *Once a Week*. The appeal lay in Millais's natural and informal grouping of figures engaged in some activity, joined to Ruskin's doctrine of truth to nature seen in his accurate depiction of flora and fauna. Although the breezy impressionism employed by the Americans was perhaps not what Ruskin had in mind, their rapid brushwork was ideally suited both to the white line wood-engraving employing photography on the block and the new process half-tone of the magazines for which they worked.

Frederic Remington (1861–1909) welcomed process reproduction. 'These engravers are all right when they do good work', he wrote to the editor of *Harper's Weekly*, 'but they need a good deal of dispensation to purge their sins – process is the coming thing.'[1] In the summer of 1881 he was travelling westwards into Montana in search of material for his illustrations to *Harper's* and *Century Magazine*.

Evening overtook me one night in Montana and I by good luck made the camp-fire of an old waggon freighter who shared his bacon and coffee with me. I was nineteen years of age and he was a very old man . . . who had gone West at a very early age. His West was Iowa. Thence during a long life he had followed the receding frontiers, always further and further West. 'And now,' said he, 'there is no more West. In a few more years the railway will come along the Yellowstone and a poor man cannot make a living at all.'[2]

In his lively portrayal of this way of life, with its prospectors, cowboys, Indians and soldiers, Remington amply shared the coffee and bacon of his talents with a younger generation who eagerly awaited each issue of the illustrated magazines or, for those who could afford them, the numerous books he illustrated. Typical of these are *Ranch Life and the Hunting Trail* by Theodore Roosevelt (1888), *Tenting on the Plains* (1887), and the Houghton Mifflin edition of Longfellow's *Song of Hiawatha* (1891). It may be objected that Remington was not an illustrator in the sense of someone who contemplated how he might best illuminate a given text with a sensitivity to typographic considerations, and there is some truth in this. For he was at all times both a reporter energetically recording a rapidly vanishing world and a painter with a gift for inventing memorable images. From the endless reproduction of these images has come the commonly accepted view of the Old West. It is to his credit that he drew always with great candour: the later romanticism of Hollywood is not to be laid at his door.

The combination of artistic inspiration and a zest for the adventurous life was to become a characteristic of American illustration, and nowhere more so than in the work of Rockwell Kent (1882–1971). Kent had a passion for boats and the sea, and had trained in early life as an architect. This draughtsman's training and a

seaman's love of tidiness are clearly in evidence in his work. Like Homer he had a love of the Maine coast, and had built himself a house on Monhegan Island. In 1918 he spent the winter in a cabin on Fox Island in Alaska and all this experience bore fruit in his illustrations to such classics as *Moby Dick* (1930). The Alaskan sojourn in particular was the subject of his own *Wilderness* (1920), based on the diary he kept through the dark winter months. The drawings, with their heavy white-on-black emphasis, giant figures and star-filled skies, are certainly powerful but are not typical, and he is better known for the books in which he had considerable control over design. These include *N by E* (1930) and *Salamina* (1935), both of which ran to many trade and special editions.[3] The icy precision of these drawings, whilst they blend well with the printed page, is something of an acquired taste. His illustrations to *Candide* (1928), *A Birthday Book* and *Venus and Adonis* (1931) show his affinity with the art deco style of that time. Throughout a long working life he remained amazingly constant to his earliest enthusiasms; *A Treasury of Sea Stories* (1948) contains some of the best of Kent's work, and distils a lifetime's study of the sea equalled only perhaps by Winslow Homer.

Preoccupied as they had been with the Civil War and as they still were with the problems of opening up a mighty continent, Americans looked to Europe for cultural stimulation, which they found not only in magazines but also in the highly popular Victorian poets and novelists.[4] No one enjoyed these writers more than Howard Pyle (1853–1911), who from his first illustration for *Harper's* in 1876 until his death in 1911 was responsible for laying the foundations of a tradition of American illustration. His great

---

1. For an account of his relationship to process reproduction see *Visual Communication and the Graphic Arts* by Estelle Jussim (Bowker, 1974), p. 195.
2. *Collier's* XXXIV (18 March 1905), p. 16.
3. For details of these see: *The Illustrations of Rockwell Kent* by F. Johnson (Dover, 1976).
4. Oscar Wilde enjoyed a hero's welcome on his American lecture tour of 1882 which took him into Remington's still slightly wild West.

love was Americana, and his knowledge of colonial and revolutionary history was deep and informed. His taste was for the large and colourful depiction of stirring events of earlier days, and much of his best work in this vein can be found in the magazines that sprang up as a result of the possibilities of the new processes. Indeed it must be admitted that illustrative talent in America seemed most at home in these journals or working for commercial publicity. This is not to say that America produced no quality book illustration of its own; it did, but such work does not compare with the tremendous outpourings of the British school. Conversely, British periodicals often pale beside their American counterparts. This position does not appear to have changed over the years. Writing in 1961 Lynton Lamb observed: 'In America, book illustrators are thought little of by the general public, but the prestige of magazine illustrators as well as the prices they can command are high.'[5] According to Percy Muir[6] one very likely reason for there being no American school of English proportions was the lack of American illustrated periodicals in the nineteenth century, *The Illustrated London News*, *Punch* and many others having provided, in his view, a seed-bed for the growth of English illustrative talent. A more prosaic reason probably lay in the fact that America was not a signatory to the Berne copyright convention; this circumstance led to a flood of 'legally' pirated English illustrated books on the American market.

Pyle's reputation must rest largely upon his early work in black and white, in which his admiration for the British school was fused with his love of Dürer, as shown by his two books *The Wonder Clock* (1887) and *Otto of the Silver Hand* (1888). This last is an excellent production which even met with Walter Crane's grudging admiration, for Crane included it in his *Of the Decorative Illustration of Books* (1896), choosing a plate which showed Pyle uncomfortably close in style to Dürer. Pyle's vivid imagination and tremendous energy employed anything that was to hand, from which he fashioned a bustling world of heroes, kings, princes, robber barons and pirates that was to breathe new life into the previously rather gloomy world of American children's books. His prodigious output was due in part to his secretary, to whom he dictated the stories whilst working at his easel – a habit he shared with William Morris, who took a pride in composing poetry whilst working at his loom. In 1903 Scribner published *The Story of King Arthur and his Knights*, the first of a quartet on the Arthurian theme which Pyle produced over a period of seven years. The last of these, *The Grail and the Passing of Arthur* (1910), appeared when Pyle was fifty-seven and approaching the end of his life. The drawings have a crude child-like simplicity which may disappoint the sophisticated but proved popular with children. His prose too has an archaic, wooden quality, rather like an authentic voice from the fourteenth century and again reminiscent of Morris. At times it can be irritatingly repetitive. In the foreword to the last volume, for example, we are assured:

Much in this is sad, but much is not sad; for all endings are sad, and the passing of a hero is a sad thing to tell of; but the events and the adventures and the achievements of such a man are not sad. Thus it is here said that much of this is sad, but much is not sad.

Pyle was later to become famous for his colour illustrations to the great American magazines, particularly for *Harper's*, to whom he supplied swashbuckling scenes. His marked enthusiasm for the pirates of the Spanish Main encompassed many things for which he felt a special affinity – old costume, the sea and ships, villainy, heroism and the desperate search for hidden treasure in tropic latitudes. All of these elements were contained in the posthumously published quarto *Howard Pyle's Book of Pirates* (1921). This volume displays many of his best stories and drawings, including 'Marooned', which made such a memorable double page in *Harper's* in 1887.

5. Lynton Lamb, *Drawing for Illustration* (1962), p. 94.
6. Percy Muir, *Victorian Illustrated Books* (Batsford, 1971), p. 266.

Having by his own efforts set the trend and mapped the new frontiers, Pyle set out to recruit a band of artists to cultivate the new terrain. His pupils, as befits pioneers, were a hardy breed; the soil was fresh and before long America had a crop of illustrative talent with a distinctive American flavour. Pyle's strong belief in the need for American artists to train in their own land was contrary to the accepted convention of that time when so many gifted Americans migrated to Europe. His own success only brought home to him more sharply how poor were the contemporary standards of illustration. The lack of adequate training and the European migration were the despair of the editors of many magazines. In 1894 Pyle decided to teach illustration, first at the Drexel Institute at Philadelphia, then at the Art Students' League in New York and finally, disappointed with conventional art schools, at his own school at Chadd's Ford, Pennsylvania.

Here in the Brandywine country Pyle set a cracking pace. Standards were high, numbers few, and by all accounts it was an exciting, if arduous, time for his pupils. No fees were charged or records kept. Money was short and the select few admitted were expected to share in the chores. In this venture he was assisted by two former pupils from the Drexel days, Stanley Arthurs and Frank Schoonover, who both shared his love for the colonial past and the still fairly wild West. The originality of Pyle's teaching lay not only in his unconventional approach but also in his basic intention, which was to make illustration a fertile ground for the growth of an American school of painters – 'not essentially the production of illustrators of books but rather the production of pictures',[7] as he once wrote to Edward Penfield. In this he was successful, although full recognition of the achievement has been long delayed by the American post-war enthusiasm for Abstract Expressionism and the more recent advances towards nihilistic Minimalism. As these clouds of Abstraction have dissolved we can see that Pyle's original landscape has been there all the time, and we look yet again at the bright landscapes of Maxfield Parrish and Andrew Wyeth. Andrew's father, Newell Convers Wyeth (1882–1945) was one of Pyle's star pupils and the line still continues unbroken, for James Wyeth, Andrew's son, is a painter in the same tradition.

Maxfield Parrish (1870–1966) has also recently been 'rediscovered', bearing further witness to the strength of the Pyle tradition. Parrish was always interested in experimenting with new techniques and different media – prepared boards, cut-outs and collage, indeed anything that would help to speed the emergence of his desired effects. His work for books and magazines was only part of an enormous production of designs of all kinds – paintings, murals, commercial publicity, package design and the colour reproductions which were to bring him international fame in the 1920s.

In his earliest book, *Mother Goose in Prose* (1897), Parrish used for backgrounds Rossboard, a commercially produced board printed with dots on lines in various tones. More original and satisfactory was the stippled effect he achieved with lithographic crayon on Steinbach paper; this can be seen in his illustrations to Washington Irving's *Knickerbocker's History of New York* of 1900. These are open-pen drawings with litho crayon added, giving a sandy, grainy effect and a sharp chiaroscuro similar to the fading of early photographs. He frequently used the camera and was often his own model for the photographs which he turned into illustrations. Something of this technique can be detected in *The Golden Age* (1899) by Kenneth Grahame, which brought him overnight fame and a notice in *The Studio*[8] quoting Hubert Herkomer: 'he has combined the photographic vision with the Pre-Raphaelite feeling. He is poetic without ever being maudlin, and has the saving clause of humour . . .[;] his work recognises the fact that photography has come and intends to remain.' The sequel, Grahame's *Dream Days* (1902) in the same format was almost as good, but like many other second attempts added nothing to

7. H. C. Pitz, *The Brandywine Tradition* (Houghton Mifflin, Boston, 1969), p. 149.
8. *The Studio*, vol. 38 (1906), p. 35.

the original. *The Golden Age* must be regarded as one of the most successful combinations of author and artist, for both caught perfectly the child's vision: Grahame with his fresh and original prose and Parrish with his low view-points and clear bright delineation creating images with a disturbing snapshot quality. The success of *Dream Days*, originally printed in monochrome half-tone (in photogravure), led to a reissue of *The Golden Age* in the same format, also by photogravure, and in an identical gold-blocked binding also by Parrish. The original illustrations were made in colour, which explains how one of the plates from *Dream Days* reproduced in *King Albert's Book* (1915) appears in colour.

With the *Arabian Nights* of 1909 Parrish found a wonderful outlet for his inventive genius. The twelve colour plates (previously issued in *Collins' Magazine*) combine all his best qualities – unusual perspectives, a taste for fantasy and bright surrealism. His sleeping woolly-haired giant with claw-like fingers is so monstrous that it is tempting to turn the page quietly lest he be disturbed.

Parrish's book illustrations are not numerous as most of his work was for magazines – *Harper's*, *Collier's*, *Century* and *Life*.[9] Commercial work was to become increasingly important to him as his work steadily declined in popularity in the world of 'high art'.

With the passion for authenticity that was one of Pyle's chief Pre-Raphaelite legacies to his pupils, Frank Schoonover (1877–1972) made two treks into the wastes of Canada, by dog-team in 1903 and by canoe in 1911. The results are apparent in his convincing illustrations of Red Indian and trapper life. No less authentic are the colourful illustrations provided by Newell Convers Wyeth. Indeed, Wyeth has more claim to the Pyle mantle than perhaps any of the others, and his illustrated books reflect a similar enthusiasm for the rumbustious life of pirates, trappers, Indians and cowboys. Outstanding in this genre are the titles he illustrated for Scribner's Classics Series. Stoutly bound and well printed, with colour plates printed on art paper, these are attractive but unpretentious books.

They are books to read and Wyeth's pictures add to rather than detract from that purpose. The series included such old favourites as James Fenimore Cooper's *The Last of the Mohicans* (1919) and *The Deerslayer* (1925), Jules Verne's *Mysterious Island* (1918), *Westward Ho!* (1920) and a series of R. L. Stevenson's adventure stories: *The Black Arrow* (1916), *David Balfour* (1924), *Kidnapped* (1913) and *Treasure Island* (1911). Here are all the well-known figures of childhood dreams – or nightmares: Blind Pew tap-tapping along the cliff road in the frosty moonlight, his gnarled hand groping out to us from the page, Israel Hands taking that last fatal step up the *Hispaniola*'s rigging, or that vicious swing of Billy Bone's cutlass that chips the sign-board of the 'Admiral Benbow'. This has always been a popular book with illustrators, attracting such diverse talents as Rowland Hilder, Edmund Dulac, Wal Paget, Mervyn Peake and John Minton. Although others might not agree[10], the Wyeth must have a strong claim to outstrip all rival editions, unless, of course, it is argued that the pictures are not book illustrations in the strict sense of the term. The originals were painted in oil on canvas 50 by 40 inches and were reproduced by four-colour half-tone on coated paper. In America there has never been quite the exclusiveness about book illustration that has typified the British approach. American book illustration, as in this case, is often indistinguishable from magazine illustration and this, in turn, is very close in style to the artwork of advertisement pages.

Something of Pyle's enthusiasm for the swash-buckling life appears in the work of many of these pupils and followers. Following on (or so it seems) from his own *Book of Pirates* came another classic of buccaneering history – *Iron Men and Wooden Ships* (1924) by Edward Wilson. This contains bold workmanlike wood-

9. A full list is given in *Maxfield Parrish* by Coy Ludwig (Watson-Guptill, New York, 1973).
10. Rigby Graham, in his *Romantic Book Illustration 1943–1955* (Private Libraries Association, 1965), gives the laurels to John Minton for his Camden Classics drawings.

cuts glinting with a cruel light and curiously sympathetic to their subject. The style is far from Pyle's, being more akin to the chap-book look of William Nicholson, though with a whiff of eighteenth-century brimstone. Later Wilson commissions included most of the great seafaring tales – his own *Pirate's Treasure*, then *Robinson Crusoe*, *Treasure Island* and *Two Years Before the Mast*. In all, he illustrated well over sixty books, including many for the Limited Editions Club.

Not all Pyle's students were horny-handed backwoodsmen. One group that is now less well known than it ought to be includes Elizabeth Shippen Green, Edith Penwill Brown, Violet Oakley, Jessie Wilcox Smith and Charlotte Harding. Their graceful illustrations reveal a shared delight in linear pattern-making. Their favourite medium was charcoal outlines sprayed with fixative and then washed with pale watercolours, and their subject matter the usual fairy-tales, folk-tales and classics, but seen always through the eyes of the well-scrubbed, pinafored and decorous little ladies that play throughout their pages. Of these artists Jessie Wilcox Smith (1863–1935) is both the best known and the most representative. The amount of her work for books and magazines was considerable, with early commissions to illustrate the novels of Louisa M. Alcott. Her own little women went on to proliferate in a growing number of titles, such as Frances Hodgson Burnett's *In The Closed Room* (1904) and Stevenson's *A Child's Garden of Verses* (1905). The first of these books is typical of her style. With text printed in black within apple-green decorations, it contains eight full-page colour plates on cream-coated paper. Here, looking like Lewis Carroll's child photographs come to life, are Judith and Jane peeping round doors, tiptoeing upstairs or holding willow-pattern tea parties for their limp dolls.

Not all American illustrators were stylistic descendants of Pyle; more than a few were indebted more directly to Edwin Austin Abbey (1852–1911), whom Joseph Pennell regarded as not only 'the greatest English-speaking illustrator, but the greatest living illustrator.'[11] Abbey's influence was strongly felt in Britain, where he made his home. His legendary passion for historical accuracy in his illustrations first brought him to England, for here the authentic props and models for his art could be found.

Abbey began his career in Philadelphia in a wood-engraver's office, graduating to *Harper's* in 1871 where he helped to produce small black-and-white magazine illustrations before providing for them his best illustrated book. *Selections from the Poetry of Robert Herrick* (1882) appeared in a luxurious *art nouveau* cloth binding of green, gold and cream. The drawings were based on Abbey's own observations of English country life during an extended visit to Britain, and, although reproduced by wood-engraving, the freshness of the original pen line was not obscured. This almost sketchy line had the breath of a new era about it and was ideally suited to the process line block. His passion for all things English, including cricket,[12] led to his acceptance by the most exclusive cultural circles. He became a member of various clubs including the Athenaeum, was elected to the Royal Academy and found himself in constant demand to teach, paint, write, design, sit on committees and judge competitions. The wonder is that he sustained all this and yet made time for illustration.

Together with his American friends J. A. M. Whistler, Henry James, John Sargent and Joseph Pennell, Abbey gave to late Victorian culture an indefinable sense of freshness and modernity that was uniquely part of the Nineties mixture. The books which he illustrated reflected his discovery of and liking for England – particularly of 'Old England'. They include *The Rivals*, *The School for Scandal*, Shakespeare's *Comedies*, and *She Stoops to Conquer* – all titles which gave him the chance to indulge his passion for old costume and scenery in fine line drawings. In this he was sometimes joined by his friend Alfred Parsons, who

11. *Pen Drawing and Pen Draughtsmen* (Macmillan, 1899), p. 203.
12. J. M. Barrie once remarked: 'In Autumn and Winter Abbey painted, but in Spring he oiled his bat and in May he put on his pads.'

collaborated with him in providing illustrations to several books including *The School for Scandal* and *The Quiet Life* in a similar wiry style.

The effect of such drawings was quickly felt and Abbey's lead was followed by Fred Pegram, F. H. Townsend, Sidney Paget, C. A. Shepperson, the Brocks and other 'costume' artists. Like them he was not always well treated by the blockmakers, his fine lines often disappearing through over-reduction. On the appearance of his *Deserted Village* in book form in 1902 he wrote to *Harper's*: 'I never dreamed that you intended to put forth the cheap and vulgar edition that you have published, in type that is simply barbarous, with a cover that is an eyesore . . . the pictures were far better printed in the *Magazine* than they were in the book.' His fame as an illustrator was even exceeded in his own day by his fame as a painter and muralist, which makes it all the more surprising that he is almost forgotten today, having experienced a rise and fall perhaps only equalled by that of Frank Brangwyn.

Although long out of fashion, Charles Dana Gibson (1867–1944) has never been quite forgotten, for he had a personal trade-mark with which he was always associated. As Louis Wain had his cats, Mabel Lucie Attwell her dimpled kiddies, and H. M. Bateman his apoplectic colonels, Gibson had his 'girls'. The Gibson girls seldom varied: pertly beautiful with sloping shoulders and high piled hair, escorted by dashing young men nearly always in evening dress, they became the rage and the mirror of smart fashion. A virtuoso of the pen, Gibson produced gigantic drawings which were occasionally issued as folio volumes by Russell in America and Lane in Britain – *Pictures of People, Sketches and Cartoons, The Americans, The Education of Mr Pipp*, among other titles. These won him many followers, of whom H. C. Christy, Henry Hutt and Hamilton Fisher became fairly well known. Gibson was enormously popular, and at the height of his fame in 1904 he accepted a contract from *Collier's Weekly* to provide a hundred double-page drawings over four years for the staggering sum of $100,000 – worth about £500,000 today. No wonder the magazines scooped up most of the best talent, and no wonder Gibson stayed with magazine work, apart from a brief flirtation with painting. With him 'black and white' had arrived – in America at least.

Reginald Birch (1856–1943) has been called the 'children's Gibson', for his illustrative style shows clearly that he followed the Gibson style rather than that of the Pyle faction. Gibson and Pyle were quite opposite in their style, Pyle careful and particular, his 'romance' springing from a concentration upon the particular, whilst Gibson achieved his effects with a flourish and panache that skipped over detail. Birch sprang into prominence with his illustrations to *Little Lord Fauntleroy* (1886) by Frances Hodgson Burnett. As so often at this period the book contains a mixture of line blocks and wood-engravings. Birch's depiction of the repellent boy-hero with his velvet suits and lace collars was soon as well known as Tenniel's Alice, and the book sold almost as well. The artist's full indebtedness to Gibson can be found in the same author's *The Captain's Youngest* (1899), also published by Warne. During a long working life of almost sixty years, he carried on steadfastly with careful and often spirited drawings which in their modesty do not claim attention for themselves but well illustrate their texts.

Gibson's influence, so potent in the Nineties, was largely felt in the world of magazine illustration, which in America took more readily to process than did book publishing. Joseph Pennell also undertook a considerable amount of illustration for process reproduction, although he was always very attached to lithography and etching. His chief claim to fame lay in his writings and encouragement to others. Beardsley, if not exactly 'discovered' by Pennell, was certainly launched on his short career by Pennell's *Studio* article of 1893. The work of Will Bradley (1868–1962) also suggests the exchange of ideas between Britain and America which gave such impetus to the graphic arts at the turn of the century. His early books, including *Fringilla* (1895), clearly reflect the inspiration of both

Morris and Beardsley; the results are a refreshing rejection of the assumption that the two styles were incompatible. As Bradley moved into commercial work, magazine covers, posters, and so on, he used both sources of inspiration to create some of the most lavish expressions of *art nouveau* taste. Like Edward Penfield and Maxfield Parrish, his talents were too large for books alone. In 1895 he founded his own Wayside Press in Springfield, Massachusetts, and there developed a love of letterforms and book design which was to have a strong an impact on American taste. *Peter Poodle, Toy Maker to the King* shows his talents in this direction – a children's book which he wrote and illustrated himself and printed in type of his own design in 1906. W. A. Dwiggins shared this enthusiasm for typography – he had studied under the great typographer Frederic W. Goudy – and brought to the books he illustrated a nice sense of weight

and fitness to the printed page, whether using spatter, as in *Tales by Edgar Allan Poe* for the Lakeside Press, or hatched lines, as in *Dr Jekyll and Mr Hyde* for Random House. Random House also published a *Tom Sawyer* in 1930 with free, even loose, line drawings by Donald McKay well in the 'typographic' tradition, for the drawings, although matching the colour and weight of the type, are more in the nature of decorations than illustrations.

The accent upon the suitability of illustration to type became, in the Thirties, part of a wider movement towards creating books in which all parts merged to form a harmonious whole. With the arrival of the more self-conscious approach, the book illustrator could no longer confine himself to a simple relationship to the text but had other factors to take into account. Such inhibitions were perhaps another reason for the relative decline of the illustrated book at this time.

CHAPTER 7

Fantasy and Fairyland

Any account of the 'process' illustrators of the latter years of the nineteenth century must acknowledge the tremendous contribution of Aubrey Beardsley (1872–98), for no one can be said to have better explored the possibilities of black and white. He was, in the words of the plaque beside the front door of his Brighton birthplace, a 'Master of Line'. Max Beerbohm once remarked that he belonged to the Beardsley period; it was no small achievement for one limited to so short a working life to give the title to a decade. Beardsley's work has a unique and distinctive flavour, but he worked in a number of styles, each of which he rapidly perfected and then discarded; he was an artist always in the process of evolution. The drawings for his *Morte d'Arthur* (1893) show him moving from a lean Pre-Raphaelitism in the Burne-Jones manner towards the abstraction and two-dimensional qualities of Japanese art. It may have been the publisher's desire to compete with William Morris's Kelmscott Press in this large-scale undertaking that prompted Beardsley to devise the involved border decorations and initials of these volumes. Nearly four hundred drawings were required, and it is not surprising that their production marked the stages of his rapidly developing talent. By the end of 1893 he had, in addition, begun the drawings for Wilde's *Salomé*, illustrated Dent's *Bon-Mots* series and completed much other work for a variety of publications. He had also given up his position as a clerk with the Guardian Life and Fire Assurance Company. That year also saw his introduction to the world at large via the pages of the new *Studio* magazine and the consequent vogue for his work which is still with us. The *Salomé* drawings are darkly brooding and full of *fin de siècle* languor. They are quite different from his *Rape of the Lock* illustrations[1] (1896), which in their delicate hatching and stippling provide a witty parallel with the work of the French copper-engravers of the eighteenth century. A third style is evident in his *Lysistrata* of the same year, produced for Leonard Smithers – a solicitor turned publisher and a good friend to Beardsley following the scandals of the Wilde trials. These drawings reflect Beardsley's interest in Greek vase painting with its graceful, simplified and sometimes erotic figures and broad areas of black and white. Such an interest, both in vase paintings and in rococo engravings, shows how his thinking was refreshingly distant from the orthodox Aestheticism or late Pre-Raphaelitism of the period. By the end of 1896 he was very conscious of working against time and his letters are full of talk of 'my old friend blood'. 'Beardsley', wrote Arthur Symons, 'ended a long career at the age of twenty-six.'

Unfortunately original editions of Beardsley's illustrated books are hard to find, and some of the later reprints of the line blocks leave much to be desired. But his drawings are to be found everywhere reproduced on carrier bags, aprons, dinner mats and as posters – perhaps the last survivors of the great poster craze of the late 1960s. It is difficult to conjecture as to how, had he lived, he would have fitted into the developing

1. Edward Hodnett, *Image and Text* (Scolar Press, 1982), p. 219.

gift book market. His eclectic list of titles was peculiarly his own and his comments, by way of 'embellishments' as they were sometimes called, were an expression of a unique personality. He belonged to no school and had no serious rivals: his period was all but extinguished by his death.

The next decade saw the rise of other stars – the Robinsons and Arthur Rackham.

In recent years a more just assessment of the work of Heath Robinson, and to some extent that of his older brothers Tom and Charles, has become possible through the writings of John Lewis and Leo de Freitas.[2] Of the three brothers Heath Robinson alone has been constantly remembered, although in the Nineties, in the heyday of John Lane's Bodley Head, the drawings of Charles were as celebrated as those of Beardsley. Mastery of the new process medium was common to them all, however, and their early books show many similarities. For example the black-and-white illustrations to W. Heath Robinson's *A Midsummer Night's Dream* (1914) show Beardsley's Savoy style carried forward to a rich maturity: the crowded textural patterning of flowers and foliage which dominate the full plates provides exactly that feeling of verdant boskiness which the play exudes. Gone are the *art nouveau* flourishes of Edgar Allan Poe's *Poems* (1900) and the elaborately drawn frames of *The Talking Thrush* (1899). Skill at hatching and shading with the pen to provide textures and middle tones is not easily obtained. Heath Robinson's progress in this difficult art may be studied by comparing the clouds and trees in Poe's *Poems* with those in *A Midsummer Night's Dream*. His mature style was apparent by 1909 with Kipling's *A Song of the English*, which appeared in a variety of styles and bindings. From then until the outbreak of the First World War he produced his finest books and those for which he is best remembered, including the unsurpassed *Bill the Minder* of 1912: a nonsense fairytale of his own devising featuring the King of Troy and a bootcleaner called Bill who 'minds' children – a gentleman whose quaint solemnity became something of a prototype for all those

balding, bespectacled elderly gentlemen that populated the pages of his later humorous books.

It was with books such as *The Saintly Hun* (1917), *Humours of Golf* (1923) and *Absurdities* (1934) that Heath Robinson became famous as an inventor of absurd machinery. It was as well that he had this second string to his bow, for the gift book market did not long survive the First World War, and the inter-war years were often lean ones for the professional illustrator. Besides book work he undertook during this time a wide variety of what we would now call graphic design but which then was termed commercial art.

Heath Robinson's greatness lay not only in his artistic ability but also in the capacity to invest everything he touched with his own sensitive and kindly personality, and as a consequence his illustrations appeal to people of all ages. Indeed it might not be too fanciful to suggest that for the generation born in the Nineties his books provided a lifetime's companionship: *The Giant Crab and Other Tales* wonderfully suitable for nursery amusement, *Uncle Lubin* for the early teens, *Chaucer* for the late school years, *Hunlikely* for the martial twenties, *The Home Made Car* perhaps for the thirties, *Professor Branestawm* to amuse one's middle age and *How to Make the Best of Things* as solace for the later years.

The name of Arthur Rackham (1867–1939) is now almost synonymous with the illustrated gift book, and so lavish has been the attention given to him, so plentiful the reproduction of his works and so high the continuing excitement about his art, that it is difficult to see him in perspective and to take a balanced view of his work in relation to that of his contemporaries. Despite the undoubted charms of Edmund Dulac and the gentle and prolific arts of the Robinson brothers and many others discussed here, Rackham must be considered the most successful, as his books are the most typical of the gift book market.

Rackham was by inclination a line artist, and

2. John Lewis, *Heath Robinson: Artist and Comic Genius* (Constable, 1973), and L. de Freitas, *Charles Robinson* (Academy Editions, 1976).

his earliest commissions for such magazines as *The Pall Mall Budget* and *The Westminster Budget* were usually made in black and white with the addition perhaps of a mechanical tint. His early style was quite unremarkable and reflected the prevailing influences of Phil May, Howard Pyle and E. A. Abbey. The delicate intricacy of his individual style of pen drawing developed rapidly, however, and was fully fledged by 1900, as we can see in his *Fairy Tales of the Brothers Grimm. Rip Van Winkle* (1905) and *Peter Pan in Kensington Gardens* (1906) reveal his tinted line drawings in their full maturity and signalled the beginning of his popular success, although, as we have noted in an earlier chapter, success did not come easily. The all-over wash, often in ochre or sepia, gave to Rackham's illustrations an 'antique' feel which became one hallmark of his style. Nevertheless it was a technique employed by many of his contemporaries, notably W. Heath Robinson and Edmund Dulac. As well as pulling the drawing together and softening the effect of the pen line, the wash had the advantage of providing a ground for the addition of further tints. If the wash contained a little white, the resulting semiopacity when dry allowed for the indication of highlights by its removal with a clean brush and water, revealing (if only partially) the paper beneath. Such a technique, which quickly produced the effect of full colour, was extremely useful to artists whose commissions sometimes stipulated as many as forty full-page colour plates and perhaps as many line illustrations. For the 1909 edition of *Fairy Tales of the Brothers Grimm* Rackham provided forty colour plates, and for the two Wagner volumes *The Rhinegold and the Valkyrie* (1910) and *Siegfried and the Twilight of the Gods* (1911) a total of sixty colour plates. His last book, *The Wind in the Willows* (1940), showed no fading of his talent, and the images of Rat, Mole and Toad going about their adventures in a world of gnarled willows and quivering aspen trees is very much in the Rackham manner. The drawings are numerous and delightful, though the characters look somewhat haggard and tatterdemalion relative to the

Shepard illustrations of the same text with which it invites comparison. It is also larger in format and perhaps a more adult version than the Shepard. With such industry over so long a period and with such a marked style it was inevitable that some of his mannerisms – the writhing tree roots, clutching branches, wrinkled faces, gesturing hands, skinny legs and outsize feet – should become clichés, yet there is no repetitiveness; all seems to reflect his own comprehensive imaginary world.

It must be admitted that some of Rackham's books are over-lavish: the demands of the gift book market with its trade, limited and *de luxe* editions, variously and often expensively bound, produced books which were to be looked at rather than read. Many of them were little more than collections of three- or four-colour reproductions of watercolours, of which the originals, in Rackham's case, were usually sold through exhibitions at the Leicester Galleries at the time of publication. The passion for collecting his illustrated editions shows no sign of abating, and prices have leapt dramatically in recent years. An ordinary trade edition of *Peter Pan in Kensington Gardens* (1906), which might have cost £10 in 1970, realised £65 in a Sotheby's sale five years later, while the signed vellum-bound *de luxe* edition fetched £210. Even these sums seem inexpensive by present-day standards.

In 1960 his old publishers Heinemann brought out Derek Hudson's monograph *Arthur Rackham: his Life and Work*. This was re-issued by Heinemann in 1973 with a revised checklist, but so prolific was the artist's output that even this is not quite complete, and fugitive drawings still remain to be discovered in sets of old magazines and children's annuals. The publication in 1975 of Fred Getting's *Arthur Rackham* has corrected many bibliographical errors and provides the most complete picture of Rackham's output. It is also the most detailed analysis of his work yet attempted.

Understandably Rackham's imitators were legion, but on the whole they were strangely unsuccessful and are now little remembered. In his early work Edmund Dulac undoubtedly picked up a trick or two from him, but his own talents were real and individual. Slightly better known than most, Warwick Goble (died 1943) was responsible for a number of gift books in the Edwardian manner, but they are generally rather feeble despite the attempts of his publishers to dress them up with fancy bindings, wash mounts and tissue overlays. Typical of these are the *Stories from the Pentamerone* by Basile (Macmillan, 1911), where the thirty-two colour plates are unsympathetically mounted on heavy brown paper, and *The Fairy Book* from Macmillan in 1913. Though decorative, Goble's drawings lack the power and descriptive skill of Rackham or Dulac, and show a recurring inability to relate figures convincingly – his distant figures always seem small rather than far away. Nevertheless he seems to have been reasonably successful and well patronised by leading publishers. He worked also for magazines including *Pearson's* and *McClure's* in America before going on to illustrate fairy and adventure stories. He had been apprenticed as a chromolithographer and studied art at evening classes in London schools, in which he resembled Charles Robinson.

Charles Folkard (1878–1963) is best known for his *Teddy Tail* children's feature in *The Daily Mail*, which he drew for seventeen years. He entered the world of illustration in a curious way, designing programmes for his own conjuring act at the Egyptian Hall, Piccadilly. After moving to book illustration, his speciality was the fairy story. *Mother Goose* and *Grimms' Fairy Tales* were his ideal subjects, and in 1911 he produced a particularly appealing *Pinocchio*. Other Rackhamesque illustrators included George Soper, who produced drawings for many popular classics, *The Water Babies* and *Lamb's Tales from Shakespeare* amongst them, the American Milo Winter (b. 1888) and a late arrival, Edmund Blampied. Blampied's *Peter Pan* (Hodder and Stoughton, 1939) must represent the tail-end of the illustrated gift book market and shows how long the vogue lasted, despite claims that it had exhausted itself twenty-five years earlier. Winter's work is not

to be fairly compared with Rackham's, but it had considerable colour and spirit and his drawings were doubtless very acceptable to children. These volumes, issued by Rand McNally in Chicago and Duckworth in London, were usually well if unpretentiously printed. Winter's *Arabian Nights* (1914) is particularly bright and cheerful with some amusingly grotesque heads. His taste was for adventure rather than fairy stories but his *Treasure Island, Robinson Crusoe, Gulliver's Travels* and *The Three Musketeers* are outside the area of this study.

The second giant of the gift book world during the first decade of this century was Edmund Dulac (1882–1953). Born in Toulouse, he was sent by his parents to study law, which he did with some reluctance at Toulouse University before breaking free to spend three much more congenial years at the local art school. His liking for art had been excited early on by the Oriental collection formed by his uncle, an importer of goods from the Far East. This and other family encouragement he found invaluable. Writing in *Nash's Magazine* in 1926 he remembered with gratitude:

My father had the tastes and temperament of an artist, and my childhood was spent in an atmosphere of Saturday evening chamber music against a background of Old Masters and old china. The desire to draw and paint came to me when still a tiny child.

He began to illustrate books in 1905, the year of Rackham's big success with *Rip Van Winkle*, starting with a series of small and not very exciting editions of Brontë novels for J. M. Dent. His *Arabian Nights* for Hodder and Stoughton in 1907 proved to be one of the most popular editions of these tales. The drawings are a *tour de force*, ranging from the charming to the quite astonishing. His talent for invoking the decorative styles of the Far and Near East was to be given further opportunity in *The Rubáiyát of Omar Khayyám* (1909), *Ali Baba* (1911) and *Princess Badoura* (1913), all from Hodder and Stoughton and issued in a variety of editions and bindings, and in one of his most lavish books, the large quarto *The Kingdom of the Pearl* (Nisbet, 1920).

Dulac's taste for fantasy is best seen in his fairyland illustrations to *Hans Andersen* (1911) or his own *Fairy Book* (1916). In these he played Hans Andersen to Rackham's Grimm. All his books display the same blend of gentle good humour and a quietly expressed scholarship. In his *Fairy Book*, a collection of fairy tales of different origin (Flemish, English, Belgian, French, Japanese, Chinese, and others), he manages to express something of the spirit and art of each country. Thus we are reminded of Brueghel by the organ grinder illustrating 'White Caroline and Black Caroline'; the Russian tale of 'Ivan and the Chestnut Horse' is illustrated with all the splendour of Russian folk art, while 'Urashima Taro' from Japan has the elegant simplicity of Hokusai or Hiroshige; and in the English tale the peasants of medieval psalters have come to life. For his native French tales he creates a special elegance: in his illustration to 'The Green Serpent' we find dandified French aristocrats of the old régime stepping impossibly into the flat lacquered landscape of a Chinese screen, an illusion which is the very essence of French *chinoiserie*.

Apart from his book illustrations[3] Dulac's decorative talents were always in demand, from chocolate boxes (for Cadbury's) to the decoration of ocean liners. His connection with the Royal Mint began in 1935 with a commission to design the Poetry Medal. In 1937 he designed Coronation stamps with Eric Gill, who undertook the lettering and emblems. The Free French Colonial stamps of 1940 were his, and he was also in demand for banknotes, caricatures, stage sets and costumes (for his friend W. B. Yeats amongst others) as well as murals and designs of all kinds. His ingenious mind seemed to respond to any challenge. R. H. Wilenski described him as

a man in love with craftsmanship. When you went to his studio if he was not at work on one of his several well known activities, you would find him making a nose flute, or binding a book, or cutting an intricate stencil, or modelling a rose in gesso for a tiny locket as a present to a friend.[4]

Nothing seemed to escape him. Sociable, energetic, a gourmet with a taste for casseroles, he liked to talk and amuse and he lectured widely on art and music – Eastern naturally, for Western music he professed to find coarse and unsubtle. His illustrative talents appear to have declined after about 1920 and *The Green Lacquer Pavilion* (1926) literally and figuratively lacks colour. His *Treasure Island* of the following year with its aerial perspectives is original and competent, but not to be compared with Rowland Hilder's evocative illustrations of 1929. *A Fairy Garland* (1928) is pleasant but uninspired and the rococo figures in ferny landscapes lack the original magic. In eighteenth-century revivalism Dulac was soon to be overtaken by Rex Whistler, whose period illustrations disposed of sentiment and combined authenticity with lyricism.

We can only regret that the books of Kay Nielsen (1886–1957) were not more numerous, for he like Rackham, Dulac and Heath Robinson was able to create his own world of fantasy. A Dane with parental connections in the theatre (his mother was an actress at the Royal Theatre and his father a Director of the Dagmartheater, Copenhagen), he soon turned from book illustration to the theatrical world, ending a long career as set designer, actor and muralist in Hollywood. He went to California[5] in 1936 to design sets for Johannes Poulson's *Everyman* and remained to work for Walt Disney, designing amongst other things the Bald Mountain for Disney's *Fantasia*.

Nielsen's visions of fairyland are best realised in his illustrated versions of Grimm and Hans Andersen, Sir Arthur Quiller-Couch's book of stories *In Powder and Crinoline* (1913) and the unsurpassed *East of the Sun and West of the Moon* by Asbjörnsen and Moe (1914). These are romantic illustrations full of fine drawing and tremendous energy. They are compounds of

3. Details of these are given in: Colin White, *Edmund Dulac* (Studio Vista, 1976).
4. *The Times*, 3 June 1953.
5. For an account of Nielsen in America see: D. Larkin, ed., *The Unknown Paintings of Kay Nielsen* (Pan Books, 1977).

many influences (Beardsley, Bakst, 'Alastair' and Jessie King, to mention the more obvious), but the results are far from plagiarism. Take the muscular nude of the North Wind striding over the sea in *East of the Sun and West of the Moon*. His hair streaming behind him, the glint in his eye, the smoking clouds veiling an angry sun and the great Hokusai wave that carries him forward – all convey a strongly Oriental mood. Clearly the art of the East, the heady world of the Russian Ballet and childhood memories of Northern folklore – the world of Ibsen and Grieg – have combined to create this powerful imaginative art. The skill with which the various notes are orchestrated is beyond praise. Not surprisingly this is a book that is now hard to find and expensive to buy. Nielsen seems to have created for himself that air of mystery which was the essential prerequisite for the aesthete at that time. Amidst much lyrical praise *The Studio* magazine noted in November 1913: 'Young and curly, impulsive and pessimistic, his history is probably yet to make. Rumour, however, has it that with no mean attractions of outward person, the young Dane is indebted to his mother – a famous actress – for his talent.'

Hollywood also eventually claimed another of the best of the gift book illustrators, the Hungarian Willy Pogány (1882–1955). Like Nielsen, with whose style his had so much in common, Pogány graduated to London via early training in Paris. He was also heavily influenced by Chinese and Japanese art, illuminated manuscripts and Hungarian peasant art. He worked in London between 1906 and 1915 before making his home in America and was thus in London at the time of the greatest opportunity for the illustrator. During these years he became well known for a succession of books (usually from Harrap), most of them fairy stories and favourite 'classics'. His illustrations to Wagner's *Tannäuser* (1911), *Parsifal* (1912) and *Lohengrin* (1913) may be preferred to Rackham's Wagner illustrations as they have a strong Germanic *fin de siècle* feel about them. A mixture of colour plates, lithographs and line drawings on heavy grey paper, they were a popular

and unusual feature of the Christmas market of those years.

Pogány, Rackham, Nielsen and Dulac all enjoyed great popularity in their own time and were never forgotten. This has not been the case with Jessie M. King (1875–1949), who seems to have been quite neglected until the pioneering researches of John Russell Taylor's *Art Nouveau Book in Britain*, published in 1966. Since then her work has become increasingly familiar, and it is now almost impossible to enter a bookseller's or stationer's shop without coming across reproductions of her work in the form of posters and postcards, for her wispy fairytale world has caught the imagination of a generation born since her death. Her fragile illustrations have always appealed to a small band of discerning collectors. The 1971 Arts Council travelling exhibition catalogue of her work lists some seventy books with which she was associated, including forty for which she designed bindings or paper wrappers.[6] Her other work in the applied arts – needlework, batik, jewellery, pottery, fabric and wallpaper design – is proof enough of the energy and vivacity with which her talents were applied. Stylistically she kept very close to her roots – the linear *art nouveau* of the Mackintosh circle at Glasgow School of Art. In 1902 this group exhibited together at the Turin International Exhibition of Decorative Art, where King won a Gold Medal. From then until 1928 *The Studio* kept her name before the public. In 1902 it published an article on her work by Walter Watson which, despite some high-flown prose, showed a keen sensitivity to her work: 'To this artist a rose bush is not a plant bearing flowers, but a bower whose green columns bearing coloured lights make a palace where bright beings walk dreamily about.'[7] This could almost be a description of the designs she made for *L'Évangile de l'Enfance* (1902), which clearly show her debt to Mackintosh's wife

6. The number of her cover designs is probably nearer to sixty. See Robin de Beaumont, 'Towards a Check-List of Books Illustrated by Jessie M. King', in *The Private Library*, vol. 10, no. 3 (1977).
7. *The Studio*, vol. 26 (1902), pp. 176–88.

COLOUR PLATE VI. A selection of gift books for children from the late 1890s

HER·FACE·WAS·VEILED·WITH·A·VEIL·OF·GAUZE·BUT·HER·FEET·WERE·NAKED·

COLOUR PLATE VII. Jessie M. King
A House of Pomegranates by Oscar Wilde, Methuen, 1915

Margaret Macdonald; the basic geometrical composition of rectangles, triangles, verticals, ball flowers and haloes linking consumptive figures with pale faces and abundant Pre-Raphaelite hair, reveals all the elements of the Macdonald style.

The following year Jessie King's own personality overrode these mannerisms and the looser, powder-fine quality of her own mature style made its appearance with books which must have been very much to her liking: Sebastian Evans's *High History of the Holy Grail* (for which she received £30) and two Broadway Booklets for Routledge, the *Morte d'Arthur* and *The Rubáiyát of Omar Khayyám*. Her next commission, for John Lane, was William Morris's *Defence of Guenevere* (1904),[8] which allowed her genius full play. Morris's poem has seldom appeared in happier dress. The twenty-two full-page illustrations, each illustrating a line from the poem, are well chosen, and 'She threw her wet hair backward from her brow' and the frontispiece 'But she stood sideways listening' are closely sympathetic to Morris in feeling if quite unlike his own art. One wonders what he might have thought of these drawings had he lived to see them, for her medievalism has a quaint diaphanous quality far removed from that of his beloved Burne-Jones. As a production the book is something of a disappointment, especially from so fastidious a publisher, being small in size with an indifferent cloth cover, drawings over-reduced and printed on an unpleasant coated paper. Much more satisfactory reproduction was obtained in the *Comus* of 1906, published in Routledge's Photogravure and Colour series – a happy choice of process for her delicate drawings. In 1906 she was commissioned by T. C. & E. C. Jack to provide the plates for two small books, *Shelley* by Churton Collins and *Spenser* by W. B. Yates. Although they contain some of her most attractive drawings they are undistinguished productions.

At about this time also Jessie King began her long association with two Scottish publishers, T. N. Foulis and Gowans & Gray. Both special-ised in tiny gift books and booklets ranging in price from a few pence to half a crown according to the binding material, which might have been paper, cloth, Japanese vellum or limp calf. The Foulis books were often in the tall format popularised by Laurence Housman, their Envelope Books being even narrower and taller than their prototypes. She produced one outstandingly good collection of drawings with *Budding Life* (1906), a book of plant drawings of almost Japanese simplicity. By 1915, when her *House of Pomegranates* was published, her work was showing a marked change of style and had become stronger and more colourful. Wilde's story is enriched with sixteen colour plates that reflect perhaps the brightness of Bakst and the Russian Ballet. It is interesting to see how subtly her style evolved with the changing artistic climate, linking her early Glasgow style of the 1890s with an almost abstract style during the 1920s and yet always retaining her unique qualities of decoration. An interesting example of this change can be seen if one compares two covers which she designed for *R. L. Stevenson Memories*. For the first, in 1912, she drew a view of cottages at Sanston within a crucifix of wiry double lines very much in the Glasgow style; for the second version, the reprint of 1922, she translated this same drawing into a mosaic of interlocking shapes of an almost abstract beauty. She was, like many of her compatriots, temperamentally very close to the Continent. France became almost a second home, and for a time she and her husband E. A. Taylor, the furniture designer, ran an art school in Paris.

In Britain, King has often been regarded as a follower of Aubrey Beardsley, but this is too simple an assessment of her work, although initially she doubtless learnt something from him, and an examination of her illustrations reveals her as a person of cosmopolitan tastes. According to received opinion she was herself something of a fairy-tale character, and it is true that she had a penchant for wide-brimmed hats, gauntlets, cloaks and shoes with silver buckles.

8. Reprinted in facsimile by Scolar Press, 1979.

In a letter written in the 1920s to Elizabeth Kyle she explained: 'I believe in fairies . . .[;] once when I was 16 I fell asleep on a hill in Argyllshire and I felt wee hands come up out of the ground and touch my eyes and when I awoke I knew I could do detail like I do in my pictures.' Fortunate owners of *Comus* or *The Defence of Guenevere* might well believe her. Early influences are also recalled in her introduction to *The Little White Town of Never Weary* (1917). In this book she describes, by means of drawings and photographs of her own models, how to make a cardboard village; she also shows how easily she was able to conjure enchantment from ordinariness.

Long ago in a country village, among hills rather bare and barren, lived a little girl, one of many children in an old world house set in an older-world garden, and although many children mean much fun and jollity, sometimes one child can be very lonely among a lot of others, just as one can, when older, feel alone in a crowd.

So this child dreamed day dreams alone of fairy castles and palaces and knights in armour and maidens in distress rescued by the same knights, and the stream which ran past the foot of the old world garden held for her enchanted princes and water-kelpies, and out of the materials to be had she made little models of those day dreams and peopled them, first with her fancies and afterwards with these fancies made real and tangible.

For someone of so strongly individual a talent Jessie King had surprisingly few emulators. Annie French, for example, seems to have illustrated only one book; many other Glasgow artists took to embroidery, which might, in their eyes at least, have seemed a sister art. Closest to Jessie King's was the work of another Scottish artist, Katherine Cameron (1874–1965), whose rather crude drawings have a strong *art nouveau* quality. Her drawing of faces and figures was often extremely weak, but what she lacked in draughtsmanship she more than made up for in feeling and expressive use of colour. Most of her work was published by the Edinburgh firm of Jack, who commissioned illustrations for books of myths, legends and fairy tales, which all gave

ample opportunity for the display of her gifts. In these books her sad figures, dressed in vivid blues and yellows, wander in almost Fauvist landscapes, or perch on hard chairs in Baillie–Scott rooms.

Another artist who showed distinct traces of Arts and Crafts as well as *art nouveau* influence, was Anne Anderson (fl. 1910–30). Her illustrations to the tales of the Grimms and Hans Andersen have been frequently reprinted, but her large picture books – *Old French Nursery Songs*, *Old English Nursery Songs* and *The Sleepy Song Book* – are less well known. Her wide-eyed children, goblins and rather gloomy medieval grown-ups inhabit a world of plasticine palaces and cottages seemingly made from sweets; her landscapes often evolve into highly decorative whiplash lines that trail around, to frame the text. She was in constant demand for embellishments for the popular children's annuals of the inter-war years and seems never to have quite gone out of favour. Her style was eminently suitable to process reproduction and was followed by many minor artists – notably L. A. Govey and M. S. Reeve.

Linking fantasy and fairyland with a sense of whimsy all his own is the work of Vernon Hill (b. 1887). Hill was a Yorkshireman who left school at the age of thirteen and was apprenticed to a lithographer, a common beginning for illustrators who came up the hard way. At eighteen he was teaching mill-hands as a pupil-teacher in a local night school, and at twenty-three was launched by John Lane with his drawings for *The Arcadian Calendar* (1909), to which he also contributed a short text for each month. The lithographed plates are of highly fantastic landscapes with elongated and emaciated figures posturing or capering about, each month having a representative figure such as the 'old speckled May-man dancing round the hawthorn, piping and jolly', or the bag-piping Fool of July in a chestnut glade. Hill illustrated several other books for Lane, of which the large quarto *Ballads Weird and Wonderful* is outstanding with its pale pencil drawings, reminiscent of Dulac, showing a highly developed sense of design. In

1921 he began working for John Hassall as a poster artist, and after this date seems to have illustrated only one book.

Fairy illustration has old roots, and both Arthur Rackham and Jessie King remind us, to some extent, of the part played by Pre-Raphaelitism in shaping its evolution. In their art it is as though the brilliantly coloured world of Tennyson, Millais and Hughes was seen only slightly dimmed through the mists of a Celtic twilight. Contemporary with Rackham and King, however, there evolved other, darker worlds of fantasy which owed their origin to the conscious attitudes of decadence prevalent in the Nineties. Aubrey Beardsley has duly received credit for his part in this development, but there were others, often obscure, who followed his lead and his *á rebours* view of life: 'Alastair' (Hans Henning Voight) (1887–1969), Harry Clarke, Austin Osman Spare, Alan Odle, Jean de Bosschère, and, in his early years, John Austen. Their comparative obscurity does not always appear to have been due to the vagaries of fortune, for in some cases it seems to have been deliberately cultivated. P. G. Konody, writing in the introduction to Walter Pater's *Sebastian Van Storck* (1927), illustrated by Alastair, commented suggestively that 'the few who met him there [Munich] had strange things to tell about his personality and manner of life', but he does not tell us what they were. Robert Ross, introducing another of the artist's books,[9] was even less help, but added darkly: 'I cannot promise for him or collectors an early death.' (Ross also wrote for Wilde's *The Sphinx* (1920) a note shot through with spurious mystery.) Alastair's books from English publishers are not numerous. Apart from the *Forty-Three Drawings* (1914), *The Sphinx* (1920) and Pater's *Sebastian Van Storck* (1927), all from John Lane, there were a number of smaller books of the late Twenties from the Black Sun Press of Paris. In all of these are present the same spidery beings of indeterminate sex likened by Ross to the art of Beardsley, but in reality closer to Harry Clarke or even Egon Schiele. Wilde did not live to see Alastair's version of *The Sphinx* but

would presumably have enjoyed his rendering of 'that Young God the Tyrian who was more amorous than the dove of Ashtaroth'.

More substance is to be found in the work of Harry Clarke (1890–1931), whose career, like Beardsley's, was cut short by tuberculosis. If Beardsley had an heir it was Clarke, for he had great gifts as a draughtsman; these can be seen to the full in his version of Poe's *Tales of Mystery and Imagination* (1919). Clarke was trained as a boy in his father's stained glass business in Dublin. At the age of twenty he was admitted to the Dublin Metropolitan School of Art, where his work attracted the attention of the celebrated judges Selwyn Image, Byam Shaw and Walter Crane. His study of stained glass was helped by a travelling scholarship to France which enabled him to see the cathedrals and helped to prepare him for the commissions which later came his way. Whilst working on the Honan Chapel windows for University College, Cork, in 1916, he was also producing the drawings for a startlingly original edition of Hans Andersen's *Fairy Tales*. In these drawings the vivid colours of the Russian Ballet are mixed with the dark mystery of Symbolist painting. The gaunt standing figures, their heavily made-up eyes and the strongly patterned backgrounds of rich colours go beyond Beardsley and have the luminous colour of stained glass. His real feeling for Gothic horror is in his Poe illustrations, where tubercular figures rise in agony from pools of black ink or subside like M. Valdemar, whose suppurating corpse decomposes on a couch. With his illustrations to Perrault's *Fairy Tales* (1922), by contrast, the sun comes out: here the spirit of the old French tales is picked out in elegant patterns.

Clarke, Odle, Spare and John Austen knew each other, and so some exchange of ideas is to be expected. Compare, for instance, John Austen's first book, *The Little Ape* by R. H. Keen, with Clarke's Poe. Austen was to outgrow this early 1890s style and adopt a more severe decorative style in the art deco manner, with

9. *Forty-Three Drawings by Alastair* (Lane, 1914).

stiff figure drawings looking like fashion plates made in paper sculpture – as in his *Manon Lescaut* (1928) from Bles. This style was applied by him so indiscriminately that his later work is more decorative than illustrative.

There was nothing fashionable about the work of Alan Odle (1888–1948), whose fantastic designs billow, or belch, in great baroque curves filled with closely-drawn and ingenious incident. For all its horror his work has a distinctly rococo charm, and his surrealism contains an element of uproarious farce – as in the drawing of 'The Infuriated Trousers' reproduced in *The Studio* in 1928. With their baggy shape, wobbling gait, flying buttons and braces lashing at terror-stricken people, they appear to have stepped out of Walt Disney's *Fantasia*, and induce the same half-fearful hilarity.

The two numbers of *The Gypsy* (1915 and 1916) contain some of Odle's best illustrations, although they are not always well reproduced, partly because of his habit of making enormous drawings in ink and soft pencil on tracing paper. The influence of Beardsley is strong: there are contrasts of texture brought about by stippling, hatching and shading that bring them very close to Beardsley's *Rape of the Lock*. In appearance and manner also he gave the impression of being a reincarnation of that consumptive genius. Writing in 1972 his sister-in-law Rose Odle described how he 'walked every night to the Café Royal, where as Prince of Bohemia, he held his court. His fair hair swathed round the top of a long narrow face, slender pointed ears, the rapid gliding walk, all combined to give a fawn-like appearance. He wore a dark velvet jacket and a flowing black ribbon bow.'[10] Emulation is one thing, but one wonders what Odle might have thought had he lived to see the Beardsley exhibition held at the Victoria and Albert Museum in 1966, where a portrait of him by Adrian Allinson was catalogued as 'reputed to be a natural son of Aubrey Beardsley' and (as if that weren't enough) labelled 'Mr Watkins'.

There is little humour in the work of Austin Spare (1888–1956), as can be seen from his illustrations to *The Starlit Mire* (1911), a book of Wildean aphorisms. In his linear style he owes something to Sullivan, but the drawings are richly imaginative with a pervasive sense of evil. He shared with Beardsley the ability to arrange the picture space into contrasting areas of black and white, and there is in his work a tendency towards the vertical. Spare dabbled in the occult, having been initiated into witchcraft during his teens. He also engaged in automatic drawing (i.e. drawing done with the conscious mind held in suspension), the results of which G. B. Shaw found 'too strong meat for normal'. In addition to illustrating Spare wrote several books on philosophy and the occult.

Strong meat, too, was provided by the Belgian Jean de Bosschère (1878–1953), whose grotesque and often erotic fancy initially owed more to Bosch than to Beardsley. The Russian choreographer Leonid Massine once declared that he found himself unable to express the modern world without being grotesque: 'Look at the chief figures of today. Take the Kaiser and Charlie Chaplin. Both are grotesque.' In this sense Bosschère's work too was modern. He was the ideal illustrator for a number of the older classics – *Ovid*, *The Golden Asse* and *The Satyricon*. The drawings of John Kettlewell and M. Watson-Williams for those facetious but once popular satires on Pepys, *The Diary of the Great Warr* and *A Second Diary of the Great Warr* (1917), appear to be strong evidence of the influence of his style on his contemporaries. It is strange that an artist of such importance has been so long neglected, but this may in part be due to the erotic nature of his later work (particularly for the Fortune Press) which in Britain has banished many of his books to booksellers' more unreachable shelves.

The work of Sidney Sime (1867–1941) suffered a similar eclipse but has now been restored to popularity owing to a post-Tolkien interest in fantasy – a term difficult to define, as what appears fantastical to one may appear merely absurd to another. About most of Sime's work

10. Rose Odle, *Salt of our Youth* (Worden's of Cornwall, 1972).

there can be little doubt, for at his best he produced disturbing drawings that were highly fantastic and often contained a vein of quiet humour. Finding these drawings presents problems, as most of them were published in old periodicals such as *The Idler*, *Pick-me-up*, *Eureka*, *The Butterfly*, *Queen*, *Strand*, *The Sketch* and *The Tatler*. His book illustrations were mostly confined to the writings of Lord Dunsany: *The Gods of Pegana* (1905), *Time and the Gods* (1906), *The Sword of Welleran* (1908), *A Dreamer's Tales* (1910), *The Book of Wonder* (1912) and *Tales of Wonder* (1916). These collections of fantastic stories concerning imaginary worlds, part Celtic and part Oriental, were not produced in large editions, and Dunsany once remarked, 'the number of people who have bought my first editions could be counted on the thumbs of one hand.'[11] The illustrations to these books, in a style that owes something to Blake and Beardsley, arouse an interest in the artist that cannot be easily satisfied. The recent researches of George Locke have helped to rectify this situation and his *From an Ultimate Dim Thule*[12] contains an invaluable record of Sime's work for magazines. From interviews he gave to the press it emerges that Sime started life as a coal miner in Yorkshire, having 'rather a severe time of it'.[13] He was put to work removing the newly-mined coal from the coal face by means of small heavily-laden trolleys, or 'scoops', which he had to push down tunnels less than three feet high. It was a life more black than white ('one did get a good deal too much of the shade') and poor training for an illustrator, although it may have stimulated the sense of alarm and drama present in much of his work. Not surprisingly he escaped as soon as he could to study at Liverpool School of Art, before going on to work for the London illustrated papers. His work for these expressed 'a distinctive mood of the period', as Holbrook Jackson remarked,[14] and Sime must be considered as a Nineties artist. In 1923 he wrote the jingles and drew the pictures for *Bogey Beasts*, a weird musical treat for children with strong nerves. Josef Holbrook's musical scores are accompanied by full-page

drawings of 'The Seekim', 'The Prapsnot' and thirteen other nightmare creatures, along with some curious comic verse with a satirical edge.

There are many other illustrators who if space allowed would merit inclusion here. Some have long been familiar from childhood and their illustrations are still in print. One case in point is Henry Ford (1860–1941), who illustrated Andrew Lang's famous collections of fairy stories, the *Blue*, *Red*, *Green*, *Yellow*, *Pink*, *Grey*, *Violet*, *Brown*, *Orange* and *Olive Fairy Books*. He was occasionally aided in this by Lancelot Speed and Jacomb Hood. His drawings are always crammed with incident, which pleases children, but they are thinly drawn. Much stronger work was produced by John Batten (1871–1932), the illustrator of Joseph Jacobs' collections of tales. *English*, *Celtic*, and *Indian Fairy Tales* were issued in a variety of bindings, from luxurious large paper copies to cheaper, ordinary editions. The illustrations are firmly drawn and show a sympathy with the Oriental and Celtic decorative styles then fashionable at Liberty's store in London. If his giants and monsters possess an authentic horror his damsels and maidens seem somewhat sexless, but then, as Sketchley had observed, 'the passionate figures of Greek and Celtic epics need translation before they can figure in fairy-tale books.'[15]

It may be claimed that the work of these artists exploited the line block to its limits, and sometimes, as with Harry Clarke, Beardsley and Jessie King, almost beyond those limits, as their drawings with pen and brush produced ever more complex shadings, hatchings and stipplings with sudden contrasts of hair-fine lines and flooding blacks. By 1918 their best work was past and the gift book market which sustained them had collapsed under changing social conditions following the First World War. However, this may not be the whole story, for the rise of

11. Letter to Margaret Coats, 7 November 1923.
12. Ferret Fantasy Ltd., 1973.
13. *The Idler*, January 1898.
14. *The Eighteen Nineties* (Grant Richards, 1913), p. 262.
15. R. E. D. Sketchley, *English Book Illustration of Today* (Kegan Paul, 1903), p. 110.

the cinema at about this time provided another and more powerful outlet for the human longing for the fantastic. This too was noticeably at first a black-and-white medium, also capable of emotional impact through strong chiaroscuro and textural effects. The books that followed in the Twenties and Thirties were on the whole fewer and feebler. The magazines, too, which had provided many of these artists with a livelihood, began to decline as their readers turned their attentions to the rival attractions of radio and cinema.

CHAPTER 8

Mainly for Children

Even before the advent of process reproduction there had been a plentiful supply of gay and colourful picture books for children. The wood-engraved books of Edmund Evans had been matched by the chromolithographic splendours of Ernest Nister imported from Bavaria, Marcus Ward and Raphael Tuck in London and McLoughlin and others in New York. In all of these the text, if present at all, played a very subsidiary role, which allowed the artist considerable scope.

The simplest picture books were often the alphabet books, but there were many other types which required a minimum of words: animal and zoo books, farm books, books about the town or countryside or books giving simple pictorial instruction on the customs and costumes of foreign peoples, or those with a strong social bent that described the habits and appearances of different trades and professions, of which early examples in process reproduction were the books illustrated by Francis Bedford (1864–1954) for E. V. Lucas. *Four and Twenty Toilers* (1900) has twenty-four colour plates showing the happy toilers at work, among them the builder, knife-grinder, carpenter, gamekeeper, chimney-sweep and school teacher. The accompanying poems are amusing and occasionally pointed, as in this extract from the verse about the speculative builder:

> It's very hard upon the field
>   On which a builder gazes
> For brick and stone are more to him
>   Than buttercups and daisies.

At first glance this book appears to be yet another in the Greenaway tradition, but closer inspection reveals that the key block and the colour blocks are all photo-engraved in skilful imitation of the earlier process and printed with the same light ochres, apple greens, creams and terracottas. Grant Richards published another of Bedford's best efforts in this style – *The Book of Shops* (1899), also by E. V. Lucas. While superficially similar to the *Toilers*, this appears to have been printed lithographically, yet retains the traditional appearance of tinted line illustration. Born in 1864, Bedford trained at the Royal College of Art Architectural Schools before becoming a pupil of Arthur Blomfield, and this early training has naturally left its mark on his convincing interiors and architectural details.

The technique of introducing a subject through a child's exploration was popular. As in the work of Charles Robinson, Bedford's little children are central to the book's purpose: they are seen wandering hand in hand through a garden of the imagination, looking at this and that with wide-eyed curiosity.

> For dear little children go romping about
> With dollies and tin-tops and drums,
> And, my! how they frolic and scamper and shout
> Till bedtime too speedily comes![1]

Quite what vein of 'perverse' sentiment gave rise to this orgy of infantilism in the Nineties is hard to say, but the gift book market, fed by the

1. Eugene Field, *Lullaby Land* (Lane, 1898), p. 62.

work of R. L. Stevenson, Eugene Field and Evelyn Sharp, faithfully reflected it. Other artists who catered for the cult included Celia Levetus, L. E. Wright, E. Richardson and Mrs Arthur Gaskin. Mabel Dearmer (1872–1915), best known for her illustrations to *The Book of Penny Toys* (1899) – illustrations with the bright simplicity of wooden toys – was, according to Laurence Housman,

one of the most amusing people I have ever met. She wrote good Nursery Rhymes, with illustrations rather crudely drawn, but of the right kind. These I admired and corrected for her as far as correctness was desirable and we had great fun together. . . . [She] turned to writing sombre novels, gradually became 'good' and when she started producing her plays by committees including archbishops and bishops, I was not of the company.[2]

Apart from Beardsley, who was not in the 'frolicsome baby' market, the chief of Lane's illustrators at this time was Charles Robinson (1870–1937). His contemporary following was enormous, but since the First World War his reputation has been eclipsed by that of his brother, W. Heath Robinson. Despite a recent revival of interest his work is still not well known to the general public, which is unfortunate, because he was one of the most prolific of British book illustrators and an imaginative and original watercolourist.

Between 1895 and 1900 he was busy on behalf of John Lane illustrating a succession of titles of which the ever-popular *A Child's Garden of Verses* (1895) is typical. The popularity of this book must be due in part to its immense readability, Stevenson's verses being part of the experience of several generations of children. Lines such as: 'The rain is falling all around,/It falls on field and tree' and 'The moon has a face like the clock in the hall,/She shines on the thieves on the garden wall' are not easily forgotten. Much of Stevenson's verse has this reflective quality: the world is seen through the half-shut eyes of a child hovering between dream and waking, whose drowsy fancy wanders over the world of counterpane 'into fairy land, where all the children dine at five,/And all the

playthings come alive.' The illustrations are a little uneven in style, owing in part to the blockmaker's over-reduction, but what is remarkable is the diversity of invention they display. His children seem to be the authentic denizens of Stevenson's dreamland; flocks of them play about the text dressed in nightgowns tied with enormous bows, their hair crisply waved in the manner of *amorini* by Bernini, their chubby hands clutching sunflowers, pop-guns or candlesticks. Eugene Field's *Lullaby Land* (1898) is almost a companion volume, so similar is it in style and format. Here again the poets sing of Shut-Eye Town and Wynken, Blynken and Nod, but carry Stevenson's charm to an extreme sentimentality: 'And here is a kiss on your winkyblink eyes,/And here is a kiss on your dumple-down cheek.' Other excellent small books in a similar vein include Gabriel Setoun's *The Child World* and *Make Believe* by H. D. Lowry (both 1896), and, perhaps the most attractive of them all, the fairy story *King Longbeard* (1898) by Barrington MacGregor. Dedicated by the author to the Duchess of York, its dedication page carries a drawing of the infant Prince Edward playing with toy scales in which the English crown is outweighed by a pile of soldiers, sailors and guns. More important than the cloudy symbolism of this is the realisation of the royal babe as a fashionable Robinson type – Charles had arrived.

Charles had been trained as a lithographic artist with Waterlow & Sons, and it was not until the end of his seven-year apprenticeship in 1894 that he could devote himself to his desired career as an illustrator, which makes his rapid rise to the top the more remarkable. Evidence of this rise is provided by *The Studio* for July 1895, which devoted several pages to him under the title 'A new book illustrator: Charles Robinson' – a service previously performed for Aubrey Beardsley.

Of his days at Waterlow's he could recall lying with two or three other apprentices across the enormous lithographic stones drawing railway

2. Laurence Housman, *The Unexpected Years* (Cape, 1937), p. 129.

posters. Pay was almost nonexistent and lunch consisted of a sixpenny steak pie with a cup of tea from a dark urn which was emptied only once a week. His obvious talents so impressed one of the Waterlow brothers that he paid for Charles to enter the Royal Academy Schools, to which his brothers, Will and Tom, had won scholarships. His finances improved considerably with his early commissions from John Lane, and in 1896 he was able to marry on the strength of his earnings from *A Child's Garden of Verses*. He seems always to have been fortunate in his friendships: John Lane helped him in many ways and the principal of Heatherley's School formed a 'black-and-white' class for him to teach. In 1898 he was at the height of his early success and taking work from other publishers – Wells Gardner Darton, Gowans and Gray and Blackie's. Arnold Bennett, who met him at this time, has left us a picture of a deceptively fragile person:

Dunn brought to lunch Charles Robinson, who has designed the cover of *Journalism for Women*: a very young unkempt, pale, nervous man, with tremulous eyes. One could see that not long since he had been more nervous than he is today. Contact with the world is making him less like a startled fawn. He told me that his designs for my book[3] had been so much liked that it had resulted in orders for twenty others.[4]

Certainly his health was never strong but his output was enormous and the strain must have been great. In the years immediately preceding the First World War he turned from exclusively black-and-white work to the newly perfected colour process and produced some of his most memorable illustrations. These included *Bee* by Anatole France (Dent, 1912), Shelley's *Sensitive Plant* (Heinemann, 1911) and Frances Hodgson Burnett's last book *The Secret Garden* (1911), which can only make one wish he had illustrated *Little Lord Fauntleroy*. In 1963 the plates were wearing thin and the publishers circulated booksellers on the advisability of finding a new illustrator for *The Secret Garden*. Their unanimous verdict, however, was that no other illustrations would do and so the plates had to be remade.

Continuously in print, the delicate watercolours he modelled on his own children have been familiar for nearly seventy years and are still appropriate today. In 1974 the BBC made a successful film version of the story drawing on Robinson's remarkable illustrations for inspiration.

Just before the outbreak of the First World War Robinson was busy on some of his finest colour illustrations, the plates for Oscar Wilde's fairy tale *The Happy Prince* (Duckworth, 1913). In the same year he also made the drawings for Shakespeare's *Songs and Sonnets* (Duckworth), but the war prevented publication and, unfortunately, payment to the artist. The book was eventually published in 1915.

The war put paid to the market which supported so many artists, and not all of them were capable of turning adversity to advantage. But W. Heath Robinson applied his comic talents to ridiculing the Hun with drawings that were originally published in magazines like *The Sketch* and *The Bystander*, and eventually collected under such titles as *Some Frightful War Pictures*, *Hunlikely* and *The Saintly Hun*. Their popularity launched him on a second career as a humorous artist, bringing him international prestige.

For Charles the problem was solved less easily and he turned to watercolour painting, commercial work and the occasional contribution to children's annuals. In later years his watercolours were frequently exhibited at the Royal Academy and he was made a member of the Royal Institute of Painters in Watercolours. Thus the hobby of his old London Sketch Club days became his chief occupation and support. In these pictures the imaginative quality of his early books is still to be found – crowds of curly-haired children cling to the masts of sailing ships that press through light rococo spray, all drawn in a mist of delicate colouring. He never tired of painting ships, and they appear in many of his illustrations. Robinson's work was always

3. *Journalism for Women: a practical guide* (Lane, 1898).
4. *Journal*, 2 March 1898.

brilliantly imaginative, and while he had many imitators his own style seems to have arrived almost overnight. An early critic in *The Studio* noted: 'He seems so far to have escaped the influence of three of his contemporaries ... Charles Ricketts, R. Anning Bell and Aubrey Beardsley.'[5] Nor does he owe anything to Vierge: only in the work of the Frenchmen Boutet de Monvel and Eugène Grasset and in the brittle rococo of Leon Solon is there any hint of his fluid style. He was a master of the curling, trailing line travelling in graceful arabesques, and had developed the knack of allowing the ink to flow easily from his pen without pressure or variation.

Robinson's imitators, though numerous, need not detain us long. To some extent Francis Bedford was one of them; *Nursery Rhymes* (Methuen, 1897), printed in colour by Edmund Evans, has the dolls'-world landscapes, the stiff wooden trees, giant sunflowers and children in billowing smocks that were so much a part of the Nineties 'nursery world'. In the decorative patterning of the foliage and simple branching leaves there is a hint too of the precision of the Gaskins and the Birmingham School – Mrs Gaskin's *A.B.C.* of the previous year is worth comparison. Both Margaret Tarrant and Helen Stratton owe more than a little to him: the former's version of Robert Louis Stevenson's *A Child's Garden of Verses* (1918) has many black-and-white illustrations which would not look out of place in Charles Robinson's 1896 forerunner. Helen Stratton's *Songs for Little People* by Norman Gale (Constable, 1896) swarms with Robinson babies and the verse is even more extreme:

> Bartholomew
> Is hugged and kissed
> He loves a flower
> In either fist.

Working in a similar vein for John Lane, Griselda Wedderburn produced some memorable black-and-white drawings for W. B. Rand's *Lilliput Revels* (1905). Grant Richards also published large coloured picture books of the baby variety, some of them illustrated in the same wooden style by Will Kidd.

Of all children's picture books, animal books, particularly baby-animal books, have proved the most popular, and none more so than those of Cecil Aldin (1870–1935). By their skill, anatomical knowledge and insight into animal behaviour, his drawings manage to avoid sentimentality. His output over a long working life was extensive, and appropriately for an M.F.H. of the South Berkshire Hunt, included many hunting pictures, which are still to be found decorating the bars of country pubs and the bedrooms of small hotels. As well as his puppy-dog and hunting books he produced some marvellous Christmas books in the Caldecott tradition. *Christmas Eve* (c.1910), which he did for Hodder & Stoughton, is typical. Washington Irving may have had more celebrated illustrators but few caught better his spirit of old Christmas. The colour plates are mounted on stiffish brown paper, as was then the fashion, and sometimes comprised two or three pictures in one, divided horizontally – a useful device for making more than one statement on the same page, and allied to the comic tradition. By the First World War his puppy-dogs and horses were well known and the puppies in particular seem in retrospect to have been almost a canine equivalent to Mabel Lucie Attwell's sturdy children. From *Ten Little Puppy Dogs* (1902) to the *Bobtail Puppy Book* (1914) their appeal was endless. Aldin was undoubtedly happiest at this kind of work and his illustrations to *Black Beauty* (1912) do not share the same sense of enjoyment. For some the puppies are, of course, too cute by half, and the parallel with Mabel Lucie Attwell may be taken further; like Aldin's puppies, her little girls seemed to arouse extremes of affection or dislike. But in fairness it must be remembered that they were drawn in the first place for the entertainment of small children, though Attwell postcards were later produced by Valentines in vast numbers in answer to

5. *The Studio*, vol. 5 (1895), p. 150.

what must have been substantial adult demand.

Children drawn by Mabel Lucie Attwell (1879–1964) may still be found in the shops today, as the 'Boo Boos' industry was successfully carried on by her late daughter. The strength of their appeal is amazing, as all the other Edwardian Baby types have been killed off by two World Wars and changes in public taste. Mabel Lucie Attwell was one of those who suffered the wearisome copying of casts at Heatherley's Art School. She took to illustrating her own fairy stories to relieve the tedium and it was not long before Raphael Tuck was employing her to illustrate the old fairy-tales of the Grimms and Hans Andersen. She drew easily from her imagination and never seems to have had resource to models for details of rooms and furniture. Her husband Harold Earnshaw, who was also illustrating children's books, supplied her with such details where required. Of her books, *Peter Pan* (1921) and *The Water Babies* (1915) are perhaps the best known and most typical. Their illustrations are sprinkled with the myriad tiny fairy folk with the pear-shaped heads and antennae of the green-coated Boo Boos. They bear a passing resemblance to the *Peek-a-Boos* picture books of Chloë Preston, and may even owe something to the Dutch dolls of Bertha and Florence Upton's *Golliwog Books*. At any rate they were soon to be found almost everywhere: on Sefton's handkerchiefs, Shelley Tableware (used by royalty) and on a wide range of commercial publicity. In 1919 she illustrated *Peeping Pansy* by Mary, Queen of Roumania, which entailed a visit to the rather threadbare Royal Palace at Bucharest. This crowned head employed many of the best book illustrators to embellish her own fairy stories, including Edmund Dulac and Helen Stratton.

Alice Woodward (1862–1911) is best remembered today for her sympathetic illustrations to *The Story of Peter Pan*, first published by Bell in 1907 and almost continuously in print ever since. Less idiosyncratic than Mabel Lucie Attwell's version, and distinctly less worrying than that of Arthur Rackham, it contains some of her finest illustrations in watercolours. It was issued in a variety of editions, the cheapest bound in cloth for ninepence; very much the same format was used for an edition for 'little folks' printed in large type. There was also a collection of the plates with a short introduction, *The Peter Pan Picture Book*, and 'for the nursery or schoolroom' *The Peter Pan Pictures*. There were four to choose from, printed on stout paper 30 by 20 inches, framed and glazed for 7s. 6d.

She drew with a lightly dancing line in which descriptive purpose was never quite overridden by a love of pattern and shapes. Her drawings have a sense of ease and good humour – her Captain Hook and Queen of Hearts look more mischievous than malicious. Her childhood was spent at home in London where her father, Dr Henry Woodward, was Keeper of Geology at the British Museum. Always fond of drawing, she was one of a number of little girls to whom Ruskin gave drawing lessons. Naturally the Museum provided her with subjects, and in later life she recalled drawing there at the age of eight: 'From our earliest childhood we all wanted to be artists and drew pictures to all our games and the stories we read or invented. We also easily drew diagrams for my father's lectures and made scientific drawings for him and his friends.'[6] For one such friend, Henry Knipe, she joined six other artists[7] in providing the illustrations for an interminable poem *Nebula to Man* (1905). As the title suggests the poem took as its subject a rather wide span of prehistoric evolution and it cannot have been the easiest of commissions, for the author's purpose was didactic and no creature of the muddy long-ago was neglected by his Miltonic muse.

With her sisters, Alice Woodward formed the '91 Club' for lady artists at their home in Manresa Road, Chelsea. Some early designs for invitations to 'At Homes' of the Club show how curiously unformed her style was as late as 1894, when she was thirty-two.[8] She studied at the

6. B. E. Mahony, *Illustrators of Children's Books 1745–1945* (Horn Book Inc., Boston, 1947), p. 374.
7. Including Charles Whymper and Edward Wilson, the Antarctic watercolourist.
8. *The Studio*, vol. 3 (1894), p. 96.

Westminster School of Art and in Paris and was noticed as a promising student by Joseph Pennell, Whistler's somewhat cranky biographer and amateur talent-spotter, with the result that in 1895 she was given two commissions – *Eric, Prince of Lorlonia* by the Countess of Jersey for Macmillan and *Banbury Cross and other Nursery Rhymes* for J. M. Dent. But it was with Blackie and Sons that she was to become well known with *The Princess of Hearts* (1899) and *To Tell the King the Sky is Falling* (1896), both by Sheila Braine. The latter book earned her a mention in R. E. D. Sketchley's *English Book Illustration of Today* (1903): 'When most successful she can draw a pleasing child with lines almost as few as those used by any modern artist.' (Presumably Charles Robinson held the record, for at this time he was busy drawing ballooning babies almost devoid of features.) Blackie's books for children were then of very high quality and in this case the stout buckram, gleaming gilt edges and smooth heavy paper are redolent of a more opulent era. For Bell in 1908 she illustrated *The Pinafore Picture Book* by W. S. Gilbert, which together with *The Story of the Mikado* (1921), publication of which was delayed by the war, formed perhaps her best-known work for the adult gift book market. In many of her children's books she developed the intriguing habit of hiding her monogram in the drawings. Her initials were stylised in the fashion of Whistler's butterfly and can be found, for example, in *The Brownies and other Tales*[9] of 1910 embroidered on a gnome's sleeve, carved on a beam in a hayloft and decorating a chair seat. Although her gentle art places her in the front rank of children's illustrators, more robust outlets for her talents included the restoration of prehistoric animals for *The Illustrated London News* and map-drawing for naval intelligence in the First World War.

The work of Susan Beatrice Pearse (1878–1980) is firmly in the Mabel Lucie Attwell camp. Her books were mostly for little children and she is well known for the small *Ameliaranne* series from Harrap, featuring the dimpled lady playing games with her friends and dolls. Even better, or worse according to one's taste, were the *Josephine* stories written and illustrated by Honor Appleton (Mrs Cradock) and published by Blackie. There were about a dozen of these, and they employed that favourite idea of an eight-year old playing mother to a family of dolls: in this case Dora, Rachel, Big Teddy, the egregious sailor-suited Quackie-Jack and others. They belong to an Edwardian ideal nursery world ruled by a benevolent Nanny where grown-ups appear only from the knees downwards and bedtime terminates all adventures.

Mention should be made of three other illustrators whose work was often very similar: Millicent Sowerby, Cecily Barker and Margaret Tarrant. Millicent Sowerby (1878–1967) brought a light touch to the classics which is particularly evident in her treatment of *Alice's Adventures in Wonderland* (1907) and *A Child's Garden of Verses* (1908). Her books combine sensitive watercolours with strongly decorative line-drawn head- and tail-pieces. The unusual title-page decorations for both the above books – a pair of tall flamingos for the one and a high dovecote and rose briars for the other – show her decorative flair. Of her own beginnings she remarked: 'Being very fond of children, I turned naturally to painting them and for them. It has always been the beautiful in childhood that attracted, not the humorous or grotesque. I love flowers and I usually use these in the backgrounds for my paintings.'[10] Presumably the children who were the recipients of the numerous books she produced for Hodder, Frowde and Humphrey Milford between 1909 and 1930 – *The Sunny Book, The Pretty Book, The Bonnie Book, The Bright Book*, and others – destroyed or neglected most of them, for they are now almost impossible to find. Flowers attracted the other artists and Cecily Mary Barker's *Flower Fairies* has long been in print in a variety of sizes. Margaret Tarrant (1888–1959) also specialised in flowers and fairies. 'I have always wanted

---

9. One of a series published by Bell under the title 'The Queen's Treasure Series'.

10. B. E. Mahony, *Illustrators of Children's Books 1745–1945* (Horn Book Inc., Boston, 1947), p. 362.

to illustrate knights and romantic things', she wrote.[11] It cannot be pretended that these ladies have made a major contribution to the arts but their often small books were illustrated with admirable sincerity, and to satisfy children so continuously can be no easy matter.

The small-format children's book of the Edwardian period deserves a chapter to itself. Beatrix Potter (1866–1943) started her long series with the *Tale of Peter Rabbit* (1901), and the small, almost square, paper-covered boards or cloth bound editions which proliferated over the years need no introduction and are still selling well. However, it is unlikely that Helen Bannerman's *Little Black Mingo*, first published in 1901, and *Little Black Sambo* (to say nothing of *Epaminondas*) will long survive the Commission for Racial Equality. This would be a pity, as these little books have an innocent charm devoid of prejudice.

Kenneth Grahame's *Wind in the Willows*, originally published in 1908, was reissued in 1931 with illustrations by Ernest Shepard (1879–1976) and accustomed its young readers to accept a world where rats rowed boats and toads drove fast cars. Shepard's line drawings (in print ever since) and the illustrations he provided for the *Pooh* books form a strong link with the heyday of black-and-white illustration. His earliest illustrated books, *Tom Brown's Schooldays* (1904) and *Jeremy* (1919), showed his inclination and sympathy for the world of childhood, as do his last published illustrations – the coloured originals for *Winnie-the-Pooh* (1973) and *The House at Pooh Corner* (1974) – made as he approached his hundredth year.

Shepard was essentially a line artist. Trained at Heatherley's Art School and the Royal Academy Schools he came early under the influence of the American artists E. A. Abbey and J. S. Sargent, both Visitors to the Academy Schools. From them he learnt the value of work-ing from models, his lines tracing the path of the eye as it caressed the form. Drawing the figure, especially children, in movement was his great talent, and humour was never far away in all his work. In 1921 he was invited to join the permanent staff of *Punch*, where the fresh and sprightly vigour of his drawing brought new life to the traditional *Punch* style. The Twenties was a decade of increasing success for Shepard and his work for *Punch* not only brought a regular income and a weekly audience, but provided the setting for his first tentative partnership with A. A. Milne – the illustrations to *When We Were Very Young* which decorated the pages of *Punch* in January and February 1924. From this slight beginning was born the famous partnership. However, it was not in the pages of *Punch* but in his illustrated children's books of the Twenties and Thirties that his humour found its most satisfactory outlet. By this time, when Shepard's popular success was assured, his style of drawing was looking somewhat old-fashioned, but like so many illustrators he resisted the temptation to flirt with current fashions and throughout a long working life remained true to the tradition of Edwin Abbey, Charles Keene, Edmund Sullivan and Phil May. Born into their late Victorian world he worked on steadily until his death in 1976, providing for successive generations a standard of draughtsmanship by which they might measure their own. Commenting upon the illustrator's traditional faithfulness of purpose and style in his book *Line* (1922), Edmund Sullivan (who taught so many of them) concluded:

In the meantime most will plant their cabbages and cultivate their gardens, content to be old fashioned and to speak the old language – like Stacey Marks, the old R.A. painter of monks and parrots, who went down on his knees night and morning to thank God he was born before everybody was so clever.

11. Letter to Mrs Arthur Hughes, 11 April 1935.

Plates

PLATE 1. Gerald Metcalf
Poems of Coleridge, Lane, c. 1895

PLATE 2. Henry Ospovat
Tristram and Iseult from *The Poems of Matthew Arnold*, Lane, 1900

PLATE 3. Winifred Smith
Lily and Waterlily by A. Comyns Carr, Innes, 1893

PLATE 4. J. Byam Shaw
Tales from Boccaccio translated by Joseph Jacobs, Allen, 1899

PLATE 5. Robert Anning Bell
A Midsummer Night's Dream, Dent, 1895

PLATE 6. Laurence Housman
Green Arras, Lane, 1896

PLATE 7. Laurence Housman
The End of Elfin Town by Jane Barlow, Macmillan, 1894

PLATE 8. Walter Crane
Household Stories from the Brothers Grimm, Macmillan, 1882

PLATE 9. E. Fortescue-Brickdale
The Book of Old English Songs and Ballads, Hodder and Stoughton, 1915

PLATE 10. Hugh Thomson
The School for Scandal by Sheridan, Hodder and Stoughton, 1911

PLATE II. Hugh Thomson
The Story of Rosina by Austin Dobson, Kegan Paul, 1895

PLATE 12. Charles E. Brock
Penelope's English Experiences by Kate Douglas Wiggin, Gay & Bird, 1900

PLATE 13. Charles E. Brock
'Running the Gauntlet'. A pen-and-ink drawing for the Percy Bradshaw Press
Art School Course, 1918

PLATE 14. Edmund Sullivan
Lavengro by George Borrow, Macmillan, 1896

PLATE 15. Edmund Sullivan
Maud by Tennyson, Macmillan, 1922

PLATE 16. H. M. Brock
Fairy Tales by Hans Andersen, Pearson, 1905

PLATE 17. Edwin Abbey
Much Ado About Nothing from *The Comedies*, Harper, 1896

PLATE 18. Edwin Abbey
'Am I in face today?' from Goldsmith's *She Stoops to Conquer*, Harper, 1887

PLATE 19. Howard Pyle
The Man with the Hoe by Edwin Markham, Doubleday, 1900

PLATE 20. Howard Pyle
The Wonder Clock, Harper, 1887

PLATE 21. Howard Pyle
The Story of the Grail and the Passing of Arthur, Scribner, 1910

PLATE 22. Maxfield Parrish
'Tom the piper's son' from *Mother Goose in Prose* by F. L. Baum, Way & Williams, 1897

PLATE 23. Maxfield Parrish
The Golden Age by Kenneth Grahame, Lane, 1900

PLATE 24. Rockwell Kent
N by E, Brewer and Warner, 1930

PLATE 25. Rockwell Kent
The Complete Works of William Shakespeare, Doubleday, 1936

PLATE 26. Elizabeth Shippen Green
Alarmed, Curtis, c. 1901

PLATE 27. Will Bradley
Fringilla by R. D. Blackmore, Burrow, 1895

PLATE 28. Jessie Wilcox Smith
In The Closed Room by Frances Hodgson Burnett, Hodder, 1904

PLATE 29. N. C. Wyeth
Treasure Island, Scribner, 1911. 'For all the world I was led like a dancing bear'

PLATE 30. Reginald Birch
Little Lord Fauntleroy by Frances Hodgson Burnett, Scribner, 1886

PLATE 31. Frederic Remington
Ranch Life and the Hunting Trail by Theodore Roosevelt, Century, 1888

PLATE 32. Edmund Sullivan
The Rubáiyát of Omar Khayyám, Freemantle, 1900

PLATE 33. Patten Wilson
Selections from the Poets by A. Lang, Longman, 1898

PLATE 34. Patten Wilson
'A Fantasy'. *The Studio*, vol. 23, 1901, p. 196

PLATE 35. Alan Odle
Mimiambs of Herondas translated by Jack Lindsay, Fanfrolico Press, 1929

PLATE 36. Alan Odle
Candide by Voltaire, Routledge, 1922

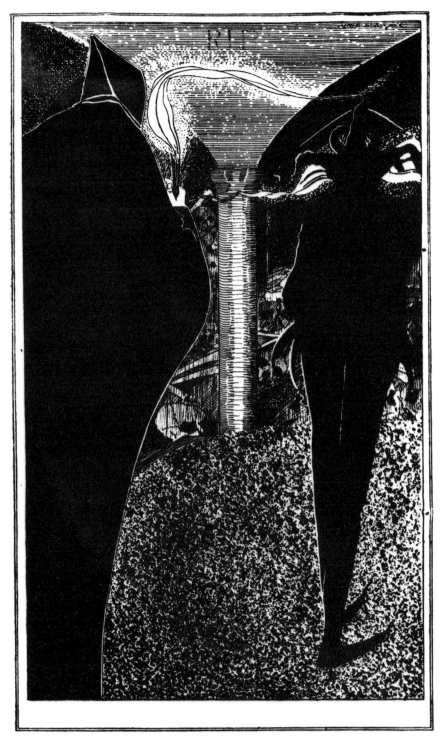

PLATE 37. W. B. Macdougall
Songs of Love and Death by Margaret Armour, Dent, 1896

PLATE 38. Vernon Hill
The Arcadian Calendar, Lane, 1909

PLATE 39. Harry Clarke
Tales of Mystery and Imagination by Poe, Harrap, 1919

PLATE 40. Harry Clarke
The Fairy Tales by Charles Perrault, Harrap, 1922

PLATE 41. Austin Osman Spare
The Starlit Mire by J. Bertram and F. Russell, Lane, 1911

PLATE 42. Austin Osman Spare
The Starlit Mire by J. Bertram and F. Russell, Lane, 1911

PLATE 43. Alastair (Hans Henning Voight)
The Sphinx by Oscar Wilde, Lane, 1920

PLATE 44. Sidney Sime
Bogey Beasts, Goodwin & Tabb, 1923

PLATE 45. Jessie M. King

A House of Pomegranates by Oscar Wilde, Methuen, 1915

BUT·STOOD·TURN'D·SIDEWAYS: LISTENING,

PLATE 46. Jessie M. King
The Defence of Guenevere and other poems by William Morris, Lane, 1904

PLATE 47. W. Heath Robinson
Uncle Lubin, Grant Richards, 1902

PLATE 48. W. Heath Robinson
Fairy Tales from Hans Christian Andersen, Dent, 1899

PLATE 49. John Batten
Indian Fairy Tales by Joseph Jacobs, Nutt, 1892

PLATE 50. J. D. Batten
English Fairy Tales by Joseph Jacobs, Nutt, 1890

PLATE 51. Edmund Dulac
Stories from Hans Andersen, Hodder & Stoughton, 1911

MERLIN TAKETH THE
CHILD ARTHVR INTO
HIS KEEPING

PLATE 52. Aubrey Beardsley
Morte d'Arthur, Dent, 1893

PLATE 53. Aubrey Beardsley
'Under the Hill': the Abbé Fanfreluche. *The Savoy*, no. 1, 1896

PLATE 54. Aubrey Beardsley
'Dieppe 1895', *The Savoy*, no. 1, 1896

PLATE 55. Arthur Rackham
Undine by La Motte Fouqué, Heinemann, 1909. 'At length they all pointed their fingers at me'

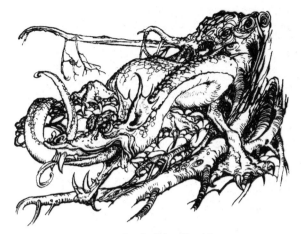

PLATE 56. Arthur Rackham
Undine by La Motte Fouqué, Heinemann, 1909. Chapter head-piece

PLATE 57. Mabel Lucie Attwell
Peter Pan and Wendy, Hodder & Stoughton, 1921

PLATE 58. Mabel Lucie Attwell
Alice in Wonderland, Tuck, 1910

PLATE 59. Ernest Aris
'Mousekin Market', *Blackie's Children's Annual*, 1925

PLATE 60. A. L. Bowley
'Busy Builders', *Father Tuck's Annual*, c. 1920

PLATE 61. Lawson Wood
Lawson Wood's Fun Fair, Arundel Prints, 1931

PLATE 62. D. R. Sexton
Alice in Wonderland, Juvenile Productions, 1932. A Thirties Alice with bobbed hair

THE SPOTTED MIMULUS.

PLATE 63. Charles Robinson
King Longbeard by B. Macgregor, Lane, 1898

PLATE 64. Charles Robinson
The Story of the Weathercock by Evelyn Sharp, Blackie, 1907

The moon
has a
face like
the
clock in
the hall;

PLATE 65. Charles Robinson
A Child's Garden of Verses by R. L. Stevenson, Lane, 1895

PLATE 66. Paul Woodroffe
Nursery Rhymes, George Allen, 1896

PLATE 67. Alice Woodward
To Tell the King the Sky is Falling by S. E. Braine, Blackie, 1896

PLATE 68. Helen Stratton
Songs for Little People by Norman Gale, Constable, 1896

PLATE 69. Honor Appleton
Josephine is Busy by Mrs Cradock, Blackie, 1918

The
Acorn Fairy.

PLATE 70. Cecily Mary Barker
Flower Fairies of the Autumn, Blackie, 1923

PLATE 71. Francis Bedford
Four and Twenty Toilers by E. V. Lucas, Grant Richards, 1900

PLATE 72. Millicent Sowerby
A Child's Garden of Verses, Chatto, 1908

With a look of scorn she put into my hand a bit of paper.

PLATE 73. S. Beatrice Pearse
The Trial of William Tinkling by Dickens, Constable, 1912

PLATE 74. Alan Wright
In Search of the Wallypug by G. E. Farrow, Pearson, 1903

PLATE 75. Harry Rountree
Uncle Remus by Joel Chandler Harris, Nelson, 1906

PLATE 76. T. H. Robinson
A Child's Book of Saints by William Canton, Dent, 1898

PLATE 77. Rowland Hilder
Treasure Island, Oxford, 1929

List of Works Consulted

All titles published in London unless stated otherwise.

Printing and Reproduction

Burton, W. K. *A Practical Guide to Photographic and Photomechanical Printing* 2nd ed. Marion 1892

Harper, C. *A Practical Handbook of Drawing for Modern Methods of Reproduction* Chapman & Hall 1901

Hentschel, C. *Pictorial Reproduction and the Art of Process Engraving* Hentschel 1901

Houfe, S. *The Dalziel Family* Sotheby 1978

Lewis, C. T. C. *The Story of Picture Printing in England during the Nineteenth Century* Sampson Low 1928

Lewis, J. *The Twentieth Century Book* Studio Vista 1967

Meisenbach & Co. Ltd. *Hints to Printers* Meisenbach 1902

Moran, J. *Printing in the Twentieth Century: a Penrose anthology* Northwood 1974

Plant, M. *The English Book Trade* Allen & Unwin 1974

Southward, J. *Practical Printing* Printers' Register 1882

—— *Progress in Printing and the Graphic Arts during the Victorian Era* Simpkin, Marshall, Hamilton & Co. 1897

Twyman, M. *Printing 1770–1970* Eyre & Spottiswode 1970

Verfasser, J. *The Halftone Process* Bradford: Lund 1894

Wakeman, G. *Victorian Book Illustration: the Technical Revolution* David & Charles 1973

Wilkinson, W. T. *Photoengraving on Zinc and Copper in Line and Halftone* Otley: Wilkinson 1886

——*Photomechanical Processes* Hampton Judd 1892

Wood, H. T. *Modern Methods of Illustrating Books* Stock 1887

Zander, C. G. *Photo-Trichromatic Printing* Leicester: Raithby Lawrence 1896

Illustration

Blackburn, H. *The Art of Illustration* Allen 1894

Blackie, A. *Blackie & Son 1809–1959* Blackie 1959

Bland, D. *A History of Book Illustration* Faber 1958

Bradshaw, P. *The Art of the Illustrator* The Press Art School [1918]

—— *Drawn from Memory* Chapman & Hall 1943

The Brooklyn Museum *A Century of American Illustration* Brooklyn: The Museum 1972

Carter, J. *New Paths in Book Collecting* Constable 1934

Cope, D. & P. *Illustrators of Postcards from the Nursery* East West Publications, 1978

Crane, W. *Of the Decorative Illustration of Books Old and New* Bell 1896

Cuppleditch, D. *The London Sketch Club* Dilke Press 1978

Dalziel, G. & E. *A Record of Fifty Years' Work* Methuen 1901

Dent, H. R. *The House of Dent* Dent 1938

Feaver, W. *When we were Young: Two Centuries of Children's Book Illustration* Thames & Hudson 1977

Hardie, M. *English Coloured Books* Bath: Kingsmead Reprints 1973

Harper, C. *English Pen Artists of Today* Chapman & Hall 1892

Harthan, J. *The History of the Illustrated Book: the Western Tradition* Thames & Hudson 1981

Hodnett, E. *Image and Text* Scolar Press 1982

Holme, C. *The Art of the Book* The Studio 1914

—— *British Book Illustration Yesterday and Today* The Studio 1923

—— *Modern Book Illustrators and their Work* The Studio 1914

—— *Modern Pen Drawings: European and American* The Studio 1901

Houfe, S. *The Dictionary of British Book Illustrators and Caricaturists, 1800–1914* Antique Collectors Club 1978

Jackson, H. *The Eighteen Nineties* Grant Richards 1913

James, P. *English Book Illustration 1800–1900* Penguin Books 1947

Jussim, E. *Visual Communication and the Graphic Arts* Bowker 1974

McLean, R. *The Reminiscences of Edmund Evans* O.U.P. 1967

—— *Victorian Book Design* Faber 1963

Mahony, B. *Illustrators of Children's Books, 1745–1945* Boston: Horn Book Inc. 1947

Meyer, S. E. *America's Great Illustrators* New York: Abrams 1978

Muir, P. *English Children's Books* Batsford 1954

—— *Victorian Illustrated Books* Batsford 1971

Pennell, J. *The Illustration of Books* Fisher Unwin 1896

—— *Modern Illustration* Bell 1895

—— *Pen Drawing and Pen Draughtsmen* Macmillan 1899

Peppin, B. *Fantasy: Book Illustration 1860–1920* Studio Vista 1975

Pitz, H. C. *200 Years of American Illustration* New York: Random House 1977

Quayle, E. *The Collector's Book of Boy's Stories* Hamlyn 1973

—— *The Collector's Book of Children's Books* Hamlyn 1973

Ray, G. N. *The Illustrator and the Book in England from 1700–1914* O.U.P. 1976

Reed, W. *Great American Illustrators* New York: Abbeyville 1979

Sketchley, R. E. D. *English Book Illustration of Today* Kegan Paul 1903

Smith, F. H. *American Illustrators* Scribner 1892

Stockham, P. *Children's Book Illustration* Tunbridge Wells: Midas 1980

Sullivan, E. J. *The Art of Illustration* Chapman & Hall 1921

—— *Line* Chapman & Hall 1922

Taylor, J. R. *The Art Nouveau Book in Britain* Methuen 1966

Thorpe, J. *English Illustration: the Nineties* Faber 1935

White, G. *Children's Books and their Illustrators* The Studio, Special Winter Number 1897–8

Illustrators

Aldin, C. *Time I was Dead* New York: Scribner 1934

Arwas, V. *Alastair: Illustrator of Decadence* Thames & Hudson 1979

Ashmolean Museum, Oxford *The Centenary Exhibition of Works by Eleanor Fortescue-Brickdale* Oxford, The Ashmolean Museum 1972

Bateman, M. *The Man who Drew the Twentieth Century* Macdonald 1972

Beare, G. *The Illustrations of W. Heath Robinson* Werner Shaw 1983

Blackburn, H. *Randolph Caldecott* Sampson Low 1870

Brighton Museum *Mabel Lucie Attwell: a Centenary Exhibition* Brighton 1980

Brooke, H. *Leslie Brooke and Johnny Crow* Warne 1982

Cole, R. V. *The Art and Life of Byam Shaw* Philadelphia: Lippincott 1932

Cuppleditch, D. *The John Hassall Lifestyle* Dilke Press 1979

Day, L. *The Life and Art of W. Heath Robinson* Joseph 1947

Engen, R. K. *Randolph Caldecott: Lord of the Nursery* Oresko 1976

Engen, R. *Walter Crane as a Book Illustrator* Academy Editions 1975

Freitas, L. de *Charles Robinson* Academy Editions 1976

Gettings, F. *Arthur Rackham* Studio Vista 1975

Gurney, J. *Margaret Tarrant and her Pictures* Medici Society 1982

Heneage, S. & Ford, H. *Sidney Sime: Master of the Mysterious* Thames & Hudson 1980

Heron, R. *Cecil Aldin* Exeter: Webb & Bower 1981

Hornung, C. P. *Will Bradley: his Graphic Art* New York: Dover 1974

Housman, L. *The Unexpected Years* Cape 1937

Hudson, D. *Arthur Rackham* Heinemann, 1960

Jensen, J. *The Man who ... and other Drawings by H. M. Bateman* Eyre Methuen 1969

Johnson, A. E. *Dudley Hardy* Black 1909

—— *John Hassall* Black 1907

—— *Lawson Wood* Black 1910

—— *Tom Browne* Black 1909

—— *W. Heath Robinson* Black 1913

Johnson, F. *Rockwell Kent: an Anthology of his Work* Collins 1982

Knox, R. *The Work of E. H. Shepard* Methuen 1979

Lane, M. *The Tale of Beatrix Potter* Warne 1947

Larkin, D. *Arthur Rackham* Pan 1975

—— *Charles and William Heath Robinson* Pan 1976

—— *Dulac* Hodder 1975

—— *The Fantastic Creatures of Edward Julius Detmold* Pan 1976

—— *The Fantastic Kingdom* Pan 1974

—— *The Unknown Paintings of Kay Nielsen* Pan 1977

Lewis, J. *Heath Robinson, Artist and Comic Genius* Constable 1973

Locke, G. *From an Ultimate Dim Thule* Ferret Fantasy 1973

Lucas, E. V. *The Life and Work of E. A. Abbey* Methuen 1921

Ludwig, C. *Maxfield Parrish* New York: Watson-Guptill 1973

Mitchell, G. *The Subject was Children: the Art of Jessie Wilcox Smith* New York: Dutton 1980

Moore, A. C. *The Art of Beatrix Potter* Warne 1967

Nicholson, K. *Kay Nielsen* Hodder 1975

Odle, R. *Salt of our Youth* Penzance: Worden's of Cornwall 1972

Ovenden, G. *The Illustrators of Alice* Academy Editions 1972

Reade, B. *Beardsley* Studio Vista 1967

Robinson, W. H. *My Line of Life* Blackie 1938

Rosenburg, J. *Dorothy Richardson: the Genius they Forgot* Duckworth 1973

Ross, R. *Forty-three Drawings by Alastair* Lane 1914

Schnessel, S. M. *Jessie Wilcox Smith* Studio Vista 1977

Scottish Arts Council *Jessie M. King* The Arts Council 1971

Sheffield City Art Galleries *Arthur Rackham 1867–1939* Sheffield 1980

—— *Edmund Dulac, Illustrator and Designer 1882–1953* Sheffield 1983

Shepard, E. *Drawn from Life* Methuen 1961

Sotheby & Co. Ltd. *Jessie M. King and E. A. Taylor* Sotheby's 1977

Southampton Art Gallery *Maxwell Armfield 1881–1972* Southampton 1978

Sparrow, W. S. *Frank Brangwyn and His Work* Kegan Paul 1910

Spencer, I. *Walter Crane* Studio Vista 1975

Spielman, M. H. & Jerrold, W. H. T. *Hugh Thomson* Black 1931

Thorpe, J. *Edmund Sullivan* Art and Technics 1948

Weintraub, S. *Aubrey Beardsley: Imp of the Perverse* State College, Pennsylvania State 1976

White, C. *Edmund Dulac* Studio Vista 1976

A Checklist of Illustrators
c. 1880–*c.* 1930

Generally this checklist does not include compilations of illustrations or those titles which were illustrated jointly with other artists or books to which the odd illustration was contributed. Nor does it include contributions to periodicals or annuals. Every attempt has been made to make the entries as full as possible, but the author is only too conscious of the number of illustrated books which have evaded the researches of auctioneers, booksellers and librarians, and would therefore be pleased to hear of any titles that may have been omitted.

ABBEY, Edwin Austin (1852–1911) American
Dickens, C. *Christmas Stories* Harper 1875
Longfellow, H. W. *The Poetical Works* Houghton 1880–3
Herrick, R. *Selections from the Poetry of Robert Herrick* Harper 1882
Black, W. *Judith Shakespeare* Harper 1884
Boughton, G. H. *Sketching Rambles in Holland* Macmillan 1885
Sheridan, R. B. *Comedies* Chatto 1885
Goldsmith, O. *She Stoops to Conquer* Harper 1887
Abbey, E. A. *Old Songs* Harper 1888
——— *The Quiet Life* Harper 1890
Shakespeare, W. *The Comedies* Harper 1896
Goldsmith, O. *The Deserted Village* Harper 1902
Stevens, L. O. *King Arthur Stories* Houghton 1908

ALASTAIR [Hans Henning Voight] (1887–1969) German
Alastair *Forty-three Drawings* Lane 1914
Wilde, O. *The Sphinx* Lane 1920
Crosby, H. *Red Skeletons* Black Sun Press 1927
Pater, W. *Sebastian Van Storck* Lane 1927
Poe, E. A. *The Fall of the House of Usher* Black Sun Press 1928
Prévost d'Exiles, A. F. *Manon Lescaut* Lane 1928
Wilde, O. *L'Anniversaire de l'Infante* Black Sun Press 1928
Choderlos de Laclos, P. A. F. *Dangerous Acquaintances* Godwin 1933

ALDIN, Cecil Charles Windsor (1870–1935) British
Hutchinson, H. N. *Prehistoric Man and Beast* Smith Elder 1896
Praed, W. *Every-day Characters* Kegan Paul 1896
Buckland, J. *Two Little Runaways* Longmans 1898

Spurr, H. A. *A Cockney in Arcadia* Allen 1899
Aldin, C. C. W. *Two Well-worn Shoe Stories* Sands 1899
Whyte-Melville, G. J. *Roy's Wife* Thacker 1900
Hayward, G. M. *The Other One* Pearson 1901
Aldin, C. C. W. *Ten Little Puppy Dogs* Sands 1902
Emanuel, W. *A Dog Day* Heinemann 1902
Aldin, C. C. W. *A Sporting Garland* Sands 1902
Emanuel, W. *The Snob* Lawrence & Bullen 1904
Aldin, C. C. W. *A Gay Dog* Heinemann 1905
Emanuel, W. *The Dogs of War* Bradbury 1906
Aldin, C. C. W. *Farm Friends for Little Folk* Blackie 1908
Irving, W. *Old Christmas* Hodder 1908
Aldin, C. C. W. *The Black Puppy Book* Hodder 1909
——— *Doggie and his Ways* Hodder 1909
——— *Farm Babies* Hodder 1909
——— *Pickles* Hodder 1909
——— *Pussy and her Ways* Hodder 1909
——— *The White Kitten Book* Hodder 1909
——— *The White Puppy Book* Hodder 1909
Irving, W. *Bachelors and A Bachelor's Confessions* Heineman 1909
——— *The Widow* Heinemann 1909
——— *Wives* Heinemann 1909
Steele, R. *The Henpecked Man* Heinemann 1909
——— *The Perverse Widow* Heinemann 1909
Surtees, R. S. *Jorrocks on 'Unting* Heinemann 1909
Irving, W. *Christmas Day* Hodder [1910]
——— *Christmas Eve* Hodder [1910]
Aldin, C. C. W. *Field Babies* Hodder 1910
——— *The Red Puppy Book* Hodder 1910
——— *Rough and Tumble* Hodder 1910
——— *The Twins* Hodder 1910
Dickens, C. *The Pickwick Papers* Chapman & Hall 1910
Aldin, C. C. W. *Merry and Bright* Frowde:Hodder 1911
Surtees, R. S. *Handley Cross* Arnold 1911
Aldin, C. C. W. *Mac* Frowde:Hodder 1912
——— *The Mongrel Puppy Book* Frowde:Hodder 1912
Byron, M. C. *Cecil Aldin's Happy Family* Frowde: Hodder 1912
Heiberg, N. *White-ear and Peter* Macmillan 1912
Sewell, A. *Black Beauty* Jarrold 1912
Waylett, R. *Puppy Tails* Lawrence 1912
Byron, M. C. *Cecil Aldin's Merry Party* Hodder 1913
Maeterlinck, M. P. M. B. *My Dog* Allen 1913
Trist, S. *The Underdog* Animal's Guardian 1913
Waylett, R. *The Playtime Picture Books* C.K.S. 1913

Aldin, C. C. W. *The Bobtail Puppy Book* Frowde : Hodder 1914

Byron, M. C. *Jack and Jill* Frowde : Hodder 1914

Emanuel, W. *The Dog who Wasn't what he Thought he Was* Tuck 1914

Aldin, C. C. W. *The Cecil Aldin Painting Book* Lawrence 1915

Byron, M. C. *Animal Revels* Frowde : Hodder 1915

Ouida *Moufflou* Jack 1915

Byron, M. C. *Animal Frolics* Frowde : Hodder 1916

Waylett, R. *Jock and Some Others* Gale 1916

Aldin, C. C. W. *Bunnyborough* Milford 1919

Davidson, G. *Gyp's Hour of Bliss* Collins 1919

Aldin, C. C. W. *Cecil Aldin Letter Book Series* Milford 1921

—— *The Great Adventure* Milford 1921

—— *Old Inns* Heinemann 1921

—— *Us* Milford 1922

Masefield, J. *Right Royal* Heinemann 1922

Aldin, C. C. W. *Old Manor Houses* Heinemann 1922

—— *Cathedrals and Abbey Churches of England* Eyre 1924

—— *Ratcatcher to Scarlet* Eyre 1926

—— *Dogs of Character* Eyre 1927

Nurse, W. H. *Berkshire Vale* Blackwell 1927

Aldin, C. C. W. *Romance of the Road* Eyre 1928

Chalmers, P. R. *A Dozen Dogs or so* Eyre 1928

Lyon, W. E. *In my Opinion* Eyre 1928

Aldin, C. C. W. *Sleeping Partners* Eyre 1929

Chalmers, P. R. *Forty Fine Ladies* Eyre 1929

Aldin, C. C. W. *An Artist's Models* Witherby 1930

Hare, K. *Road and Vagabonds* Eyre 1930

Helme, E. E. & Paul, N. *Jerry* Eyre 1930

Aldin, C. C. W. *Mrs Tickler's Caravan* Eyre 1931

Ashmore, M. *Lost Stolen or Strayed* Eyre 1931

Fleuron, S. *Flax : Police Dog* Eyre 1931

Hunloke, S. *Riding* Eyre 1931

Aldin, C. C. W. *The Cecil Aldin Book* Eyre 1932

Douglas, J. *The Bunch Book* Eyre 1932

Fife, D. *Scarlet Blue and Green* Macmillan 1932

Helme, E. E. & Paul, N. *The Joker and Jerry Again* Eyre 1932

Kipling, R. *His Apologies* Doubleday 1932

Aldin, C. C. W. *Scarlet to M.F.H.* Eyre 1933

Chalmers, P. R. *Dogs of Every Day* Eyre 1933

Fleuron, S. *The Wild Horses of Iceland* Eyre 1933

Morton, J. B. *Who's Who in the Zoo* Eyre 1933

Aldin, C. C. W. *Just Among Friends* Eyre 1934

—— *Time I was Dead* Eyre 1934

Vickerman, J. *Hotspur the Beagle* Constable 1934

Aldin, C. C. W. *Exmoor, the Riding Playground of England* Witherby 1935

—— *How to Draw Dogs* Lane 1935

—— *Hunting Scenes* Eyre 1936

Hope, W. S. *Smugglers' Gallows* Eyre 1936

Aldin, C. C. W. *The Merry Party* Milford 1938

Chalmers, P. R. *The Last Muster* Eyre 1939

ANDERSON, Anne (fl. 1910–1930) British

Anderson, A. *The Dandy Andy Book* Nelson 1911

Underdown, E. *Aucassin and Nicolette* Black 1911

Anderson, A. *The Funny Bunny A.B.C.* Nelson 1912

Underdown, E. *The Gateway to Chaucer* Nelson 1912

Mansion, H. *Old English Nursery Songs* Harrap n.d.

—— *Old French Nursery Songs* Harrap n.d.

—— *The Sleepy Song Book* Harrap n.d.

Anderson, A. *The Busy Bunny Book* Nelson 1916

Wright, A. *Two Bold Sportsmen* Nelson 1918

—— *The Naughty Neddy Book* Nelson 1918

Anderson, A. *The Patsy Book* Nelson 1919

—— *The Jackie Jackdaw Book* Nelson 1920

—— *The Jacky Horner ABC* Dean c. 1920

Eliot, E. C. *The House above the Trees* Thornton Butterworth 1921

Barnes, M. *Fireside Stories* Blackie 1922

Grimm, J. & W. *Grimm's Fairy Tales* Collins 1922

Herbertson, A. *Sing Song Stories* Milford 1922

Joan, N. *Cosy Time Tales* Nelson 1922

Anderson, A. *The Anne Anderson Fairy Tale Book* Nelson 1923

Andersen, H. C. *Fairy Tales* Collins 1924

Garrett, E. W. *Wanda and the Garden of the Red House* Milford 1924

Kingsley, C. *The Water Babies* Jack 1924

Morrison, P. *Cosy Chair Stories* Collins 1924

Spyri, J. *Heidi* Harrap 1924

Strang, Mrs H. *Little Rhymes for Little Folk* Milford 1925

Anderson, A. & Wright, A. *The Cuddly Kitty and the Busy Bunny* Nelson 1926

Heward, C. *Mr Pickles and the Party* Warne 1926

The Old Mother Goose Nursery Rhyme Book Nelson 1926

Wright, A. *The Podgy Puppy* Nelson 1927

Anderson, A. *A Series of Fairy Tales* Nelson 1928

—— *The Fairy Tale Omnibus* Collins 1929–

—— *Merry Folk* Collins 1930

—— *Playtime A.B.C.* Collins [1930]

—— *The Anne Anderson Picture Book* Collins 1943

—— *The Cosy Corner Book* Collins 1943

—— *Little Folk A.B.C.* Collins n.d.

APPLETON, Honor C. (fl. 1900–40) British

The Bad Mrs Ginger Grant Richards 1902

Dumpy Proverbs Grant Richards 1903

Cradock, H. C. *Josephine and her Dolls* Blackie 1915

—— *Josephine's Happy Family* Blackie 1916

—— *Josephine is Busy* Blackie 1918

—— *Big Book of Josephine* Blackie [1919]

—— *Josephine's Birthday* Blackie 1919

—— *Where the Dolls Lived* S.P.C.K. [1919]

Perrault, C. *Fairy Tales* Simpkin Marshall 1919

Cradock, H. C. *Josephine, John and the Puppy* Blackie 1920

Appleton, H. C. *Babies Three* Nelson 1921

—— *Me and My Pussies* Nelson 1924

Cradock, H. C. *Josephine Keeps School* Blackie 1925

—— *The Bonny Book of Josephine* Blackie [1926]

—— *Josephine Goes Shopping* Blackie 1926

Edgar, M. C. *A Treasury of Verse for School and Home* Harrap 1926

Cradock, H. C. *Josephine's Christmas Party* Blackie 1927

—— *Josephine Keeps House* Blackie 1931

Cruse, A. *The Golden Road in English Literature* Harrap 1931

Southwold, S. *The Book of Animal Tales* Harrap 1932

Cradock, H. C. *Josephine's Pantomine* Blackie 1939

—— *Josephine Goes Travelling* Blackie 1940

Appleton, H. C. *Towlocks and his Wooden House* Chatto n.d.
Tyrrell, E. *How I Trained the Wild Squirrels* Harrap n.d.
The World's Best Stories for Children n.d.

ARMFIELD, Maxwell Ashby (1881–1972) British

Augustine *The Confessions* Chatto 1909
Hutton, E. *Rome* Methuen 1909
Lees, F. *A Summer in Touraine* Methuen 1909
Faery Tales from Hans Andersen Dent 1910
Mason, E. *Aucassin and Nicolette* Dent 1910
Smedley, A. C. *The Flower Book* Chatto 1910
Hutton, E. *Venice and Venetia* Methuen 1911
Rossetti, H. M. *Shelley and his Friends in Italy* Methuen 1911
Smedley, A. C. *Sylvia's Travels* Dent 1911
Gray, A. *Cambridge and its Story* Methuen 1912
Hutton, E. *The Cities of Lombardy* Methuen 1912
Andersen, H. C. *The Ugly Duckling and other Tales* Dent 1913
Armfield, M. A. *The Hanging Garden and other verse* Simpkin 1914
Lee, V. *The Ballet of the Nations* Chatto 1915
Mackenzie, D. *Indian Fairy Stories* Blackie 1915
Morris, W. *The Life and Death of Jason* Headley 1915
Smedley, A. C. *Wonder Tales of the World* Harcourt 1920
Shakespeare, W. *The Winter's Tale* Dent 1922
Smedley, A. C. *The Armfield's Animal Book* Duckworth 1922
—— *Greenleaf Theatre Plays* Duckworth 1922–5
Armfield, M. A. *White Horses* Blackwell 1923
Smedley, A. C. *Tales from Timbuktu* Chatto 1923
Armfield, M. A. *Artist in America* Methuen 1925
—— *Artist in Italy* Methuen 1926
Armfield, M. A. *Stencil Printing* Dryad 1927
Smedley, A. C. *The Blue Bus Route* Oxford 1927
—— *A Manual of Tempera Painting* Allen 1930

ATTWELL, Mabel Lucie (1879–1964) British

Baldwin, M. *That Little Lamb* Chambers c. 1905
—— *Dora, a High School Girl* Chambers 1906
Mar, G. *The Little Tin Soldier* Chambers 1909
Carroll, L. *Alice's Adventures in Wonderland* Tuck 1910
Nursery Tales Nelson c. 1910
Grimm, J. L. C. & W. C. *Fairy Tales* Tuck n.d.
Mother Goose *Fairy Tales* Tuck n.d.
Jacbern, R. *Tabitha Smallways, Schoolgirl* Chambers 1912
Andersen, H. C. *Fairy Tales* [1914]
Kingsley, C. *The Water Babies* Tuck 1915
Meade, L. T. *A Band of Mirth* Chambers 1917
Ashley, M. *Children's Stories from French Fairy Tales* Tuck 1917
Mary, Queen of Roumania *Peeping Pansy* Hodder 1919
Marshall, A. W. *Wooden* Collins 1920
Attwell, M. L. *The Boo Boos Series* Valentine 1921–
—— *Peggy: Cut-out Dressing Doll* Valentine 1921
Barrie, J. M. *Peter Pan and Wendy* Hodder 1921
Attwell, M. L. *Baby's Book* Tuck 1922
—— *The Lucie Attwell Annual* Dean 1922–
—— *Lucie Attwell's Painting Books* Dean 1934
—— *Lucie Attwell's Great Big Midget Book* Dean 1935
—— *Playtime Pictures* Carlton 1935

AUSTEN, John (1886–1948) British

Keen, R. H. *The Little Ape and other Stories* Hendersons 1921
Fausset, H. I'A. *The Condemned, etc.* Selwyn 1922
Lefroy, C. *Echoes from Theocritus* Selwyn 1922
Perrault, C. *Tales of Passed Times* Selwyn & Blount 1922
Shakespeare, W. *Hamlet* Selwyn & Blount 1922
Bickley, F. L. *The Adventures of Harlequin* Selwyn & Blount 1923
Eça de Queiroz, J. M. de *Perfection* Selwyn & Blount 1923
Moult, T. *The Best Poems of 1922* Cape 1923
Allison, J. M. *The Five Black Cousins* 1924
Austen, J. *Rogues in Porcelain* Chapman & Hall 1924
Disraeli, B. *Ixion in Heaven* Cape 1925
Everyman and other plays Chapman & Hall 1925
France, A. *The Works of Anatole France* Lane 1925
Longus *Daphnis and Chloe* Bles 1925
Byron, G. G. N. *Don Juan* Lane 1926
Flaubert, G. *Madame Bovary* Lane 1928
Prévost d'Exiles, A. F. *Manon Lescaut* Bles 1928
Sterne, L. *The Life and Opinions of Tristram Shandy* Lane 1928
Defoe, D. *The Fortunes and Misfortunes of Moll Flanders* Lane 1929
Disraeli, B. *The Infernal Marriage* Jackson 1929
Bates, H. E. *The Hessian Prisoner* Jackson 1930
David, V. P. *The Guardsman and Cupid's Daughter* Toulmin 1930
Richardson, D. *John Austen and the Inseparables* 1930
Shakespeare, W. *As You Like It* Jackson 1930
Cooper, A. B. *Poets in Pinafores* Alston Rivers 1931
Thackeray, W. M. *Vanity Fair* O.U.P. 1931
Ratcliffe, D. *Gypsy Dorelia* Lane 1932
Dickens, C. *Posthumous Papers of the Pickwick Club* O.U.P. 1933
France, A. *The Gods Are Athirst* Bodley Head 1933
Dickens, C. *David Copperfield* Heritage 1935
Smollett, T. G. *The Adventures of Peregrine Pickle* O.U.P. 1936
Aristophanes *The Frogs* Enschedé 1937
Le Sage, A. R. *The Adventures of Gil Blas* O.U.P. 1937
Goldsmith, O. *The Vicar of Wakefield* Heritage 1939
Shakespeare, W. *The Comedies, Histories and Tragedies* Limited Editions Club 1939

BATTEN, John Dickson (1871–1932) British

Seaman, Sir O. *Oedipus the Wreck* Johnson 1888
Jacobs, J. *English Fairy Tales* Nutt 1890
—— *Celtic Fairy Tales* Nutt 1892
—— *Indian Fairy Tales* Nutt 1892
Dixon, E. *Fairy Tales from the Arabian Nights* Dent 1893
Jacobs, J. *More English Fairy Tales* Nutt 1893
—— *More Celtic Fairy Tales* Nutt 1894
Ogilvie, G. S. *Hypatia: a play* Heinemann 1894
Dixon, E. *More Fairy Tales from the Arabian Nights* Dent 1895
Hewlett, M. *A Masque of Dead Florentines* Dent 1895
Dickson, M. *The Saga of the Sea-Swallow* Innes 1896
Jacobs, J. *The Book of Wonder Voyages* Nutt 1896
Batten, J. D. *An Approach to Winged Flight* Dolphin Press 1928

Dante *Inferno* O.U.P. 1933

BAUMER, Lewis (1870–1963) British
Baumer, L. *Jumbles* Pearson 1897
Molesworth, Mrs *Hoodie* Chambers 1897
Whishaw, F. *Elsie's Magician* Chambers 1897
Berridge, R. *The Baby Philosopher* Jarrold 1898
Molesworth, Mrs *Hermy. The Boys and I. The Three Witches* Chambers 1898–1900
—— *Miss Bouverie* Chambers 1901
Baumer, L. *Did You Ever?* Pearson 1903
Meade, L. T. *The Hilltop Girl* Chambers 1906
Spielmann, M. H. *The Rainbow Book* Chatto 1909
Graham, H. J. C. *Deportmental Ditties* Mills & Boon 1909
Browning, R. *The Last Ride Together* Foulis 1909
Graham, H. J. C. *The Bolster Book* Arnold 1910
Cherry Ripe and other famous lyrics Foulis 1911
Graham, H. J. C. *Canned Classics and other verses* Mills & Boon 1911
Hyatt, A. H. *The Gift of Love, etc.* Foulis 1911
Graham, H. J. C. *The Perfect Gentleman* Arnold 1912
——*The Motley Muse* Arnold 1913
Thackeray, W. M. *Vanity Fair* Hodder & Stoughton 1913
Graham, H. J. C. *The Complete Sportsman* Arnold 1914
Hay, I. *The Lighter Side of School Life* Foulis 1914
Norton, F. *An Elegy on the Death of a Mad Dog* Warne 1914
Calthrop, D. C. & Barker, H. G. *The Harlequinade* Sidgwick & Jackson 1918
Irving, W. *Old Christmas and Bracebridge Hall* Constable 1918
Hay, I. *The Shallow End* Hodder & Stoughton 1924
Baumer, L. *Bright Young Things* Methuen 1928
Arkell, T. R. *Winter Sportings* Jenkins 1929
Emtage, J. B. *Ski Fever* Methuen 1936

BEDFORD, Francis Donkin (1864–1954) British
Gould, S. B. *Old Country Life* Methuen 1890
—— *The Deserts of Southern France* Methuen 1894
Homer *The Battle of the Frogs and Mice* Methuen 1894
Gould, S. B. *Old English Fairy Tales* Methuen 1895
A Book of Nursery Rhymes Methuen 1897
Goldsmith, O. *The Vicar of Wakefield* Dent 1898
Thackeray, W. M. *The History of Henry Esmond* Dent 1898
Lucas, E. V. *The Book of Shops* Richards 1899
—— *Four and Twenty Toilers* Richards 1900
Troutbeck, G. E. *Westminster Abbey* Methuen 1900
Lucas, E. V. *The Visit to London* Methuen 1902
Clinch, G. *Kent* Methuen 1903
Gilbert, A. *The 'Original Poems' and others* Wells Gardner 1903
Roscoe, E. S. *Buckinghamshire* Methuen 1903
Clinch, G. *The Isle of Wight* Methuen 1904
Field, L. *Two are Company* Wells Gardner 1905
Lucas, E. V. *Old Fashioned Tales* Wells Gardner 1905
Bedford, F. D. *A Night of Wonders* Richards 1906
Lucas, E. V. *Forgotten Tales of Long Ago* Wells Gardner 1906
—— *A Book of Verses for Children* Wells Gardner 1907
—— *Another Book of Verses for Children* Wells Gardner 1907

—— *Runaways and Castaways* Wells Gardner 1908
Barrie, J. M. *Peter Pan and Wendy* Hodder & Stoughton 1911
Langbridge, R. *The Land of the Ever Young* S.P.C.K. 1920
Dickens, C. *The Magic Fishbone* Warne 1921
MacDonald, G. *Billy Barnicote* 1923
—— *At the Back of the North Wind* Macmillan 1924
—— *The Princess and the Goblin* Macmillan 1926
Dickens, C. *The Cricket on the Hearth* Warne 1927
Macdonald, G. M. *Count Billy* Dent 1928
Stevens, F. L. *Through Merrie England* Warne 1928
Dickens, C. *A Christmas Carol* 1931
Kelman, J. H. *Stories from the Life of Christ* Nelson n.d.

BELL, Robert Anning (1863–1933) British
Mack, R. E. *The Golden Treasury of Art and Song* Nister 1890
Bell, R. A. & Paget, H. M. *Burns Pictures* Nister 1891
Rhys, G. *Jack the Giant Killer and Beauty and the Beast* Dent 1894
Rhys, G. *The Sleeping Beauty and Dick Whittington* Dent 1894
Keble, J. *The Christian Year* Methuen 1895
Shakespeare, W. *A Midsummer Night's Dream* Dent 1895
Keats, J. *Poems* Bell 1897
Bunyan, J. *Pilgrim's Progress* Methuen 1898
Dennis, J. *English Lyrics from Spenser to Milton* Bell 1898
Lamb, C. & M. *Tales from Shakespeare* Freemantle 1899
Grimm, J. L. C. & W. C. *Grimm's Household Tales* Dent 1901
Keats, J. *The Odes of John Keats* Bell 1901
Shakespeare, W. *The Tempest* Freemantle 1901
Keats, J. *Isabella and the Eve of St Agnes* Bell 1902
The Rubáiyát of Omar Khayyám Bell 1902
Shelley, P. B. *Poems* Bell 1902
Jameson, A. B. *Shakespeare's Heroines* Dent 1905
Palgrave, F. T. *Golden Treasury* Dent 1907
Meynell, A. C. *Mary the Mother of Jesus* Lee Warner 1912
Rhys, E. C. *English Fairy Tales* Dent 1913

BIRCH, Reginald Bathurst (1856–1943) American
Baldwin, J. *The Story of Roland* Scribner 1883
Stockton, F. R. *The Story of Viteau* Scribner 1884
Burnett, F. H. *Little Lord Fauntleroy* Scribner 1886
—— *Sarah Crew and Editha's Burglar* Warne 1888
—— *Little Saint Elizabeth* Warne 1890
Fletcher, R. H. *Marjorie and her Papa* Century Co. 1891
Jamison, C. V. *Lady Jane* Century Co. 1891
Carryl, C. E. *Admiral's Caravan* Century Co. 1892
Jamison, C. V. *Toinette's Philip* Century Co. 1894
Stearns, A. *Sindbad, Smith and Co.* Century Co. 1896
Bennett, J. *Master Skylark* Century Co. 1897
Cloud, V. W. *Down Durley Lane and other ballads* Century Co. 1898
Sheard, V. *Trevelyan's Little Daughters* Briggs 1898
Burnett, F. H. *The Captain's Youngest* Warne 1899
Dix, B. M. *Soldier Rigdale* Macmillan 1899
Stockton, F. R. *The Vizier of the Two-horned Alexander* Century Co. 1899

Alcott, L. M. *Little Men* Little 1901
Brown, A. F. *Lucky Stone* Century Co. 1914
Bowen, W. A. *The Old Tobacco Shop* Macmillan 1921
Untermeyer, L. *Last Pirate* Harcourt 1934
—— *Rainbow in the Sky* Harcourt 1935
Nash, O. *The Bad Parents' Garden of Verse* Simon 1936
Stockton, F. R. *The Reformed Pirate* Scribner 1936
Moore, C. C. *The Night Before Christmas* Harcourt 1937
Richards, L. E. *Harry in England* Appleton 1937
Burnett, F. H. *A Little Princess* Scribner 1938
Richards, L. E. *I Have a Song to Sing You* Appleton-Century 1938
Burns, T. *Terrence O'Hara* Harcourt 1939
Dickens, C. *Five Christmas Novels* Heritage Club 1939

BOSSCHÈRE, Jean de (1878–1953) Belgian
Bosschère, J. de *Twelve Occupations* Elkin Mathews 1916
—— *The Closed Door* Lane 1917
—— *Christmas Tales of Flanders* Heinemann 1917
—— *Beasts and Men* Heinemann 1918
—— *The City Curious* Heinemann 1920
Swift, J. *Gulliver's Travels* Heinemann 1920
Bosschère, J. de *Weird Islands* Chapman & Hall 1921
—— *Le Bourg* Paris 1922
—— *Job le Pauvre* Lane 1922
Cervantes, M. de *The History of Don Quixote* Constable 1922
Apuleius, L. *The Golden Asse* Lane 1923
Sinclair, M. *Uncanny Stories* Hutchinson 1923
Flaubert, G. *The First Temptation of St Anthony* Lane 1924
Anthony, E. & J. *The Fairies Up-to-Date* Thornton Butterworth 1925
Ovid *The Love Books of Ovid* Lane 1925
Balzac, H. de *Ten Droll Tales* Lane 1926
Wilde, O. *Poems* New York: Boni & Liveright 1927
Aristophanes *The Plays* New York: Boni & Liveright 1928
Baudelaire, C. *Little Poems in Prose* Paris: Black Manikin 1928
Bosschère, J. de *Marthe and the Madman* New York: Covici Friede 1928
Putnam, S. *Rabelais* New York: Covici Friede 1929
Balzac, H. de *Droll Tales (The Second Decade)* New York: Covici Friede 1929
Boccaccio, G. *The Decameron* Putnam 1930
Plato *Plato's Symposium, or Supper* Fortune Press 1932
Putnam, S. *The World of Jean de Bosschère* Fortune Press 1932
Strato's Boyish Muse Fortune Press 1932
Louys, P. *The Songs of Bilitis* Fortune Press 1933
Petronius *The Satyricon* Fortune Press 1934
Pickard, W. B. *The Adventures of Alcassim* Cape 1936
Aymé, M. *The Green Mare* Fortune Press 1938
Bosschère, J. de *Peacocks and other Mysteries* New York 1941
—— *The House of Forsaken Hope* Fortune Press 1942

BRADLEY, William H. (1868–1962) American
Blackmore, R. D. *Fringilla* Burrow 1895
Bradley, W. H. *Bradley: his book* Springfield, Mass. 1896
Irving, W. *Rip Van Winkle* Russell 1897
Crane, S. *War is Kind* Stokes 1899

Shards of the Silver Sword 1902
Bradley, W. H. *Peter Poodle, Toy Maker to the King* Dodd 1906
—— *The Wonderbox Stories* Century Co. 1916
—— *Launcelot and the Ladies* Harper 1927

BRANGWYN, Frank (1867–1956) British
Russell, W. C. *Collingwood* Methuen 1891
Hyne, C. J. *The Captured Cruiser* Blackie 1893
Leighton, R. *The Wreck of the Golden Fleece* Blackie [1893]
Scott, M. *Tom Cringle's Log* 2 v. [1894]
Cervantes, M. de *Don Quixote* Gibbings 1895
Crockett, S. R. *et al. Tales of Our Coast* Chatto 1896
The Arabian Nights Gibbings 1896
Scott, M. *The Cruise of the Midge* Gibbings 1898
Cupples, G. *A Spliced Yarn* Gibbings 1899
Long, W. H. *Naval Yarns* Gibbings 1899
Cervantes, M. de *Exemplary Novels* Gibbings 1900
Brangwyn, F. *The Spirit of the Age* Hodder 1905
Raleigh, W. *The Last Fight of the Revenge* Gibbings 1908
The Rubáiyát of Omar Khayyám Foulis 1910
Southey, R. *The Life of Nelson* Gibbings 1911
Kinglake, A. W. *Eöthen* Sampson 1913
Sparrow, W. S. *A Book of Bridges* Lane 1915
Kitchener, H. H. *Facsimile of Lord Kitchener's Letter* Tuck 1916
Phillpotts, E. *The Girl and the Faun* Palmer 1916
Stokes, H. *Belgium* Kegan 1916
Binyon, L. *Bruges* Morland 1919
Hutton, E. *The Pageant of Venice* Lane 1922
The Thousand and One Nights Palmer 1922
Brangwyn, F. *Some Architectural Etchings* Architectural Press 1923
—— & Preston, H. *Windmills* Lane 1923
The Pageant of Empire Fleetway 1924
Barman, C. *The Bridge* Lane 1926
Brangwyn, F. & Walcot, W. *Nero and Modern Time* [1930?]
Shebbeare, C. E. *Sir Thomas More* Harding 1930
Taylor, F. I. *Sacrifice* Ingper 1930
Chesterton, G. K. *The Way of the Cross* Hodder 1935

BROCK, Charles Edmund (1870–1938) British
Johnson, J. R. *The Parachute and other Bad Shots* Routledge 1891
Atkinson, Canon *Scenes in Fairyland* Macmillan 1893
Hartland, E. S. *English Fairy and Folk Tales* Scott 1893
Barr, J. *The Humour of America* Scott 1893
Hood, T. *Humorous Poems* Macmillan 1893
Johnson, J. R. *The Knight of Grazinbrook* Routledge 1893
Mueller-Casenov, H. *The Humour of Germany* Scott 1893
Swift, J. *Travels of Lemuel Gulliver* Macmillan 1894
Galt, J. *Annals of Parish and Ayrshire Legatees* Macmillan 1894
Peek, H. *Nema and other stories* Chapman & Hall 1895
Canton, W. *W.V. her book* Isbister 1896
Austen, J. *Pride and Prejudice* Macmillan 1896
Kingsley, C. *Westward Ho!* Macmillan 1896
Peek, H. *The Poetry of Sport* Longman 1896
Canton, W. *The Invisible Playmate* Isbister 1897
Scott, W. *Ivanhoe* Service & Paton 1897

Austen, J. *The Novels of Jane Austen* Dent 1898
Cowper, W. *John Gilpin* Aldine House 1898
Defoe, D. *Robinson Crusoe* Service & Paton 1898
Dent's Second French Book Dent 1898
Goldsmith, O. *The Vicar of Wakefield* Service & Paton 1898
Scott, W. *The Lady of the Lake* Service & Paton 1898
Hohler, A. V. *The Bravest of them All* Macmillan 1899
Scott, W. *Ivanhoe* Dent 1899
Whyte-Melville, G. J. *M or N* Thacker 1899
Dickens, C. *The Holly Tree and the Seven Poor Travellers* Dent 1900
Cooper, J. F. *The Pathfinder* Macmillan 1900
Cooper, J. F. *The Prairie* Macmillan 1900
Lamb, C. *The Essays of Elia* Dent 1900
Scott, W. *Ivanhoe* (Temple Classics) Dent 1900
Une Joyeuse Nichée (Modern Language Series) Dent 1900
Wiggins, K. D. *Penelope's English Experiences* Gay & Bird 1900
—— *A Cathedral Courtship* Gay & Bird 1901
Wiggin, K. D. *Penelope's Irish Experiences* Gay & Bird 1902
Thackeray, W. M. *The Works of W. M. Thackeray* Dent 1902–3
Lamb, C. *The Works of Charles Lamb* Dent 1903
Gaskell, E. *Cranford* Dent 1904
Goldsmith, O. *The Vicar of Wakefield* Dent 1904
Lamb, C. *Mrs Leicester's School* Wells Gardner 1904
Mitford, M. R. *Our Village* Dent 1904
Dickens, C. *The Cricket on the Hearth* Dent 1905
—— *A Christmas Carol* Dent 1905
—— *The Chimes* Dent 1905
Eliot, G. *Silas Marner* Dent 1905
Nesbit, E. *Oswald Bastable and others* Wells Gardner 1905
Manning, A. *The Household of Sir Thomas More* Dent 1906
Irving, W. *Christmas at Bracebridge Hall* Dent 1906
Austen, J. *Northanger Abbey* Dent 1907
—— *Pride and Prejudice* Dent 1907
Dickens, C. *The Battle of Life* Dent 1907
—— *The Haunted Man* Dent 1907
Atlas Assurance Company *Atlas Reminiscent* Dent 1908
Austen, J. *Mansfield Park* Dent 1908
—— *Sense and Sensibility* Dent 1908
Dickens, C. *Dr Marigold* Foulis 1908
Masters, M. S. *The Knights of Compassion* Wells Gardner 1908
A Day Book for Girls Frowde:Hodder 1909
Austen, J. *Emma* Dent 1909
—— *Persuasion* Dent 1909
Malet, L. *Little Peter* Frowde:Hodder 1909
Oppenheim, E. P. *Jeanne of the Marshes* Lock 1909
Tolstoy, L. *The Vow* 1909
Blackmore, R. D. *Lorna Doone* Sampson Low 1910
Byron, M. *The Garden of Love* Hodder 1910
Irving, W. *The Sketchbook* Cassell 1910
Kipling, R. *Rewards and Fairies* Macmillan 1910
Orpen, T. H. *The Rain Children* S.P.C.K. 1910
Clare, M. *Days with Great Writers* Hodder 1911
Craik, Mrs *John Halifax, Gentleman* Cassell 1911
Dickens, C. *A Christmas Tree* Hodder 1911
Ewing, J. H. *Mrs. Overtheway's Remembrances* Frowde: Hodder 1911

Lee, C. *The Widow Woman* Dent 1911
Bradby, V. *The Capel Cousins* Frowde:Hodder 1912
Crockett, S. R. *Sweethearts at Home* Hodder 1912
Farnol, J. J. *The Broad Highway* Sampson Low 1912
Masters, M. S. *The King's Scout* Wells Gardner 1912
Raymond, W. *Tryphena in Love* Dent 1912
Farnol, J. J. *The Honorable Mr Tawnish* Sampson Low 1913
Hay, I. *Happy Go Lucky* Blackwood 1913
(Delafield, E. M.) *The Unlucky Family* Frowde:Hodder 1914
Quiller-Couch, A. *Troy Town* Dent 1914
Stockton, F. *Rudder Grange* Dent 1914
Farnol, J. J. *The Amateur Gentleman* Sampson Low 1916
(Gardiner, A. G.) *Pebbles on the Shore* Dent 1917
Rhys, E. *The Old Country* Dent 1917
Strang, H. *Bright Ideas* O.U.P. 1920
Cook, H. *Littleman's Book of Courtesy* Dent 1920
Dickens, C. *A Christmas Carol* Dent 1920
Girvin, B. *Jenny Wren* O.U.P. 1920
Bird, R. *The Rival Captains* Frowde:Hodder 1922
Cleaver, H. *The Old Order* O.U.P. 1922
Strang, H. *Winning his Name* Milford 1922
Gaster, M. *Children's Stories from Roumanian Legends and Fairy Stories* Tuck 1923
Reid, A. *Off the High Road* Heffer 1923
Strang, H. *True as Steel* O.U.P. 1923
Corkey, E. *The Magic Circle* Blackie 1924
Burnett, F. H. *Little Lord Fauntleroy* Warne 1925
Farjeon, E. *Martin Pippin in the Apple Orchard* Collins 1926
Dickens, C. *Christmas Stories* Ginn 1927
Dickens, C. *The Cricket on the Hearth* Dent 1927
Irving, W. *The Keeping of Christmas at Bracebridge Hall* Dent 1927
Vredenburg, E. *The Book for Boys* Tuck 1927
Chisholm, L. *The Golden Staircase* Jack 1928
Gilbert, W. S. *The Mikado* Macmillan 1928
—— *The Yeoman of the Guard* Macmillan 1928
Stevenson, R. L. *Catriona* Macmillan 1928
Lamb, C. *Collected Essays* Dent 1929
Dickens, C. *Pickwick Papers* Harrap 1930
Keary, A. *The Heroes of Asgard* Macmillan 1930
Dickens, C. *Nicholas Nickleby* Harrap 1931
Molesworth, Mrs *The Cuckoo Clock* Macmillan 1931
Dickens, C. *Martin Chuzzlewit* Harrap 1932
Phillpotts, E. *Nancy Owlett* Tuck 1933
Galt, J. *The Works of John Galt* Grant 1936
Wilson, T. W. *Through the Bible* Collins 1938

BROCK, Henry Matthew (1875–1960) British
Marryat, Capt. *Japhet in Search of a Father* Macmillan 1895
—— *Jacob Faithful* Macmillan 1895
Pollock, R. *Tales of the Covenanters* Anderson 1895
Watson, A. G. T. *Racing and Chasing* Longman (1896)
Lover, S. *Handy Andy* Macmillan 1896
Thackeray, W. M. *Ballads and Songs* Cassell 1896
Austen, J. *The Novels* Dent 1898
Gaskell, E. *Cranford* Service & Paton 1898
Grove, L. *Scenes from Child Life* Macmillan 1898
—— *Scenes from Familiar Life* Macmillan 1898
Scott, W. *Waverley* Service & Paton 1899

Shakespeare, W. *The Swan Shakespeare* Longmans 1899 etc.
Whyte-Melville, G. J. *Black But Comely* Thacker 1899
—— *Songs and Verses* Thacker 1899
Bunyan, J. *The Pilgrim's Progress* Pearson 1900
Cooper, J. F. *The Deerslayer* Macmillan 1900
—— *The Last of the Mohicans* Macmillan 1900
—— *The Pioneers* Macmillan 1900
Frazer, J. G. *Asinette* Dent 1900
Scott, W. *Ivanhoe* Dent 1900
Whyte-Melville, G. J. *Digby Grand* Thacker 1900
Wotton, M. E. *The Little Browns* Blackie 1900
Bradley, M. C. *Private Bobs and the New Recruit* Dent 1901
W., M. C. E. *All About All of Us* Dent 1901
Wallace, L. *Ben Hur* Pearson 1901
Blundell, M. *North, South and Over the Sea* Newnes 1902
Holmes, O. *The Autocrat of the Breakfast-Table* Dent 1902
—— *The Poet at the Breakfast-Table* Dent 1902
—— *The Professor at the Breakfast-Table* Dent 1902
Hunt, J. H. L. *The Essays of Leigh Hunt* Dent 1903
Jerrold, D. W. *The Essays of Douglas Jerrold* Dent 1903
Kingsley, C. *Westward Ho!* Pearson 1903
Alcott, L. *Little Women* Seeley 1904
Defoe, D. *Robinson Crusoe* Pearson 1904
F. J. G. *An Historical Sketch and Argument of Molière's* LES FEMMES SAVANTES Heffer 1904
Aguilar, G. *The Days of Bruce* Pearson 1905
Andersen, H. C. *Fairy Tales and Stories* Pearson 1905
Cervantes, M. de *Don Quixote* Pearson 1905
The Spectator *Sir Roger de Coverley and other essays* Dent 1905
Mallett, W. E. *An Introduction to Old English Furniture* Newnes 1906
The Fairy Library Newnes 1907
Irving, W. *The Old English Christmas* Foulis [1909]
Orczy, E. *The Emperor's Candlesticks* Greening 1909
—— *The Old Man in the Corner* Greening 1909
Grove, L. *Histoire de Monsieur Blanc* Macmillan 1910
Dickens, C. *A Christmas Tree* Hodder & Stoughton 1911
—— *The Holly-Tree Inn* Hodder & Stoughton 1911
Hughes, T. *Tom Brown's Schooldays* Seeley 1911
A Knight Errant and his Doughty Deeds. The Story of Amadis of Gaul Seeley 1911
Goldsmith, O. *The Vicar of Wakefield* Seeley 1912
Harding, T. *Tales of Madingley* Bowes & Bowes 1912
Siepmann, O. *A Primary German Course* Macmillan 1912
Cooke, W. B. *The Cragsmen* Cassell 1913
Ewing, J. H. *Jackanapes and other tales* C. K. S. 1913
The Old Fairy Tales Warne 1913–16
The Book of Fairy Tales Warne 1914
Grove, L. *La Maison aux panonceaux* C.U.P. 1914
Rhys, E. *The Old Country* Dent 1917
Coke, D. F. T. *Youth, Youth . . .!* Chapman & Hall 1919
Foss, K. *'Till Our Ship Comes In'* Grant Richards 1919
Frazer, J. G. *Leaves from the Golden Bough* Macmillan 1924
Drinkwater, J. *All About Me* Collins 1928
Kingsley, C. *The Heroes* Macmillan 1928
Stevenson, R. L. *The Black Arrow* Macmillan 1928
—— *Treasure Island* Macmillan 1928
Drinkwater, J. *More About Me* Collins 1929

Ceppi, M. *Bell's New French Picture Cards* Bell 1928
Borrow, G. *Lavengro* Nelson 1932
Gilbert, H. F. B. *Robin Hood* Nelson 1932
Meyer, P. *Bell's German Picture Cards* Bell 1932 etc.
The Book of Nursery Tales Warne 1934
Mackenzie, C. *The Book of Nursery Tales* Warne [1934]
Nichols, B. *A Book of Old Ballads* Hutchinson 1934
Frazer, J. G. *Pasha the Pom* Blackie 1937
Through the Bible Collins 1938
Steedman, A. *Bible Pictures and Stories* Nelson 1939
Stuart, D. M. *The Young Clavengers* Univ. of London Press 1947

BROOKE, Leonard Leslie (1862–1940) British

Everett-Green, E. *Miriam's Ambition* Blackie 1889
—— *The Secret of the Old House* Blackie 1890
MacDonald, G. *The Light Princess* Blackie 1890
Rowsell, M. *Thorndyke Manor* Blackie 1890
Armstrong, A. *Marian* Blackie 1892
Thorn, I. *Bab* Blackie 1892
White, R. *Brownies and Rose Leaves* Innes 1892
Knatchbull-Hugessen, E. *A Hit and a Miss* Innes 1893
White, R. *Moonbeams and Brownies* Innes 1894
Strain, E. H. *School in Fairyland* Fisher Unwin 1896
Walton, A. *Penelope and the Others* Blackie 1896
Molesworth, Mrs *Nurse Heatherdale's Story* Macmillan 1891
—— *The Girls and I* Macmillan 1892
—— *Mary* Macmillan 1893
—— *My New Home* Macmillan 1894
—— *Sheila's Mystery* Macmillan 1895
—— *The Carved Lions* Macmillan 1895
—— *The Oriel Window* Macmillan 1896
—— *Miss Mouse and Her Boys* Macmillan 1897
Lang, A. *The Nursery Rhyme Book* Warne 1897
Browning, R. *Pippa Passes* Duckworth 1898
Nash, T. *A Spring Song* Dent 1898
Lear, E. *The Jumblies* Warne 1900
—— *The Pelican Chorus* Warne 1900
Hayden, E. G. *Travels Round Our Village* Constable 1901
Shakespeare, W. *Works* Constable 1902
Brooke, L. L. *Johnny Crow's Garden* Warne 1903
Trollope, A. *Barchester Towers* Blackie 1903
The Story of the Three Little Pigs Warne 1904
Tom Thumb Warne 1904
Brooke, L. L. *The Golden Goose Book* Warne 1905
—— *Johnny Crow's Party* Warne 1907
—— *The House in the Wood* Warne 1909
Hill, G. F. *The Truth About Old King Cole* Warne 1910
Brooke, L. L. *The Tailor and the Crow* Warne 1911
—— *The Man in the Moon* Warne 1913
—— *Oranges and Lemons* Warne 1913
—— *Nursery Rhymes* Warne 1916
—— *Ring O' Roses* Warne 1922
Jacks, L. P. *Mad Shepherds* Williams & Norgate 1923
Charles, R. H. *A Roundabout Turn* Warne 1930
Brooke, L. L. *Johnny Crow's New Garden* Warne 1935
—— *Leslie Brooke's Little Books* Warne 1950

BROWNE, Gordon Frederick (1858–1932) British

Cook, J. *The Voyages* Routledge 1882
Hope, A. R. *Stories of Old Renown* Blackie 1883
Wood, K. *A Wait of the Sea* Blackie 1884

Defoe, D. *The Life and Surprising Adventures of Robinson Crusoe* Blackie 1885

Farjeon, B. L. *Christmas Angel* Ward 1885

Hodder, E. *Thrown on the World* Hodder 1885

Hodgetts, J. F. *The Champion of Odin* Cassell 1885

O'Reilly, R. *Kirk's Mill* Hatchard 1885

Stuart, E. *Miss Fenwick's Failures* Blackie 1885

Wood, K. *Winnie's Secret* Blackie 1885

Ewing, J. H. *Melchior's Dream* S.P.C.K. 1886

—— *Mary's Meadow* S.P.C.K. 1886

Halse, G. *The Legend of Sir Juvenis* Hamilton 1886

Hope, A. R. *The Hermit's Apprentice* Nimmo 1886

Hutcheson, J. C. *Fritz and Eric* Hodder 1886

Irving, W. *Rip Van Winkle* Blackie 1886

Richards, L. *Gordon Browne's Old Fairy Tales* Blackie 1886–7

Swift, J. *Gulliver's Travels* Blackie 1886

Collingwood, H. *The Log of the Flying Fish* Blackie 1887

Corkran, A. *Down the Snow Stairs* Blackie 1887

Ewing, J. H. *Dandelion Clocks* S.P.C.K. 1887

—— *The Peace Egg* S.P.C.K. 1887

Fenn, G. M. *Devon Boys* Blackie 1887

Henty, G. A. *With Wolfe in Canada* Blackie 1887

Hope, A. R. *The Seven Wise Scholars* Blackie 1887

Atteridge, H. *Bunty and the Boys* Cassell 1888

Aulnoy, Countess de *Fairy Tales* Routledge 1888

Banks, A. *Chirp and Chatter* Blackie 1888

Edgcumbe, S. B. *Claimed at Last* Cassell 1888

Ewing, J. H. *Snap Dragons* S.P.C.K. 1888

Hodgetts, J. F. *Harold the Boy Earl* R.T.S. 1888

—— *Tom's Nugget* S.S.U. 1888

Searchfield, E. *Claimed at Last* Cassell 1888

Shakespeare, W. *Works* Blackie 1888

Thorn, I. *A Golden Age* Hatchard 1888

Hudson, F. *The Origin of Plum Pudding* Ward 1889

Lang, A. *Prince Prigio* Arrowsmith 1889

Molesworth, M. L. *Great Uncle Hoot-Toot* C.K.S. 1889

Reed, T. B. *My Friend Smith* R.T.S. 1889

Thorn, I. *A Flock of Four* Wells Gardner 1889

—— *Jim* Wells Gardner 1889

—— *Captain Geoff* Wells Gardner n.d.

Browne, G. *A. Apple Pie* Evans 1890

Fenn, G. M. *Syd Belton* Methuen 1891

Molesworth, M. L. *The Red Grange* Methuen 1891

Russell, W. C. *Master Rockafeller's Voyage* Methuen 1891

Synge, G. M. *Great Grandmama* Cassell 1891

Collingwood, H. *The Doctor of the 'Juliet'* Methuen 1892

Walford, L. B. *A Pinch of Experience* Methuen 1892

Hitopadesa *The Book of Good Counsels* Allen 1893

Hocking, S. K. *One in Charity* Warne 1893

Lang, A. *Prince Ricardo of Pantouflia* Arrowsmith 1893

Meade, L. T. *A Young Mutineer* Wells Gardner 1893

Pain, B. *Graeme and Cyril* Hodder 1893

Pemberton, M. *The Iron Pirate* Cassell 1893

Synge, G. M. *Beryl* Skeffington 1894

Grimm, J. L. C. & W. C. *Fairy Tales* Wells Gardner 1895

Lang, A. *My Own Fairy Book* Arrowsmith 1895

Nobody, A. (G. Browne) *Nonsense for Somebody, Anybody or Everybody* Wells Gardner 1895

Jones, H. *Prince Boo Hoo and Little Smuts* Wells Gardner 1896

La Motte Fouqué, F. H. K. de *Sintram and his Companions* Wells Gardner 1896

Nobody, A. (G. Browne) *Some More Nonsense for the same Bodies as Before* Wells Gardner 1896

Allen, G. *An African Millionaire* Grant Richards 1897

Crockett, S. *The Surprising Adventures of Sir Toady Lion* Wells Gardner 1897

Anstey, F. *Paleface and Redskin* Richards 1898

Atteridge, H. *Butterfly Ballads* Milne 1898

Farrar, F. W. *Eric, or Little by Little* Black 1898

Dr Jollyboy's A.B.C. Wells Gardner 1898

Lee, C. J. *Paul Carah Cornishman* Bowden 1898

Allen, C. G. B. *Miss Cayley's Adventures* Richards 1899

Froissart, J. *Stories from Froissart* Wells Gardner 1899

Nesbit, E. *The Story of the Treasure Seekers* Fisher Unwin 1899

Shakespeare, W. *Macbeth* Longmans 1899

Allen, C. G. B. *Hilda Wade* Richards 1900

Collins, W. W. *After Dark* Gresham 1900

Farrar, F. W. *St Winifred's* Black 1900

Andersen, H. C. *Fairy Tales* Wells Gardner 1901

Gallon, T. *The Man Who Knew Better* Constable 1901

Meade, L. T. *Daddy's Girl* Newnes 1901

Proverbial Sayings Illustrated Wells Gardner 1901

Begbie, E. H. *Bundy in the Greenwood* Sunday Mag. 1902

Gallon, T. *The Charity Ghost* Hutchinson 1902

Macleod, M. *The Shakespeare Story Book* Gardner 1902

Begbie, E. H. *Bundy on the Sea* Isbister 1903

Bell, R. S. W. *J. O. Jones* Black 1903

Crockett, S. R. *The Adventurer in Spain* Isbister 1903

—— *Sir Toady Crusoe* Gardner 1905

—— *Sweetheart Travellers* Gardner n.d.

Brown Linhet (pseud.) *Why-Why and Tom Cat* Gardner 1906

Barham, R. *Tales of Mirth and Marvel from the Ingoldsby Legends* Gardner 1907

Farrow, G. E. *The Escape of the Mullingong* Blackie 1907

Burns, R. *Auld Lang Syne and other poems* Nister 1908

Sharp, E. *The Hill That Fell Down* Blackie c. 1908

Spielmann, M. H. *Margery Redford and Her Friends* Chatto 1908

The Bells of London Town S.P.C.K. 1909

Farrow, G. E. *The Dwindleberry Zoo* Blackie 1909

Hope, A. R. *Seeing the World* Gardner 1909

Thackeray, W. M. *The Rose and the Ring* Chatto 1909

Burns, R. *The Cotter's Saturday Night* Nister 1910

Chamisso de Boncourt *The Shadowless Man* Chatto 1910

Masefield, J. *A Book of Discoveries* Wells Gardner 1910

Blackmore, R. D. *Lorna Doone* Chambers 1911

Hoffman, A. *Heroes and Heroines of English History* Nister 1912

Reade, C. *The Cloister and the Hearth* Chambers 1912

Wood, W. *Grant the Grenadier* Routledge 1912

Cowper, E. E. *The Strange Story of Kittiwake's Castle* S.P.C.K. 1913

Eliot, G. *Adam Bede* Chambers 1913

Hoffman, A. S. *The Book of the Sagas* Nister 1913

Hollis, G. *Jem Forster's Revenge* C.K.S. 1913

Stevenson, R. L. *The Pavilion on the Links* Chatto 1913

Wilson, T. *The Children of Trafalgar Square* Blackie [1915]

Browne, E. A. *The Queen of Hearts* Hodder 1919

Cervantes M. de *Don Quixote* Wells Gardner 1920

Corkey, E. *Mollie's Good Intentions* R.T.S. 1920
Kennett, E. F. B. *Three Little Sisters* Wells Gardner 1920
Wynne, M. *Little Ladyship* R.T.S. 1921
Johnson, R. *The Seven Champions of Christendom* Blackie 1926
Browne, G. *The Tale of the Cauldron* Macleod 1927
Hayens, H. *Play Up!* Collins 1928
Little Children of the Great Round World Blackie 1930

CAMERON, Katherine (1874–1965) British
Chisholm, L. *In Fairyland* Jack 1904
Kingsley, C. *The Water Babies* Jack 1905
Macgregor, M. *Stories of King Arthur's Knights* Jack 1905
Chisholm, L. *The Enchanted Land* Jack 1906
Steedman, A. *Legends and Stories of Italy for Children* Jack 1909
Chisholm, L. *Celtic Tales* Jack 1910
Aitken, J. R. *In a City Garden* Foulis 1913
Thomas, P. E. *The Flowers of Love* Jack 1916
Grierson, F. *Haunting Edinburgh* Lane 1929
Williams, I. A. *Where the Bee Sucks* Medici 1929
Cameron, K. *Iain the Happy Puppy* Moray 1934
Chisholm, L. *Cinderella and other stories* Jack n.d.

CLARKE, Harry (1890–1931) Irish
Andersen, H. C. *Fairy Tales* Harrap [1916]
Poe, E. A. *Tales of Mystery and Imagination* Harrap 1919
Walters, L. d'O. *The Year's at the Spring* Harrap 1920
Perrault, C. *The Fairy Tales* Harrap 1922
Jameson *The Origin of John Jameson Whiskey* Jameson 1924
—— *The Elixir of Life* Jameson 1925
Goethe, J. W. von *Faust* Harrap 1925
Swinburne, A. C. *Selected Poems* Lane 1928

COLE, Herbert (1867–1930) British
Nelson, W. *Wood-working Positions* Chapman 1893
Coleridge, S. T. *The Rime of the Ancient Mariner* Gay & Bird 1900
Swift, J. *Gulliver's Travels* Lane 1900
The Nut Brown Maid Lane 1901
Cole, H. *Queen Mab's Fairy Realm* Newnes 1901
The Rubáiyát of Omar Khayyám Lane 1901
Suckling, J. *A Ballade Upon a Wedding* Lane 1901
Watts, W. T. *Christmas at the Mermaid* Lane 1902
Barham, R. *The Ingoldsby Legends* Lane 1903
Rhys, E. *Fairy Gold* Dent 1906
B., H. H. *The Village of Eynsford* Simpkin 1908
Froissart, J. *The Chronicles* Dent 1908
Jackson, V. *English Melodies from the 13th to the 18th Century* Dent 1910
Hare, C. *The Story of Bayard* Dent 1911
Hutchinson, W. *The Sunset of the Heroes* Dent 1911
Canton, W. *A Child's Book of Warriors* Dent 1912
Raymond, W. *The Book of Simple Delights* Dent 1912
Rhys, E. *English Fairy Tales* Dent 1913

DEARMER, Jessie Mabel (1872–1915) British
Sharp, E. *Wymps* Blackie 1897
Dearmer, M. *Roundabout Rhymes* Blackie 1898

Sharp, E. *All the Way to Fairyland* Lane 1898
Dearmer, M. *The Book of Penny Toys* Macmillan 1899
Housman, L. *The Story of the Seven Young Goslings* Blackie 1899
Dearmer, M. *A Noah's Ark Geography* Macmillan 1900
—— *Gervase* Macmillan 1909
—— *Seven Little Ducklings* 1910
—— *The Dreamer* Mowbray 1912
—— *The Cockyolly Bird* Hodder 1914

DETMOLD, Edward Julius (1883–1957) British
Detmold, M. and E. J. *Pictures from Birdland* Dent 1899
—— *16 Illustrations from Kipling's Jungle Book* Macmillan 1903
Kipling, R. *The Jungle Book* Macmillan 1908
Aesop *The Fables* Hodder 1909
Dugdale, F. E. *The Book of Baby Beasts* Hodder 1911
Lemonnier, C. *Birds and Beasts* Allen 1911
Maeterlinck, M. P. M. B. *The Life of the Bee* Allen 1911
Dugdale, F. E. *The Book of Baby Birds* Hodder 1912
Maeterlinck, M. P. M. B. *Hours of Gladness* Allen 1912
Dugdale, F. E. *The Book of Baby Pets* Hodder 1915
Kaberry, C. J. *The Book of Baby Dogs* Hodder 1915
Hudson, W. H. *Birds in Town and Village* Dent 1919
Maeterlinck, M. P. M. B. *The Children's Life of the Bee* Allen 1920
Fabre, J. H. C. *Fabre's Book of Insects* Hodder 1921
Kaberry, C. J. *Our Little Neighbours* Milford 1921
Hall, A. V. *Rainbow Houses* Cape 1923
The Arabian Nights Hodder 1924
Hall, A. V. *Poems of a South African* Longmans 1928

DIXON, Arthur A. (fl. 1892–1927) British
Dickens, C. *The Holly Tree* Nister 1899
—— *Child Characters from Dickens* Nister 1905
Irving, W. *Christmas at Bracebridge Hall* Nister 1905
Longfellow, H. W. *The Courtship of Miles Standish* Nister 1906
Kingsley, C. *The Water Babies* Nister 1908
Lefebvre-Laboulaye, E. R. *Fairy Tales* Nister 1909
Hauff, W. *Fairy Tales* Nister 1910
Wilson, T. *Stories from the Bible* Blackie 1914
Pulman, S. *Children's Stories from Russian Fairy Tales* Tuck 1917
Jones, C. M. D. *The Candle of the North* Mowbray 1924

DULAC, Edmund (1882–1953) British
Brontë, C. *The Novels of the Brontë Sisters* Dent 1905
Stawell, M. M. *Fairies I Have Met* Lane 1907
Stories from the Arabian Nights Hodder 1907
Dulac, E. *Lyrics, Pathetic and Humourous from A to Z* Warne 1908
Shakespeare, W. *The Tempest* Hodder 1908
The Rubáiyát of Omar Khayyám Hodder 1909
Couch, A. T. Q. *The Sleeping Beauty* Hodder 1910
Ali Baba and other stories Hodder 1911
Andersen, H. C. *Stories from Hans Andersen* Hodder 1911
Poe, E. A. *The Bells, and other poems* Hodder 1912
Princess Badoura Hodder 1913
Stawell, M. M. *My Days With the Fairies* Hodder 1913
Sinbad the Sailor and other stories Hodder 1914
Dulac, E. *Edmund Dulac's Picture Book* Hodder 1915

Mary, Queen of Roumania *The Dreamer of Dreams* Hodder 1915
Dulac, E. *Edmund Dulac's-Fairy Book* Hodder 1916
Hawthorne, N. *Tanglewood Tales* Hodder 1918
Rosenthal, L. *The Kingdom of the Pearl* Nisbet 1920
Yeats, W. B. *Four Plays for Dancers* Macmillan 1921
Beauclerk, H. de V. *The Green Lacquer Pavilion* Collins 1926
Yeats, W. B. *A Vision* Laurie 1926
Stevenson, R. L. *Treasure Island* Benn 1927
A Fairy Garland Cassell 1928
Williamson, H. R. *Gods and Mortals in Love* Country Life 1935
Cary, M. *The Daughter of the Stars* Hatchard 1939

EDWARDS, George Wharton (1859–1950) American
Hawthorne, N. *Tanglewood Tales* Houghton 1887
Taylor, J. *Sundry Rhymes from the Days of our Grandmothers* Randolph 1888
Dobson, A. *The Sundial* Dodd 1890
Edwards, G. W. *Thumb-nail Sketches* Century Co. 1893
—— *P'tit Matinic' and other monotones* Century Co. 1894
Holmes, O. W. *The Last Leaf* Houghton 1895
The Rivalries of the Long and Short Codiac Century Co. 1895
Spenser, E. *Epithalamion* Dodd 1895
Edwards, G. W. *Break o' Day and other stories* Century Co. 1896
A Book of Old English Love Songs Macmillan 1897
De Kay, C. *Bird Gods* Barnes 1898
Edwards, G. W. *Holland of Today* Moffat 1909
A Book of Old English Ballads Macmillan 1910
Edwards, G. W. *Brittany and the Bretons* Moffat 1910
—— *Some Old Flemish Towns* Moffat 1911
—— *Marken and its People* Moffat 1912
—— *The Forest of Arden* Stokes 1914
Watson, V. C. *The Princess Pocahontas* Penn 1916
Edwards, G. W. *Vanished Halls and Cathedrals of France* Penn 1917
—— *Alsace-Lorraine* Penn 1918
Barham, R. H. *The Jackdaw of Rheims* Houghton 1919
Edwards, G. W. *Belgium Old and New* Penn 1920
Dodge, M. E. *Hans Brinker* Scribner 1922
Edwards, G. W. *London* Penn 1922
—— *Paris* Penn 1924
—— *Spain* Penn 1926
—— *Rome* Penn 1928
—— *Constantinople* Penn 1930

FELL, Herbert Granville (1872–1951) British
Our Lady's Tumbler Dent 1894
Mary the Blessed Virgin 1894
Ali Baba and the Forty Thieves Dent 1895
The Fairy Gifts and Tom Hickathrift Dent 1895
Maud, C. E. *Wagner's Heroes* Arnold 1895
The Book of Job Dent 1896
The Song of Solomon Chapman 1897
Herodotus *Wonder Stories from Herodotus* Harper 1900
Nesbit, E. *The Book of Dragons* Harper 1900
Hood, T. *The Serious Poems of Thomas Hood* Newnes 1901
Hawthorne, N. *A Wonder Book and Tanglewood Tales* Dent 1910

FLINT, William Russell (1880–1969) British
Haggard, H. R. *King Solomon's Mines* Cassell 1905
À Kempis, T. *Of the Imitation of Christ* Chatto 1908
Aurelius, M. *The Thoughts of the Emperor Marcus Aurelius Antoninus* Warner 1909
Gilbert, W. S. *Savoy Operas* Bell 1909
The Song of Songs Warner 1909
Arnold, M. *The Scholar Gipsy and Thyrsis* Warner 1910
Gilbert, W. S. *Iolanthe and other operas* Bell 1910
Malory, T. *Le Morte D'Arthur* Warner 1910
Burns, R. *Songs and Lyrics* Warner 1911
Gilbert, W. S. *Comic Operas* Bell 1911
—— *The Gondoliers* Bell 1912
Kingsley, C. *The Heroes* Riccardi 1912
Chaucer, G. *The Canterbury Tales* Medici 1913
Malory, T. *Le Morte D'Arthur* Cape 1920
Lang, A. *Theocritus, Bion and Moschus* Riccardi 1922
Homer *The Odyssey* Mecici 1924
Judith Haymarket Press 1928
Gilbert, W. S. *The Mikado* 1928
—— *The Yeomen of the Guard* 1929
The Book of Tobit and the History of Susanna Haymarket Press 1929
Chaucer, G. *Tales from Chaucer* Medici 1930

FOLKARD, Charles (1878–1963) British
Wyss, J. D. *The Swiss Family Robinson* Dent 1910
Grimm, J. L. C. & W. C. *Grimms' Fairy Tales* Black 1911
Hoffman, A. S. *The Children's Shakespeare* Dent 1911
Lorenzini, C. *Pinocchio* Dent 1911
Aesop's Fables Black 1912
The Arabian Nights Black 1913
Barham, R. *The Jackdaw of Rheims* Gay 1913
Nyblom, H. A. *Jolly Calle and other Swedish Fairy Tales* Dent 1913
Folkard, C. *The Teddy Tail Series* Black 1915 etc.
Garnett, L. M. J. *Ottoman Wonder Tales* Black 1915
Walter, L. E. *Mother Goose's Nursery Rhymes* Black 1919
Brook, A. W. *Witch's Hollow* Black 1920
Glover, W. J. *British Fairy and Folk Tales* Black 1920
Black, D. *The Magic Egg* Black 1922
Mother Goose's Nursery Tales Black 1923
Nursery Rhymes Moring 1925
Lamb, C. & M. A. *Tales from Shakespeare* Dent 1926
Kossak-Szczucka, Z. *The Troubles of a Gnome* Black 1928
Daglish, A. & Rhys, E. *The Land of Nursery Rhyme* Dent 1932

FORD, Henry Justice (1860–1941) British
Aesop's Fables for Little Readers Unwin 1888
Lang, A. *The Blue Fairy Book* Longmans 1889
—— *The Red Fairy Book* Longmans 1890
Yorke, S. P. *When Mother was Little* Fisher Unwin 1890
Bourdillon, F. W. *A Lost God* Mathews 1891
Lang, A. *The Blue Poetry Book* Longmans 1891
—— *The Green Fairy Book* Longmans 1892
—— *The True Story Book* Longmans 1893
Weyman, S. *A Gentleman of France* Longmans 1893
Lang, A. *The Yellow Fairy Book* Longmans 1894

—— *The Red True Story Book* Longmans 1895
—— *The Animal Story Book* Longmans 1896
—— *The Blue True Story Book* Longmans 1896
—— *The Pink Fairy Book* Longmans 1897
The Arabian Nights Entertainment Longmans 1898
Lang, A. *The Red Book of Animal Stories* Longmans 1899
Taylor, U. A. *Early Italian Love Stories* Longmans 1899
Lang, A. *The Grey Fairy Book* Longmans 1900
—— *The Violet Fairy Book* Longmans 1901
—— *The Book of Romance* Longmans 1902
—— *The Disentanglers* Longmans 1902
Shakespeare, W. *Works* Constable 1902
Lang, A. *The Crimson Fairy Book* Longmans 1903
—— *The Brown Fairy Book* Longmans 1904
—— *The Red Romance Book* Longmans 1905
Tales of King Arthur Longmans 1905
Lang, A. *The Orange Fairy Book* Longmans 1906
—— *The Olive Fairy Book* Longmans 1907
—— *Tales of Troy and Greece* Longmans 1907
Scott, W. *Kenilworth* Jack 1907
Walker, G. B. *The Luck-Flower* Ellis 1907
Lang, L. B. *The Book of Princes and Princesses* Longmans 1908
Lang, A. *Marvellous Musician* Longmans 1909
—— *The Lilac Fairy Book* Longmans 1910
Fletcher, C. R. L. & Kipling, R. *A School History of England* Clarendon 1911
Lang, L. B. *The All Sorts of Stories Book* Longmans 1911
—— *The Book of Saints and Heroes* Longmans 1912
James, M. R. *Old Testament Legends* Longmans 1913
Lang, L. B. *The Strange Story Book* Longmans 1913
Greene, H. P. *Pilot and other stories* Macmillan 1916
Newbolt, H. J. *The Book of the Happy Warrior* Longmans 1917
Benson, E. F. *David Blaize and the Blue Door* Hodder 1918
The Parables S.P.C.K. 1920
Bunyan, J. *The Pilgrim's Progress* S.P.C.K. 1921
Clarke, W. *SS. Peter and Paul* S.P.C.K. 1921
Prescott, W. H. *The Conquest of Montezuma's Empire* Longmans 1932

FORTESCUE-BRICKDALE, Eleanor (1872–1945) British
Gibbs, J. A. *A Cotswold Village* Murray 1898
Scott, W. *Ivanhoe* Bell 1898
Tennyson, A. *Poems* Bell 1905
Dearmer, M. *A Child's Life of Christ* Methuen 1906
Browning, R. *Pippa Passes* Chatto 1908
—— *Dramatis Personae* Chatto 1909
Wright *Beautiful Flowers* Jack 1909
Tennyson, A. *Idylls of the King* Hodder 1911
Canton, W. *The Story of St Elizabeth of Hungary* Herbert & Daniel 1912
Fairless, M. *The Gathering of Brother Hilarius* Duckworth 1913
The Book of Old English Songs and Ballads Hodder 1915
Eleanor Fortescue-Brickdale's Golden Book of Famous Women Hodder 1919
Fleur and Blanchefleur O'Connor 1922
Palgrave, F. T. ed. *Golden Treasury* Hodder 1924
Christmas Carols Alexander Moring 1925

Calthrop, D. C. *A Diary of an Eighteenth-Century Garden* Williams & Norgate 1926
—— *The Gentle Art* Williams & Norgate 1927

FRASER, Claud Lovat (1890–1921) British
Flying Fame Booklets 1913
Macfall, H. *The Splendid Wayfaring* Simpkin Marshall 1913
Hare, W. *The Court of the Printers' Guild* Pulman 1914
Pirates Simpkin 1915
Nursery Rhymes Jack 1919
The Lute of Love Selwyn 1920
Fraser, C. L. *Sixteen Songs for Sixpence* 1921
Gay, J. *The Beggar's Opera, etc.* Heinemann 1921
Nodier, C. *The Luck of the Bean Rows* O'Connor [1921]
Goldoni, C. *The Liar: a Comedy of Three Acts* Selwyn 1922
Nodier, J. E. C. *The Woodcutter's Dog* O'Connor 1922
Preston, H. *The House of Vanities* Lane 1922
Millard, C. *The Printed Work of Claud Lovat Fraser* Danielson [1923?]
Characters from Dickens Jack 1924
De La Mare, W. *Peacock Pie* Constable 1924
Fraser, C. L. *Sixty-Three Unpublished Designs* First Editions Club 1924

GOBLE, Warwick (fl. 1900–1920) British
Crockett, S. R. *Lad's Love* Bliss Sands 1897
Van Milligen, A. *Constantinople* Black 1906
Gasquet, F. A. *The Greater Abbeys of England* Chatto 1908
Barlow, J. *Irish Ways* Allen 1909
Kingsley, C. *The Water Babies* Macmillan 1909
James, G. *Green Willow* Macmillan 1910
Basile, G. B. *Stories from the Pentamerone* Macmillan 1911
Chaucer, G. *The Modern Reader's Chaucer* Macmillan 1912
Lalavihari, De *Folk Tales of Bengal* Macmillan 1912
The Fairy Book Macmillan 1913
Mackenzie, D. *Indian Myth and Legend* Gresham 1913
Sohrabji, C. *Indian Tales of the Great Ones* Blackie 1916
Fletcher, J. *The Cistercians in Yorkshire* S.P.C.K. 1919
Owen, D. *The Book of Fairy Poetry* Longmans 1920

GREEN, Elizabeth Shippen (1871–1954) American
Smith, J. W. *The Book of the Child* Stokes 1903
Peabody, J. P. *The Book of the Little Past* Houghton 1908
Hardy, A. S. *Aurelie* Harper 1912
Le Gallienne, R. *The Maker of Rainbows* Harper 1912
Lamb, C. & M. *Tales from Shakespeare* McKay 1922
Waller, M. E. *Daughter of the Rich* Little 1924
Willcox, L. C. *The Torch* Harper 1924
Wiggin, K. D. S. *Mother Carey's Chickens* Houghton 1930

GREIFFENHAGEN, Maurice (1862–1932) British
Crowdy, W. L. *'Dorothy' Sketches* Pramitic Publishing 1887
Haggard, R. *Cleopatra* Longmans 1889
Kennedy, A. C. *Picturer in Rhyme* Longmans 1891

Lund, T. W. M. *The Religion of Art in Three Pictures* Howell 1891

Gilkes, A. H. *Kallistratus* Longmans 1897

Haggard, R. *Swallow* Longmans 1899

Jacobs, W. W. *The Lady of the Barge* Harper 1902

Pemberton, M. *The Gold Wolf* Ward 1903

Crockett, S. *Strong Mac* Ward 1904

Norway, A. H. *Naples Past and Present* Methuen 1905

Vaughan, H. *The Naples Riviera* Methuen 1907

The Rubáiyát of Omar Khayyám Foulis 1909

Forman, J. *Bianca's Daughter* Ward 1910

Parsons, C. *Some Thoughts at Eventide* Methuen 1910

Pemberton, M. *White Walls* Ward 1910

Jacobs, W. W. *Many Cargoes* Methuen 1912

Wallace, E. *Lieutenant Bones* Ward 1918

HARRISON, (Emma) Florence (fl. 1887–1914) British

Harrison, Florence *Rhymes and Reasons* Blackie 1905

—— *The Rhyme of a Run* Blackie 1907

—— *In the Fairy Ring* Blackie 1908

—— *Light of Love* Humphreys 1908

Rossetti, C. *Poems* Blackie 1910

Tennyson, A. *Guinevere and other poems* Blackie 1912

Harrison, F. *Elfin Song* Blackie 1912

Morris, W. *Early Poems* Blackie 1914

Ferguson, S. *Poems* Dublin 1916

Harrison, F. *Tales in Rhyme and Colour* Blackie 1916

Herbertson, A. *Tinkler Johnny* Blackie 1916

Harrison, F. *The Man in the Moon* Blackie 1918

—— *The Pixy Book* Blackie 1918

Syrett, N. *Godmother's Garden* Blackie 1918

Beautiful Poems Blackie 1923

HENDERSON, A. Keith (1883–?) British

Lorris, G. de *The Romaunt of the Rose* Chatto 1908

Whitworth, G. *A Book of Whimsies* Dent 1909

Hardy, T. *Under the Greenwood Tree* Chatto 1913

Henderson, K. *Letters to Helen* Chatto 1917

Prescott, W. H. *The Conquest of Mexico* Chatto 1922

Henderson, K. *Palm Groves and Humming Birds* Benn 1924

Hudson, W. H. *Green Mansions* Duckworth 1926

Pre-historic Man Chatto 1927

Hudson, W. H. *The Purple Land* Duckworth 1929

Beith, J. *Sand Castle* Hodder 1936

Burns, R. *Burns by Himself* Methuen 1938

HILDER, Rowland (1905–) British

Westerman, P. F. *The Riddle of the Air* Blackie 1925

Lesterman, J. *Adventures of a Trafalgar Lad* Cape 1926

—— *A Sailor of Napoleon* Cape 1927

Westerman, P. F. *The Junior Cadet* Blackie 1927

Lesterman, J. *A Pair of Rovers* Cape 1928

—— *The Second Mate of the Myradale* Cape 1929

Stevenson, R. L. *Treasure Island* O.U.P. 1929

Webb, M. *Precious Bane* Cape 1929

Stevenson, R. L. *Kidnapped* O.U.P. 1930

Manhood, H. A. *Little Peter the Great* Jackson 1931

Masefield, J. *The Midnight Folk* Heinemann 1931

Westerman, P. F. *The Senior Cadet* Blackie 1931

Smith, C. F. *Three Tales of the Sea* O.U.P. 1932

Watt, W. M. W. *Fire Down Below* Muller 1935

Forester, C. S. *The Happy Return* Joseph 1937

Strong, L. A. G. *They went to the Island* Dent 1940

HILL, Vernon (1887–?) British

Hill, V. *The Arcadian Calendar for 1910* Lane [1909]

Phillips, S. *The New Inferno* Lane 1911

Chope, R. P. *Ballads Weird and Wonderful* Lane 1912

Cammaerts, E. *Belgian Poems* Lane 1915

Graham, S. *Tramping with a Poet in the Rockies* Macmillan 1922

HOUSMAN, Laurence (1865–1959) British

MacDonald, G. *The Elect Lady* Kegan Paul 1888

Meredith, G. *Jump to Glory Jane* Swan Sonnenschein 1892

Lie, J. L. *Weird Tales from Northern Seas* Kegan Paul 1893

Rossetti, C. *Goblin Market* Macmillan 1893

Barlow, J. *The End of Elfin Town* Macmillan 1894

Davidson, J. *A Random Itinerary* Mathews & Lane 1894

Hinkson, K. T. *Cuckoo Songs* Mathews 1894

Housman, L. *A Farm in Fairyland* Kegan Paul 1894

—— *The House of Joy* Kegan Paul 1895

Nesbit, E. *A Pomander of Verse* Lane 1895

Newton-Robinson, C. *The Viol of Love* Lane 1895

Thompson, F. *Sister Songs* Lane 1895

Housman, C. A. *The Were Wolf* Lane 1896

Housman, L. *All Fellows* Kegan Paul 1896

—— *Green Arras* Lane 1896

Shelley, P. B. *The Sensitive Plant* Aldine House 1898

Housman, L. *The Field of Clover* Kegan Paul 1898

Arnold, T. W. *Little Flowers of St Francis* Dent 1898

À Kempis, T. *Of the Imitation of Christ* Kegan Paul 1898

Holmes, E. *The Silence of Love* Lane 1899

Housman, L. *The Little Land* Grant Richards 1899

MacDonald, G. *At the Back of the North Wind* Blackie 1900

—— *The Princess and the Goblin* Blackie 1900

Housman, L. *The Blue Moon* Murray 1904

—— *The Cloak of Friendship* Murray 1905

Tennyson, A. *Maud* Essex House 1905

Housman, L. *Prunella* Bullen 1906

—— *All Fellows and the Cloak of Friendship* Cape 1923

HUDSON, Gwynedd M. (fl. 1912–1925) British

Carroll, L. *Alice's Adventures in Wonderland* Hodder 1922

Barrie, J. M. *Peter Pan and Wendy* Hodder 1931

JACKSON, A. E. (1873–1952) British

Woolf, B. S. *The Twins of Ceylon* Duckworth 1909

—— *The Twins of Ceylon and More about the Twins* Duckworth 1913

Carroll, L. *Alice in Wonderland* Hodder 1915

Lamb, C. & M. *Tales from Shakespeare* Ward 1918

Kingsley, C. *The Water Babies* Milford 1920

Tales from the Arabian Nights Ward 1920

JONES, Alfred Garth (1872–1930) British

Peters, W. T. *The Tournament of Love* Brentano 1894

Milton, J. *The Minor Poems* Bell 1898

Queen Mab's Fairy Realm Newnes 1901

Tennyson, A. *In Memoriam* Newnes 1901

Lamb, C. *Essays of Elia* Methuen 1902

Landry, G. de la T. *The Book of Thenseygnementes* Newnes 1902

KENT, Rockwell (1882–1971) American
Kent, R. *Alaska Drawings* Knoedler 1919
—— *Wilderness* Putnam 1920
—— *Voyaging Southward from the Strait of Magellan*
Halcyon House 1924
Burke, J. *Dreams and Derisions* Limited Edition 1927
Voltaire, F. M. A. de *Candide* Random House 1928
Kent, R. *Elmer Adler* Harbor 1929
Pushkin, A. S. *Gabriel* Covici Friede 1929
Wilder, T. N. *The Bridge of San Luis Rey* Boni 1929
Chaucer, G. *Canterbury Tales* Covici Friede 1930
Kent, R. *N by E* Brewer and Warner 1930
Melville, H. *Moby Dick* Random House 1930
Kent, R. *A Birthday Book* Random House 1931
Robinson, S. *City Child* Farrar 1931
Shakespeare, W. *Venus and Adonis* Hart 1931
Beowulf Random House 1932
Casanova, G. *The Memoirs* Boni 1932
Kent, R. *Rockwellkentiana* Harcourt 1933
Alexander, L. M. *Candy* Dodd 1934
Butler, S. *Erewhon* Limited Ed. 1934
Powell, L. C. *Robinson Jeffers* Primavera 1934
Rich, E. G. *Hans the Eskimo* Houghton 1934
Vercel, R. *In Sight of Eden* Harcourt 1934
Kent, R. *Salamina* Harcourt 1935
The Saga of Gisli Harcourt 1936
Shakespeare, W. *Complete Works* Doubleday 1936
Whitman, W. *Leaves of Grass* Heritage 1936
Melville, H. *Moby Dick* Garden City 1937
Kent, R. *This is my Own* Duell 1940

KING, Jessie M. (1875–1949) British
Mendès, C. trans. *L'Évangile de l'Enfance* Glasgow:
Maclehose 1902
Buchanan, G. *Jeptha* Alex Gardner [1903]
Evans, S. *The High History of the Holy Grail* Dent 1903
The Rubáiyát of Omar Khayyám Routledge 1903
Tennyson, A. *Elaine* Routledge 1903
Spielmann, M. H. *Littledom Castle* Routledge 1903
Tennyson, A. *Morte d'Arthur* Routledge 1903
—— *Guinevere* Routledge 1903
Morris, W. *The Defence of Guenevere* Lane 1904
King, J. M. *Budding Life* Gowans & Gray 1906
Milton, J. *Comus* Routledge 1906
Spenser, E. *Poems* Jack [1906]
Keats, J. *Isabella or the Pot of Basil* Foulis 1907
Shelley, P. B. *Poems* Jack [1907]
Mantegazza, P. *The Legends of the Flowers* Foulis 1908
King, J. M. *Dwellings of an Old World Town: Culcross*
Gowans & Gray 1909
—— *The Grey City of the North* Foulis 1910
Arcambeau, E. *The Book of Bridges* Gowans & Gray
1911
Hogg, J. *Kilmenny* Foulis 1911
King, J. M. *The Grey City of the West* Foulis 1911
Arcambeau, E. *Ponts de Paris* Perche 1912
Songs and Poems of the Ettrick Shepherd Foulis 1912
R. L. Stevenson Memories Foulis 1912
The Studio *Seven Happy Days* (Christmas Supplement)
1913
Wilde, O. *A House of Pomegranates* Methuen 1915
King, J. M. *The Little White Town of Never Weary*
Harrap 1917

The Studio *Good King Wenceslas* (Christmas Supplement) 1919
'Marion' *Mummy's Bedtime Story Book* Palmer 1920–
Kipling, R. *L'Habitation Forcée* Kieffer 1921
King, J. M. *How Cinderella was able to go to the Ball*
Foulis 1924
London Transport *Whose Land? The Underground
Electric Railway* 1930
Corder, A. *Our Lady's Garland* 1934
The Fringes of Paradise Muller 1935

MACDOUGALL, W. Brown (?–1936) British
Armour, M. *The Home and Early Haunts of Robert Louis
Stevenson* White 1895
The Book of Ruth Dent 1896
Chronicles of Strathearn Philips 1896
Armour, M. *Songs of Love and Death* Dent 1896
—— *Thames Sonnets and Semblances* Mathews 1897
—— *The Fall of the Niblungs* Dent 1897
—— *The Eerie Book* Shiells 1898
—— *The Shadow of Love* Duckworth 1898
Keats, J. *Isabella* Kegan Paul 1898
Rossetti, D. G. *The Blessed Damozel* Duckworth 1898
The Rubáiyát of Omar Khayyám Macmillan 1898
The Fields of France Chapman 1905
Gudrun Dent 1928

MILLAR, H. R. (1869–1940) British
Sand, G. *The Golden Fairy Book* Hutchinson 1894
Taylor, S. *The Humour of Spain* Scott 1894
Bernhardt, S. *The Silver Fairy Book* Hutchinson 1895
—— *The Golden Fairy Book* Hutchinson n.d.
Morier, J. *The Adventures of Haji Baba* Macmillan 1895
Fairy Tales Far and Near Cassell 1895
Marryat, F. *The Phantom Ship* Macmillan 1896
Peacock, T. L. *Headlong Hall and Nightmare Abbey*
Macmillan 1896
Bellerby, I. *The Diamond Fairy Book* Hutchinson 1897
Harraden, B. *Untold Tales of the Past* Blackwood 1897
Hope, A. *Phroso* Methuen 1897
Marryat, F. *Frank Mildmay* Macmillan 1897
—— *Snarley-Yow* Macmillan 1897
Kinglake, A. W. *Eothen* Newnes 1898
Nesbit, E. *The Book of Dragons* Harper 1900
—— *Nine Unlikely Tales for Children* Unwin 1901
Hugo, V. *The Story of the Bold Pécopin* Smith 1902
Anstey, F. *Only Toys* Richards 1903
Nesbit, E. *The Phoenix and the Carpet* Newnes 1904
Hamilton, M. *Kingdoms Curious* Heinemann 1905
Nesbit, E. *The Enchanted Castle* Unwin 1907
Turley, C. *The Playmate* Heinemann 1907
Kingsley, C. *Hereward the Wake* Blackie n.d.
Nesbit, E. *The Magic City* Macmillan 1910
—— *The Wonderful Garden* Macmillan 1911
—— *Wet Magic* Laurie 1913
Harding, N. *The Little Grey Pedlar* Blackie 1914
Millar, H. R. *The Big Coloured Picture Book* Blackie 1924
—— *The Dreamland Express* Milford 1927
Hakluyt *Voyages* n.d.
Aly the Philosopher Macmillan 1930
Macmillan's Infant Readers Macmillan 1933
All the Puck Stories 1935
Walker, E. *Joyous Stories* Macmillan 1935

NELSON, Harold Edward Hughes (1871–1946) British
La Motte Fouqué, F. H. K. de *Undine and Aslauga's Knight* Newnes 1901
Sylva, C. *A Real Queen's Fairy Book* Newnes 1901
Nelson, H. *His Book of Bookplates* Schulze 1904
Thoms, W. *Early English Prose Romances* Schulze 1904

NIELSEN, Kay (1886–1957) Danish
Quiller-Couch, A. T. *In Powder and Crinoline* Hodder 1913
Asbjörnsen, P. C. & Moe, J. T. *East of the Sun and West of the Moon* Hodder 1914
Quiller-Couch, A. T. *Twelve Dancing Princesses* Doran 1923
Andersen, H. C. *Fairy Tales* Hodder 1924
Grimm, J. L. C. & W. C. *Hansel and Gretel* Hodder 1925
Wilson, R. *Red Magic* Cape 1930

ODLE, Alan (1888–1948) British
The Gypsy Nos. 1 & 2 Pomegranate Press 1915–16
Voltaire, F. M. A. de *Candide* Routledge 1922
Rabelais, F. *Works*
The Mimiambs of Herondas Fanfrolico 1929
Hanley, J. *The Last Voyage* Jackson 1931
Clemens, S. *1601: A Tudor Fireside Conversation* 1936

PAPE, Eric (1870–1938) American
Groesbeck. T. *The Incas* Putnam 1896
Woodbury, J. C. *Echoes* Putnam 1897
Wallace, L. *The Fair God* Harper 1899
Andersen, H. C. *Fairy Tales* Macmillan 1921
The Arabian Nights Macmillan 1923
Irving, W. *Rip Van Winkle* Macmillan 1925
Hugo, V. *Notre Dame de Paris* Washburn 1928

PAPÉ, Frank Cheyne (1878–?) American
Buckley, E. F. *Children of the Dawn* Gardner 1908
Andersen, H. C. *Fairy Tales* Nister 1910
Bunyan, J. *The Pilgrim's Progress* Dent 1910
Sand, G. *The Wings of Courage* Blackie 1911
Siegfried and Kriemhild Nelson 1911
Spenser, E. *The Gateway to Spenser* Nelson 1911
Carové, F. W. *The Story Without an End* Duckworth 1912
Clark, A. *As it is in Heaven* Sampson 1912
Stawell, M. M. *The Fairy of Old Spain* Dent 1912
Book of Psalms Hutchinson 1913
Wilson, R. *The Indian Fairy Book* Macmillan 1914
Homer *The Toils and Travels of Odysseus* Gardner 1916
Wilson, R. *The Russian Story Book* Macmillan 1916
MacDonald, G. *At the Back of the North Wind* Blackie [192–?]
Cabell, J. B. *Jurgen* Lane 1921
France, A. *At the Sign of the Reine Pedauque* Bodley Head 1922
Hodges, G. *When the King Came* Houghton 1923
Lamb, C. & M. *Tales from Shakespeare* Warne 1923
Tales from the Mahabharata Selwyn 1924
Cabell, J. B. *Figures of Earth* Lane 1925
France, A. *The Works of Anatole France* Lane 1925
Cabell, J. B. *The Cream of the Jest* Lane 1927
Rabelais, F. *Works* Lane 1927
Cabell, J. B. *The Silver Stallion* Lane 1928

—— *The Way of Ecben* Lane 1929
—— *Domnie* Lane 1930
Davies, R. *The Stars, the World and the Women* Jackson 1930
Suetonius *Lives of the Twelve Caesars* Argus 1930
Blackmore, R. D. *The Picture Story of Lorna Doone* Lane 1933
Defoe, D. *The Picture Story of Robinson Crusoe* Lane 1933
Wheatley, D. *Old Rowley* Hutchinson 1933
Falk, B. *Rachel the Immortal* Hutchinson 1935

PARK, Carton Moore (1877–1956) British
Park, C. M. *An Alphabet of Animals* Blackie 1899
—— *A Book of Birds* Blackie 1900
Hendry, H. *A Child's London* Sands 1900
Lever, C. J. *The Confessions of Harry Lorrequer* Gresham 1900
Norman *A Book of Elfin Rhymes* Gay 1900
The Child's Pictorial Natural History S.P.C.K. 1901
Bicknell, E. *A Dog Book* Richards 1902
The King of Beasts Blackie 1904
La Fontaine, J. *La Fontaine's Fables* Nelson 1905
The Lilliput Library for Children Allen 1907
Spielmann, M. H. *The Love Family* Allen 1908
Hyatt, S. P. *Biffel* Melrose 1909
Brown, J. *A Little Book of Dogs* Foulis 1911
Morris, A. T. *Old Friends and New Fables* Blackie 1916

PARRISH, Maxfield (1870–1966) American
Baum, F. L. *Mother Goose in Prose* Way & Williams 1897
Read, O. *Bolanyo* Way & Williams 1897
Butler, W. M. *Whist Reference Book* Yorston 1898
Grahame, K. *The Golden Age* Lane 1900
Irving, W. *Knickerbocker's History of New York* Russell 1900
Grahame, K. *Dream Days* Lane 1902
Carryl, G. W. *The Garden of Years* Putnam 1904
Field, E. *Poems of Childhood* Scribner 1904
Wharton, E. *Italian Villas and their Gardens* Century 1904
Smith, A. C. *The Turquoise Cap and The Desert* Scribner 1905
Wiggin, K. D. *The Arabian Nights* Scribner 1909
Hawthorne, N. *A Wonder Book and Tanglewood Tales* Duffield 1910
Scudder, H. *The Children's Book* Houghton Mifflin 1910
Hawthorne, H. *Lure of the Garden* Century 1911
Palgrave, F. T. *The Golden Treasury* Duffield 1911
Saunders, L. *The Knave of Hearts* Scribner 1925

PEARSE, Susan Beatrice (1878–1980) British
Dickens, C. *The Magic Fishbone* Nisbet 1911
—— *The Trial of William Tinkling* Constable 1912
Heward, C. *Ameliaranne and the Green Umbrella* Harrap 1920
—— *The Twins and Tabiffa* Harrap 1923
Dickens, C. *Captain Boldheart and the Latin Grammar Master* Macmillan 1927
Heward, C. *Ameliaranne Keeps Shop* Harrap 1928
—— *Ameliaranne Cinema Star* Harrap 1929
Joan, N. *Ameliaranne in Town* Harrap 1930
Gilmour, M. *Ameliaranne at the Circus* Harrap 1931

Joan, N. *Ameliaranne and the Big Treasure* Harrap 1932
Farjeon, E. *Ameliaranne's Prize Packet* Harrap 1933
—— *Ameliaranne's Washing Day* Harrap 1934
Gilmour, M. *Ameliaranne at the Seaside* Harrap 1935
Thompson, K. L. *Ameliaranne at the Zoo* Harrap 1936
Heward, C. *Ameliaranne at the Farm* Harrap 1937
—— *Ameliaranne Gives a Christmas Party* Harrap 1938
—— *Ameliaranne Camps Out* Harrap 1939
—— *Ameliaranne Keeps School* Harrap 1940

POGÁNY, Willy (1882–1955) Hungarian

Kunos, I. *Turkish Fairy Tales* Burt 1901
Farrow, G. E. *The Adventures of a Dodo* Unwin 1907
Thomas, W. J. *The Welsh Fairy Book* Unwin 1907
Ward, M. A. *Milly and Olly* Unwin 1907
Edgar, M. G. *A Treasury of Verse for Little Children* Harrap 1908
Goethe, J. W. von *Faust* Hutchinson 1908
Dasent, G. W. *Norse Wonder Tales* Collins 1909
Hawthorne, N. *Tanglewood Tales* Unwin 1909
The Rubáiyát of Omar Khayyám Harrap 1909
Coleridge, S. T. *The Rime of the Ancient Mariner* Harrap 1910
Gask, L. *Folk Tales from Many Lands* Harrap 1910
Young, G. *The Witch's Kitchen* Harrap 1910
Wagner, R. *Tannhäuser* Harrap 1911
Gask, L. *The Fairies and the Christmas Child* Harrap 1912
Wagner, R. *Parsifal* Harrap 1912
Heine, H. *Atta Troll* Sidgwick 1913
Kunos, I. *Forty-Four Turkish Fairy Tales* Harrap 1913
Pogány, W. *The Hungarian Fairy Book* Unwin 1913
Wagner, R. *The Tale of Lohengrin* Harrap 1913
Pogány, W. *Children* Harrap 1914
—— *A Series of Books for Children* Harrap 1915
More Tales from the Arabian Nights Holt 1915
Swift, J. *Gulliver's Travels* Macmillan 1917
Bryant, S. C. *Stories to Tell the Little Ones* Harrap 1918
Colum, P. *Adventures of Odysseus* Macmillan 1918
Olcutt, F. J. *Tales of the Persian Genii* Harrap 1919
Skinner, E. L. *Children's Plays* Appleton 1919
Colum, P. *The King of Ireland's Son* Harrap 1920
—— *The Children of Odin* Harrap 1922
The Adventures of Haroun El Raschid Holt 1923
Newman, I. *Fairy Flowers* Milford 1926
Flanders, H. H. *Looking Out of Jimmie* Dent 1928
Carroll, L. *Alice's Adventures in Wonderland* Dutton 1929
Pogány, W. *Mother Goose* Nelson 1929
Anthony, J. *Casanova Jones* Century 1930
Pogány, W. *Magyar Fairy Tales* Dutton 1930
Burton, R. F. *The Kasîdah of Hàjî Abdû El-Yezdî* McKay 1931
Huffard, G. T. *My Poetry Book* Winston 1934
Pushkin, A. *The Golden Cockerel* Nelson 1938

POTTER, Beatrix (1866–1943) British

Potter, B. *The Tale of Peter Rabbit* (privately printed, 250 copies) Warne 1901
—— *The Tale of Peter Rabbit* Warne 1902
—— *The Tailor of Gloucester* (privately printed, 500 copies) Warne 1902
—— *The Tale of Squirrel Nutkin* Warne 1902

—— *The Tailor of Gloucester* Warne 1903
—— *The Tale of Benjamin Bunny* Warne 1904
—— *The Tale of Two Bad Mice* Warne 1904
—— *The Tale of Mrs Tiggy-Winkle* Warne 1905
—— *The Pie and the Patty-pan* Warne 1905
—— *The Tale of Mr Jeremy Fisher* Warne 1906
—— *The Story of a Fierce Bad Rabbit* (in panoramic form) Warne 1906
—— *The Story of Miss Moppet* (in panoramic form) Warne 1906
—— *The Tale of Tom Kitten* Warne 1907
—— *The Tale of Jemima Puddle-Duck* Warne 1908
—— *The Roly-Poly Pudding* (larger format) Warne 1908
—— *The Tale of the Flopsy Bunnies* Warne 1909
—— *Ginger and Pickles* (larger format) Warne 1909
—— *The Tale of Mrs Tittlemouse* Warne 1910
—— *Peter Rabbit's Painting Book* Warne 1911
—— *The Tale of Timmy Tiptoes* Warne, 1911
—— *The Tale of Mr Tod* Warne 1912
—— *The Tale of Pigling Bland* Warne 1913
—— *Tom Kitten's Painting Book* Warne 1917
—— *Appley Dapply's Nursery Rhymes* Warne 1917
—— *The Tale of Johnny Town-Mouse* Warne 1918
—— *Cecily Parsley's Nursery Rhymes* Warne 1922
—— *Jemima Puddle-Duck's Painting Book* Warne 1925
—— *Peter Rabbit's Almanac for 1929* Warne 1928
—— *The Fairy Caravan* (privately printed, 100 copies) Warne 1929
—— *The Fairy Caravan* McKay 1929
—— *The Tale of Little Pig Robinson* McKay 1930
—— *The Tale of Little Pig Robinson* (larger format) Warne 1930
—— *Sister Anne* McKay 1932
—— *Wag-by-Wall* (limited edition, 100 copies) Warne 1944
—— *Wag-by-Wall* Horn Book Inc. 1944

PYLE, Howard (1853–1911) American

Yankee Doodle Dodd 1881
Tennyson, A. *The Lady of Shalott* Dodd 1881
Baldwin, M. *The Story of Siegfried* Scribner 1882
Carleton, W. *Farm Ballads* Harper 1882
Pyle, H. *The Merry Adventures of Robin Hood* Scribner 1883
Within the Capes Scribner 1885
Irving, W. *History of New York* Grolier Club 1886
Pyle, H. *Pepper and Salt* Harper 1886
Baldwin, M. *Story of the Golden Age* Scribner 1887
Pyle, H. *The Wonder Clock* Harper 1887
—— *Otto of the Silver Hand* Scribner 1888
The Rose of Paradise Harper 1888
School and Playground Lothrop 1891
Holmes, O. W. *The Autocrat of the Breakfast Table* Houghton 1892
—— *Dorothy Q together with a Ballad of the Boston Tea Party* Houghton 1892
—— *The One Hoss Shay* Houghton 1892
Pyle, H. *Men of Iron* Harper 1892
A Modern Aladdin Harper 1892
Pyle, H. *The Garden Behind the Moon* Scribner 1895
Howells, W. D. *Stops of Various Quills* Harper 1895
Pyle, H. *The Story of Jack Ballister's Fortunes* Century 1895

—— *Twilight Land* Harper 1895
Mitchell, S. W. *Hugh Wynne* Century 1896
Page *In Old Virginia* Scribner 1896
A Catalogue of Drawings Illustrating the Life of George Washington Philadelphia 1897
Van Dyke, H. *The First Christmas Tree* Scribner 1897
Longfellow, H. W. *Evangeline* Gay & Bird 1897
Lodge, H. C. *The Story of the Revolution* Scribner 1898
Deland, M. W. *Old Chester Tales* Harper 1899
The Price of Blood Badger 1899
Markham, E. *The Man with the Hoe* Doubleday 1900
Pyle, H. *Some Merry Adventures of Robin Hood* Scribner 1902
Rejected of Men Harper 1903
Pyle, H. *The Story of King Arthur and his Knights* Harper 1905
Cabell, J. B. *The Line of Love* Harper 1905
Pyle, H. *The Story of the Champions of the Round Table* Scribner 1905
—— *Stolen Treasure* Harper 1907
—— *The Story of Sir Launcelot and his Companions* Scribner 1907
The Ruby of Kishmoor Harper 1908
Pyle, H. *The Story of the Grail and the Passing of Arthur* Scribner 1910
Cabell, J. B. *The Soul of Melicent* Stokes 1913
Clemens, S. (Mark Twain) *St Joan of Arc* Harper 1919
Howard Pyle's Book of Pirates Harper 1921
Howard Pyle's Book of the American Spirit Harper 1923
Holmes, O. W. *Grandmother's Story of Bunker Hill* Houghton 1925

RACKHAM, Arthur (1867–1939) British

Beryln, A. *Sunrise Land* Jarrold 1894
Hope, A. *The Dolly Dialogues* Westminster Gazette 1894
Irving, W. *The Sketch Book* Putnam 1895
Adair-Fitzgerald, S. *The Zankiwank and the Bletherwitch* Dent 1896
Merriman, H. S. & Tallantyre, S. *The Money-spinner* Smith Elder 1896
Browne, M. *Two Old Ladies, Two Foolish Fairies and a Tom Cat* Cassell 1897
Lever, C. *Charles O'Malley* Service & Patton 1897
Merriman, H. S. *The Grey Lady* Smith Elder 1897
Barham, R. H. *The Ingoldsby Legends* Dent 1898
Burney, F. *Evelina* Newnes 1898
Dewar, G. *Wild Life in Hampshire Highlands* Dent 1899
Gray, E. *Fly Fishing* Dent 1899
Hole, S. R. *Our Gardens* Dent 1899
Lamb, C. *Tales from Shakespeare* Dent 1899
Martineau, H. *Feats on the Fjord* Dent 1899
Tate, W. J. *East Coast Scenery* Jarrold 1899
Grimm, J. L. C. & W. C. *Fairy Tales* Freemantle 1900
Herbertson, A. *The Bee-Blowaways* Cassell 1900
Nisbet, J. *Our Forest and Woodlands* Dent 1900
Paget, J. O. *Hunting* Dent 1900
Kenyon, C. R. *The Argonauts of the Amazon* Chambers 1901
Lyttleton, C. R. *Outdoor Games* Dent 1901
Selous, E. *Bird Watching* Dent 1901
Shand, A. *Shooting* Dent 1902
Greene, Mrs *The Grey House on the Hill* Nelson 1903
Henty, G. A. *Brains and Bravery* Chambers 1903

Niebuhr, B. G. *The Greek Heroes* Cassell 1903
Tod, W. M. *Farming* Dent 1903
Browne, M. *Surprising Adventures of Tuppy and Tue* Cassell 1904
Cholmondeley M. *Red Pottage* Newnes 1904
Dana, R. H. *Two Years Before the Mast* Collins 1904
Drury, W. P. *The Peradventures of Private Paget* Chapman 1904
Harbour, H. *Where Flies the Flag* Collins 1904
Haydon, A. L. *Stories of King Arthur* Cassell 1905
Irving, W. *Rip Van Winkle* Heinemann 1905
Barrie, J. M. *Peter Pan in Kensington Gardens* Hodder 1906
Kipling, R. *Puck of Pook's Hill* Doubleday 1906
Barham, R. H. *The Ingoldsby Legends* Dent 1907
Bonser, E. *The Land of Enchantment* Cassell 1907
Carroll, L. *Alice's Adventures in Wonderland* Heinemann 1907
Gates, E. *Good Night* Crowell 1907
Shakespeare, W. *A Midsummer Night's Dream* Heinemann 1908
La Motte Fouqué, F. H. K. de *Undine* Heinemann 1909
Grimm, J. L. C. & W. C. *Fairy Tales* Constable 1909
Swift, J. *Gulliver's Travels* Dent 1909
Lamb, C. & M. *Tales from Shakespeare* Dent 1909
Browne, M. *The Book of Betty Barber* Duckworth 1910
Wagner, R. *The Rhinegold and the Valkyrie* Heinemann 1910
—— *Siegfried and the Twilight of the Gods* Heinemann 1911
Aesop *Fables* Heinemann 1912
Barrie, J. M. *Peter Pan in Kensington Gardens* Hodder 1912
—— *The Peter Pan Portfolio* Hodder 1912
Mother Goose *Old Nursery Rhymes* Heinemann 1913
Rackham, A. *Arthur Rackham's Book of Pictures* Heinemann 1913
Dickens, C. *A Christmas Carol* Heinemann 1915
The Allies Fairy Book Heinemann 1916
Grimm, J. L. C. & W. C. *Little Brother and Little Sister* Constable 1917
Malory, T. *The Romance of King Arthur* Macmillan 1917
Steel, F. A. *English Fairy Tales Retold* Macmillan 1918
Swinburne, A. C. *The Springtide of Life* Heinemann 1918
Evans, C. *Cinderella* Heinemann 1919
Ford, J. E. *Snickerty Nick* Moffat & Ward 1919
Some British Ballads Constable 1919
Evans, C. S. *Sleeping Beauty* Heinemann 1919
Grimm, J. L. C. & W. C. *Hansel and Gretel* Constable 1920
—— *Snowdrop and other Tales* Constable 1920
Stephens, J. *Irish Fairy Tales* Macmillan 1920
Milton, J. *Comus* Heinemann 1921
Phillpotts, E. *A Dish of Apples* Hodder 1921
Hawthorne, N. *A Wonder Book* Hodder 1922
Morley, C. *Where the Blue Begins* Heinemann 1925
Shakespeare, W. *The Tempest* Heinemann 1926
Irving, W. *The Legend of Sleepy Hollow* Harrap 1928
Goldsmith, O. *The Vicar of Wakefield* Harrap 1929
Dickens, C. *The Chimes* Limited Editions Club 1931
Moore, C. C. *The Night Before Christmas* Harrap 1931
Walton, I. *The Compleat Angler* Harrap 1931
Andersen, H. C. *Fairy Tales* Harrap 1932
Ruskin, J. *King of the Golden River* Harrap 1932

Rackham, A. *The Arthur Rackham Fairy Book* Harrap
1933
Rossetti, C. *Goblin Market* Harrap 1933
Browning, R. *The Pied Piper of Hamelin* Harrap 1934
Poe, E. A. *Tales of Mystery and Imagination* Harrap
1935
Ibsen, H. *Peer Gynt* Harrap 1936
Shakespeare, W. *A Midsummer Night's Dream* Limited
Editions Club 1939
Grahame, K. *The Wind in the Willows* Limited Ed. 1940

ROBINSON, Charles (1870–1937) British
Aesop *Fables* Dent 1895
Stevenson, R. L. *A Child's Garden of Verses* Lane 1895
Carrington, E. *Animals in the Wrong Places* Bell 1896
Lowry, H. D. *Make Believe* Lane 1896
Setoun, G. *The Child World* Lane 1896
Bell, A. *Dobbie's Little Master* Bell 1897
Field, E. *Lullaby Land* Lane 1898
Macgregor, B. *King Longbeard* Lane 1898
Andersen, H. C. *Fairy Tales* Dent 1899
Cule, W. E. *Child Voices* Melrose 1899
Rands, W. B. *Lilliput Lyrics* Lane 1899
Bell, J. J. *Jack of all Trades* Lane 1900
―――― *The New Noah's Ark* Lane 1900
Canton, W. *The True Annals of Fairyland* Dent 1900
Dearmer, P. *The Little Lives of the Saints* Gardner 1900
Garstin, N. *The Suitors Of Aprille* Lane 1900
Homer *The Adventures of Odysseus* Dent 1900
La Motte Fouqué, F. H. K. de *Sintram and his Com-
panions* Dent 1900
―――― *Aslauga's Knight* Dent 1900
Perrault, C. *Tales of Passed Times* Dent 1900
Sand, G. *The Master Mosaic Workers* Dent 1900
Stacpoole, H. de V. *Pierrette* Lane 1900
Rhys, E. *The True Annals of Fairyland* Dent 1901
―――― *The Reign of King Cole* Dent 1901
A Book of Days for Little Ones Dent 1901
Copeland, W. *The Farm Book* Dent 1901
Bridgman, C. *The Bairn's Coronation Book* Dent 1902
―――― *The Shopping Day* Dent 1902
Burn, J. H. *The Mother's Book of Song* Gardner 1902
Copeland, W. *The Book of the Zoo* Dent 1902
Jerrold, W. *Nonsense! Nonsense!* Blackie 1902
The Coronation Autograph Book Gardner 1902
Jerrold, W. *The Big Book of Nursery Rhymes* Blackie 1903
The New Testament of Our Lord Gowans & Gray 1903
Jerrold, D. W. *Fireside Saints* Blackie 1904
A Bookful of Fun Clark 1905
Copeland, W. *The Black Cat Book* Blackie 1905
―――― *Rhymes* Blackie 1905–8
―――― *The Book of Dolly's Doings* Blackie
―――― *The Book of Dolly's House* Blackie
―――― *The Book of Ducks and Dutchies* Blackie
―――― *The Book of Other People* Blackie
―――― *The Book of Sailors* Blackie
―――― *The Book of Little Dutch Dolls* Blackie
―――― *The Cake Shop* Blackie
―――― *The Sweet Shop* Blackie
―――― *The Toy Shop* Blackie
*The Hundred Best Blank Verse Passages in the English
Language* Gowans & Gray 1905
Wallis, I. H. *The Cloud Kingdom* Lane 1905

Robinson, C. *The Silly Submarine* Blackie 1906
Picture Books for Children Dent 1906 etc
Sharp, E. *The Child's Christmas* Blackie 1906
Tynan, K. *A Little Book of Courtesies* Dent 1906
Black Bunnies Blackie 1907
Carroll, L. *Alice's Adventures in Wonderland* Cassell
1907
Matheson, A. *Songs of Love and Praise* Dent 1907
Sharp, E. *The Story of the Weathercock* Blackie 1907
Copeland, W. *Babes and Blossoms* Blackie 1908
Martinengo-Cesaresco, F. *The Fairies' Fountain* Fair-
bairns 1908
Jerrold, W. *The True Annals of Fairyland in the Reign
of King Aberon* Dent 1909
Rhys, E. *The True Annals of Fairyland in the Reign of
King Cole* Dent 1909
Arkwright, R. *Brownikens and other Fancies* Gardner
1910
Grimm, J. L. C. & W. C. *Fairy Tales* Nister 1910
Pope, J. *Babes and Birds* Blackie 1910
Syrett, N. *The Vanishing Princess* Nutt 1910
Burnett, F. H. *The Secret Garden* Heinemann 1911
Jerrold, W. *The Big Book of Fairy Tales* Blackie 1911
Pope, J. *The Baby Scouts* Blackie 1911
Shelley, P. B. *The Sensitive Plant* Heinemann [1911]
*The True Annals of Fairyland in the Reign of King
Herta* Dent 1911
France, A. *Bee* Dent 1912
Handasyde *The Four Gardens* Heinemann 1912
Jerrold, W. *The Big Book of Fables* Blackie 1912
Pope, J. *Babes and Beasts* Blackie 1912
Fielding, H. *Margaret's Book* Hutchinson 1913
Minnion, W. *Topsy Turvey* Connoisseur 1913
Perrault, C. *Fairy Tales* Dent 1913
Thurston, E. T. *The Open Window* Chapman 1913
Wilde, O. *The Happy Prince* Duckworth 1913
Castle, A. E. *Our Sentimental Garden* Heinemann 1914
Morris, A. T. *A Child's Book of Empire* Blackie 1914
Herrick, R. *Robert Herrick* Gardner 1915
Shakespeare, W. *Songs and Sonnets* Duckworth 1915
Sharp, E. *What Happened at Christmas* Blackie 1915
The Story of Prince Ahmed Gay 1915
Goldfish Bowl Hutchinson 1918
Stevenson, M. *Bridget's Fairies* R.T.S. 1919
Pan-pipes Collins n.d.
Rhys, G. *The Children's Garland of Verse* Dent 1921
Stevenson, J. G. *Father Time Stories* R.T.S. 1921
Doris and David Alone 1922
Girvin, B. & Cosens, M. *Wee Men* Hutchinson 1923
Jerrold, W. *The Book of Story Poems* Stokes 1924
Milne, A. A. *Once on a Time* Hodder 1925
Radcliffe, W. *The Saint's Garden* S.P.C.K. 1927
Mother Goose Nursery Rhymes Collins 1928
The Rubáiyát of Omar Khayyám Collins 1928
Marsh, L. *Old Time Tales* Frowde n.d.

ROBINSON, Frederick Cayley (1862–1927) British
Maeterlinck, M. P. M. B. *The Blue Bird* Methuen 1911
The First Book of Moses called Genesis Riccardi 1914
Hodgkin, L. V. *A Book of Quaker Saints* Foulis 1917
Webling, P. *Saints and their Stories* Nisbet 1919
Chesterton, G. K. *St Francis of Assisi* Hodder 1926
Trine, R. W. *In Tune with the Infinite* Foulis 1926

ROBINSON, Thomas Heath (1869–1950) British

Rinder, F. *Old World Japan* Allen 1895
Gaskell, E. *Cranford* Bliss 1896
Sylva, C. & Strettell, A. *Legends from River and Mountain* Allen 1896
Thackeray, W. M. *The History of Henry Esmond* Allen 1896
Hawthorne, N. *The Scarlet Letter* Bliss 1897
Milton, J. *Hymn on the Morning of Christ's Nativity* Allen 1897
Sterne, L. *A Sentimental Journey* Bliss 1897
Canton, W. *A Child's Book of Saints* Dent 1898
Andersen, H. C. *Fairy Tales* Dent 1899
The Arabian Nights Dent 1899
Kingsley, C. *The Heroes* Dent 1899
Minssen, B. *A Book of French Songs* Dent 1899
Hauff, W. *Lichtenstein* Nister 1900
Porter, J. *The Scottish Chiefs* Dent 1900
Aguilar, G. *The Vale of Cedars* Dent 1902
Crewick, P. *Robin Hood and His Adventures* Nister 1902
Boult, K. F. *Heroes of the Norseland* Dent 1903
Hughes, T. *Tom Brown's Schooldays* Dent 1903
Meade, E. T. *Stories from the Old Old Bible* Newnes 1903
Spenser, E. *Una and The Red Cross Knight* Dent 1905
Kelly, M. D. *The Story of Sir Walter Raleigh* Jack 1906
The Rubáiyát of Omar Khayyám Nister 1907
Coxhead, M. D. *Mexico* Jack 1909
Macy, S. B. *The Master Builders* Longmans 1911
Tales and Talks from History Blackie 1911
Macy, S. B. *The Book of the Kingdom* Longmans 1912
Tennyson, G. C. *The Song of Frithiof* Longmans 1912
Lees, G. R. *The Life of Christ* Partridge 1920
Eliot, G. *The Mill on the Floss* Gresham 1924
The Child's Bible Cassell 1928
The Story Bible Cassell 1930
Haydon, A. L. *The Book of Robin Hood* Warne 1931

ROBINSON, W. Heath (1872–1944) British

Andersen, H. C. *Danish Fairy Tales and Legends* Bliss 1897
Cervantes, M. de *Don Quixote* Bliss 1897
Rouse, W. H. D. *The Giant Crab and other tales* Nutt 1897
Bunyan, J. *The Pilgrim's Progress* Sands 1897
Gomme, G. L. *The Queen's Story Book* Constable 1898
Crooke, W. & Rouse, W. H. D. *The Talking Thrush* Dent 1899
Andersen, H. C. *Fairy Tales* Dent 1899
The Arabian Nights Entertainments Newnes 1899
Poe, E. A. *Poems* Bell 1900
Schück *Medieval Stories* Sands 1902
Rippman, W. *Dent's Andersen in German* Dent 1902
Robinson, W. H. *Uncle Lubin* Richards 1902
Cervantes, M. de *The Adventures of Don Quixote* Dent 1902
Munchausen, Baron *The Surprising Travels and Adventures* Richards 1902
Lamb, C. *Tales from Shakespeare* Sands 1902
Robinson, W. H. *The Child's Arabian Nights* Richards 1903
Hodgson, G. *Rama and the Monkeys* Dent 1903
Rabelais, F. *Works* 2v. Richards 1904

Carse, R. *The Monarchs of Merry England* Unwin 1904
Kennedy, H. A. *The Merry Multifleet and the Mounting Multicorps* Dent 1904
Kelman, J. H. *Stories from Chaucer* Jack 1906
Stories from the Odyssey Jack c. 1906
Shakespeare, W. *Twelfth Night* Hodder 1908
Kipling, R. *A Song of the English* Hodder 1909
—— *Collected Verse* Doubleday 1910
—— *The Dead King* Hodder 1910
Robinson, W. H. *Bill the Minder* Constable 1912
Andersen, H. C. *Fairy Tales* Hodder 1913
Shakespeare, W. *A Midsummer Night's Dream* Constable 1914
Kingsley, C. *The Water Babies* Constable 1915
Robinson, W. H. *Some Frightful War Pictures* Duckworth 1915
—— *Hunlikely* Duckworth 1916
De La Mare, W. *Peacock Pie* Constable 1916
Robinson, W. H. *The Saintly Hun* Duckworth 1917
—— *Flypapers* Duckworth 1919
—— *Get on With it.* G. Heath Robinson [1920?]
—— *The Home Made Car* Duckworth 1921
Perrault, C. *Old Time Stories* Constable 1921
Robinson, W. H. *Peter Quip in Search of a Friend* Partridge 1921
—— *Quaint and Selected Pictures* G. Heath Robinson 1922
—— *Humours of Golf* Methuen 1923
Smeaton, E. *Topsy Turvey Tales* Lane 1923
Hunter, N. *The Incredible Adventures of Professor Branestawm* Lane 1933
Robinson, W. H. *Absurdities* Hutchinson 1934
Lyne, G. M. *Balbus: a Latin Reading Book* Arnold 1934
Robinson, W. H. *Heath Robinson's Book of Goblins* Hutchinson 1934
Browne, K. R. G. *How to Live in a Flat* Hutchinson 1936
—— *How to be a Perfect Husband* Hutchinson 1937
—— *How to Make a Garden Grow* Hutchinson 1938
Robinson, W. H. *My Line of Life* Blackie 1938
Gledhill, J. B. & Preston, F. *Success with Stocks and Shares* Pitman 1938
Browne, K. R. G. *How to be a Motorist* Hutchinson 1939
—— *Let's Laugh* Hutchinson 1939
Patterson, R. F. *Mein Rant* Blackie 1940
Hunt, H. C. *How to Make the Best of Things* Hutchinson 1941
Robinson, W. H. *Heath Robinson at War* Methuen 1942
Hunt, H. C. *How to Run a Communal Home* Hutchinson 1943
Clopet, L. M. C. *Once Upon a Time* Muller 1944

ROUNTREE, Harry (1878–1950) Australian

The Child's Book of Knowledge Richards 1903
Hamer, S. H. *The Young Gullivers* Cassell 1906
Harris, J. *Uncle Remus* Nelson 1906
Morgan, O. & Rountree, H. *Mr Punch's Book of Birthdays* Punch 1906
Hamer, S. H. *The Story of 'The Ring'* Cassell 1907
Harry Rountree's Annual 1907
Avery, C. H. *The Little Robinson Crusoes* Nelson 1908
Carroll, L. *Alice's Adventures in Wonderland* Nelson 1908

Hamer, S. H. *The Transformations of the Truefitts* Cassell 1908
—— *The Wonderful Isles* Duckworth 1908
Hamer, S. H. & Rountree, H. *The Magic Wand, etc.* Duckworth 1908
Bright, A. D. *The Fortunate Princeling* Duckworth 1909
Hamer, S. H. *The Enchanted Wood* Duckworth 1909
—— *The Forest Foundling* Duckworth 1909
Spielmann, M. H. *The Rainbow Book* Chatto 1909
Darwin, B. *The Golf Courses of the British Isles* Duckworth 1910
Hamer, S. H. *The Dolomites* Methuen 1910
Davidson, G. *Tales from the Woods and Fields* Gardner 1911
Hamer, S. H. *The Four Glass Balls* Duckworth 1911
Harvey, B. S. *The Magic Dragon* Duckworth 1911
Hamer, S. H. *The Adventures of Spider and Co.* Duckworth 1912
Doyle, A. C. *The Poison Belt* Hodder 1913
Jefferies, J. R. *Bevis* Duckworth 1913
Macnair, J. H. *Animal Tales from Africa* Gardner 1914
Bayne, C. S. *My Book of Best Fairy Tales* Cassell 1915
Rountree, H. *Rountree's Ridiculous Rabbits* Stevenson 1916
—— *Rabbit Rhymes* Stevenson 1917
Paine, A. B. *The Arkansaw Bear* Harrap 1919
Saint Mars, F. *Pinion and Paw* Chambers 1919
—— *The Wild Unmasked* Chambers 1920
Fonhus, H. *The Trial of the Elk* Cape 1922
Seymour, M. F. *The Misadventures of Tootles and Timothy* Cassell 1922
Aesop's Fables Ward 1924
Batten, H. M. *Dramas of the Wild Folk* Partridge 1924
Dumas, A. *The Dumas Fairy Tale Book* Warne 1924
Mainland, L. G. *True Zoo Stories* Partridge 1924
Birds, Beasts and Fishes Press Art School 1929
Dearden, H. *A Wonderful Adventure* Heinemann 1929
Rountree, L. *Me and Jimmy* Warne 1929
Talbot, A. J. *The Pond Mermaid* Cassell 1929
Rountree, L. *Ronald, Rupert and Reg* Warne 1930
Balfour, R. *Animal Rhymes* Walker 1931
Bowen, O. *Beetles and Things* Mathews 1931
Rountree, L. *Dicky Duck and Wonderful Walter* Warne 1931
Rountree, H. *Jungle Tales* Warne 1934

SCHOONOVER, Frank E. (1877–1972) American
Wallace, D. *Arctic Stowaways* McClurg 1917
Madison, L. F. *Joan of Arc* Skeffington 1920
Scott, W. *Ivanhoe* Harper 1922
Munroe, K. *Flamingo Feather* Harper 1923
Schultz, J. W. *Questers of the Desert* Houghton 1925
Smith, M. P. W. *Boy Captives of Old Deerfield* Little 1929
Collier, V. M. *Roland the Warrior* Harcourt 1934

SHAW, John Byam Liston (1872–1919) British
Browning, R. *Poems* Bell 1897
Jacobs, J. *Tales from Boccaccio* Allen 1899
Hippocrates, Junior *The Predicted Plague* Simpkin 1899
Shakespeare, W. *The Chiswick Shakespeare* Bell 1899 etc.
—— *Works* Constable 1902
Lamb, C. & M. A. *Tales from Shakespeare* Bell 1903

Bunyan, J. *The Pilgrim's Progress* Jack 1904
Burke, H. F. *The Historical Record of the Coronation of King Edward VII and Queen Alexandra* Harrison 1904
Disraeli, B. *Young England* Johnson 1904
Rossetti, D. G. *The Blessed Damozel* Jack 1906
Atkinson, E. *A Garden of Shadows* Macmillan 1907
Hadden, J. C. *The Great Operas* Jack 1907
Tennyson, A. *Poems* Jack 1907
Hadden, J. C. *The Operas of Wagner* Jack 1908
Sidgwick, F. *Ballads and Lyrics of Love* Chatto 1908
—— *Legendary Ballads* Chatto 1908
Poe, E. A. *Selected Tales of Mystery* Sidgwick 1909
Reade, C. *The Cloister and the Hearth* Chatto 1909
Stories from Wagner Jack [1909]
Hadden, J. C. *Favourite Operas from Mozart and Mascagni* Jack 1910
Shaw, J. B. L. *Tableaux from Wagner's 'Parsifal'* London Coliseum [1913]
Steel, F. A. *The Adventures of Akbar* Heinemann 1913
Fellowship of Books Foulis 1914
Hope, L. *The Garden of Karma* Heinemann 1914
Shakespeare, W. *Bell's Shakespeare for Schools* Bell 1914–

SHEPARD, Ernest Howard (1879–1976) British
Hughes, T. *Tom Brown's Schooldays* Methuen 1904
Walpole, H. *Jeremy* Macmillan 1919
Benson, A. C. & Weaver, L. *Everybody's Book of the Queen's Dolls' House* Methuen 1924
Milne, A. A. *When We Were Very Young* Methuen 1924
Lucas, E. V. *Playtime and Company* Methuen 1925
Dickens, C. *The Holly Tree and other Christmas Stories* Partridge 1926
Milne, A. A. *Winnie-the-Pooh* Methuen 1926
Pepys, S. *Everybody's Pepys* Bell 1926
Agnew, G. *Let's Pretend* Saville 1927
Isaacs, E. V. *The Little One's Log* Partridge 1927
Milne, A. A. *Now We Are Six* Methuen 1927
Grahame, K. *The Golden Age* Lane 1928
Lucas, E. V. *Mr Punch's County Songs* Methuen 1928
Milne, A. A. *The Christopher Robin Calendar* Methuen 1928
—— *The House at Pooh Corner* Methuen 1928
Armstrong, A. *Livestock in Barracks* Methuen 1929
Boswell, J. *Everybody's Boswell* Bell 1930
Grahame, K. *Dream Days* Lane 1930
Milne, A. A. *The Christopher Robin Birthday Book* Methuen 1930
—— *Tales of Pooh* Methuen 1930
—— *When I was Very Young* Fountain Press 1930
Drinkwater, J. *Christmas Poems* Sidgwick 1931
Grahame, K. *The Wind in the Willows* Methuen 1931
Jefferies, J. R. *Bevis* Cape 1932
Milne, A. A. *The Christopher Robin Verses* Methuen 1932
Struther, J. *Sycamore Square* Methuen 1932
Boswell, J. *The Great Cham – Dr. Johnson* Bell 1933
Chalmers, P. R. *The Cricket in the Cage* Black 1933
Lamb, C. *Everybody's Lamb* Bell 1933
Housman, L. *Victoria Regina* Cape 1934
Shepard, E. *Fun and Fantasy* Methuen 1936
Struther, J. & Shepard, E. *The Modern Struwwelpeter* Methuen 1936
Lucas, E. V. *As The Bee Sucks* Methuen 1937
Squire, J. C. *Cheddar Gorge* Collins 1937

SIME, Sidney H. (1867–1941) British
Dunsany, Lord *The Gods of Pegana* Mathews 1905
—— *Time and the Gods* Putnam 1906
Machen, A. *The House of Souls* Richards 1906
—— *The Hill of Dreams* Richards 1907
Dunsany, Lord *The Sword of Welleran* Allen 1908
Hodgson, W. H. *The Ghost Pirates* Paul 1909
Dunsany, Lord *A Dreamer's Tales* Allen 1910
—— *The Book of Wonder* Heinemann 1912
—— *Tales of Wonder* Mathews 1916
—— *Chronicles of Rodriguez* Putnam 1922
Sime, S. H. *Bogey Beasts* Goodwin & Tabb 1923
Dunsany, Lord *The King of Elfland's Daughter* Putnam 1924

SMITH, Jessie Wilcox (1863–1935) American
Both Sides Nisbet 1887
Stephen Gilmore's Dream Nisbet 1887
Longfellow, H. W. *Evangeline* Gay & Bird 1897
Alcott, L. M. *An Old-Fashioned Girl* Little 1902
The Book of the Child Stokes 1903
Sage, B. *Rhymes of Real Children* Duffield 1903
Burnett, F. H. *In The Closed Room* Hodder 1904
Stevenson, R. L. *A Child's Garden of Verses* Longmans 1905
Smith, J. W. *A Child's Book of Old Verses* Duffield 1910
Higgins, A. C. *Dream Blocks* Chatto 1911
Dickens's Children Scribner 1912
Moore, C. C. *'Twas the Night Before Christmas* Houghton 1912
A Child's Book of Stories Chatto 1913
Mother Goose Dodd 1914
Alcott, L. M. *Little Women* Little 1915
Underwood, P. *When Christmas Comes Round* Chatto 1915
Kingsley, C. *The Water Babies* Dodd 1916
Chapin, A. A. *The Everyday Fairy Book* Harrap 1917
MacDonald, G. *At the Back of the North Wind* McKay 1919
—— *The Princess and the Goblin* McKay 1920
Stewart, M. *The Way to Wonderland* Hodder 1920
Chapin, A. A. *The Now-a-Days Fairy Book* Harrap 1922
Spyri, J. H. *Heidi* McKay 1922
Crothers, S. M. *Children of Dickens* Scribner 1925

SOWERBY, Millicent (1878–1967) British
Sowerby, G. *The Wise Book* Dent 1906
Carroll, L. *Alice's Adventures in Wonderland* Chatto 1907
Sowerby, G. *The Bumbletoes* Chatto 1907
—— *Childhood* Chatto 1907
—— *Yesterday's Children* Chatto 1908
Stevenson, R. L. *A Child's Garden of Verses* Chatto 1908
Grimm, J. L. C. & W. C. *Grimms' Fairy Tales* Richards 1909
Sowerby, G. *The Happy Book* Hodder 1909
Little Stories for Little People Hodder 1910
Sowerby, G. *Little Plays for Little People* Hodder 1910
—— *The Merry Book* Hodder 1911
—— *My Birthday* Hodder 1911
—— *Poems of Childhood* Hodder 1912
—— *Cinderella* Hodder 1915
—— *The Dainty Book* Hodder 1915
—— *The Gay Book* Hodder 1915

—— *The Pretty Book* Frowde 1915
Strang, H. *The Children's Story Book* Frowde [1915]
Sowerby, G. *The Bright Book* Hodder 1916
Fyleman, R. *The Sunny Book* Milford 1918
Sowerby, G. *The Bonnie Book* Milford 1918
Joan, N. *The Glad Book* Milford 1921
—— *The Darling Book* Milford 1922
—— *The Joyous Book* Milford 1923
Cinderella's Play-Book Milford 1927

SPARE, Austin Osman (1888–1956) British
Earth Inferno Co-op Printing Society 1905
Wheeler, E. R. *Behind the Veil* Nutt 1906
A Book of Satyrs Lane 1909
Darling, C. J. *On the Oxford Circuit* Smith 1909
Bertram, J. & Russell, F. *The Starlit Mire* Lane 1911
The Book of Pleasure Co-op Printing Society 1913
Form: a Quarterly of the Arts 1916–
The Focus of Life Morland 1920

STRATTON, Helen (fl. 1892–1925) British
Andersen, H. C. *Tales* Constable 1896
Gale, N. R. *Songs for Little People* Constable 1896
Campbell, W. D. *Beyond the Border* Constable 1898
The Arabian Nights Entertainments Newnes 1899
Selections from Le Morte D'Arthur Marshall 1902
Spenser, E. *Tales from the Faerie Queene* Speight 1902
Grimm, J. L. C. & W. C. *Grimms' Fairy Tales* Blackie 1903
Herbertson, A. G. *Heroic Legends* Blackie 1908
Mary, Queen of Roumania *The Lily of Life* Hodder 1913
Lang, J. *A Book of Myths* Jack 1915
Barnes, E. C. *As the Water Flows* Richards 1920
Stories from Andersen, Grimm and the Arabian Nights Blackie 1929

SULLIVAN, Edmund Joseph (1869–1933) British
Borrow, G. *Lavengro* Macmillan 1896
Sheridan, R. B. *The School for Scandal and The Rivals* Macmillan 1896
Hughes, T. *Tom Brown's Schooldays* Macmillan 1896
Walton, I. *The Compleat Angler* Dent 1896
Marryat, F. *Newton Forster or the Merchant Service* Macmillan 1897
—— *The Pirate and the Three Cutters* Macmillan 1897
Carlyle, T. *Sartor Resartus* Bell 1898
Scott, W. *The Pirate* Service 1898
The Rubáiyát of Omar Khayyám Freemantle 1900
Tennyson, A. *A Dream of Fair Women and other poems* Richards 1900
White, G. *The Natural History and Antiquities of Selborne* Freemantle 1900
Bunyan, J. *The Pilgrim's Progress* Newnes 1901
Burns, R. *Poems* Newnes 1901
Barr, R. *A Prince of Good Fellows* Chatto 1902
Hunt, L. *The Old Court Suburb* Freemantle 1902
Irving, W. *The Sketch Book* Newnes 1902
Lodge, T. *Rosalynde, etc.* Newnes 1902
Goldsmith, O. *Letters from a Citizen of the World* Wells Gardner 1904
Wells, H. G. *A Modern Utopia* Chapman 1905
La Motte Fouqué, F. H. K. de *Sintram and his Companions* Methuen 1908

Carlyle, T. *The French Revolution* Chapman 1910
Keats, J. *Poems of Keats* Jack 1910
Shakespeare, W. *The Works of Shakespeare* Dutton 1911
Borrow, G. H. *Lavengro* Foulis 1914
Goldsmith, O. *The Vicar of Wakefield* Constable 1914
Sullivan, E. J. *The Kaiser's Garland* Heinemann 1915
Outram, G. *Legal and other Lyrics* Foulis 1916
Sullivan, E. J. *The Art of Illustration* Chapman & Hall 1921
—— *An Art Study* Chapman & Hall 1922
—— *Line* Chapman & Hall 1922
Tennyson, A. *Maud* Macmillan 1922
Sullivan, E. J. *Still Life and Flowers* Press Art School 1929

TARRANT, Margaret Winifred (1888–1959) British

Kingsley, C. *The Water Babies* Dent 1908
Dewar, G. A. B. *The Book of the Seasons* Allen 1910
Perrault, C. *Contes de Perrault* Siegle 1910
Browning, R. *The Pied Piper of Hamelin* Dent 1912
Bigham, M. A. *Merry Animal Tales* Harrap 1913
Nursery Rhymes Ward 1914
Webb, M. St. J. *The Littlest One* Harrap 1914
Wilman, S. V. *Games for Playtimes and Parties* Jack 1914
Cole, F. *A Picture Birthday Book for Boys and Girls* Harrap 1915
Golding, H. *Fairy Tales* Ward 1915
Snell, F. J. *The Girlhood of Famous Women* Harrap 1915
Carroll, L. *Alice's Adventures in Wonderland* Ward 1916
Andersen, H. C. *Fairy Stories from Hans C. Andersen* Ward 1917
Webb, M. St. J. *Knock Three Times!* Harrap 1917
Golding, H. *Verses for Children* Ward 1918
Rhys, G. *In Wheelabout and Cockalone* Harrap 1918
Stevenson, R. L. *Songs with Music from A Child's Garden of Verses* Jack [1918]
Golding, H. *Zoo Days* Ward 1919
Rudolf, R. de M. *The Tookey and Alice Mary Tales* Harrap 1919
Webb, M. St. J. *Elizabeth Phil and Me* Harrap 1919
Golding, H. *The Animal A.B.C.* Ward 1920
Our Day Ward 1923
Rhymes of Old Times Medici 1925
The Tales the Letters Tell Grant 1925
Webb, M. St. J. *The Forest Fairies* Modern Art Society 1925
—— *The House Fairies* Modern Art Society 1925
—— *The Insect Fairies* Modern Art Society 1925
—— *The Pond Fairies* Modern Art Society 1925
—— *The Sea Shore Fairies* Modern Art Society 1925
—— *The Wild Fruit Fairies* Modern Art Society 1925
—— *The Magic Lamplighter* Medici 1926
Farjeon, E. *An Alphabet of Magic* Medici 1928
Webb, M. St. J. *The Orchard Fairies* Modern Art Society 1928
—— *The Twilight Fairies* Modern Art Society 1928
Mother Goose : Nursery Rhymes Ward 1929
D., S. N. *Simple Composition Steps* Grant 1930
—— *The Songs the Letters Sing* Grant 1930
Golding, H. *Our Animal Friends* Ward 1930
Mackenzie, E. *Simple Reading Steps* Grant 1930–32
Oxenham, J. *The Hidden Years* Longmans 1931

Tarrant, M. *The Margaret Tarrant Birthday Book* Medici 1932
Todd, B. *Magic Flowers* Medici 1933
Tarrant, M. & Dutton, L. *Joan in Flowerland* Warne 1935
Gann, M. *Dreamland Fairies* Duckworth 1936
Flowers of the Countryside Medici 1943
Tarrant, M. *The Margaret Tarrant Nursery Rhyme Book* Collins 1944

THOMSON, Hugh (1860–1920) British

Days with Sir Roger de Coverley Macmillan 1886
Tristram, W. O. *Coaching Days and Coaching Ways* Macmillan 1888
Goldsmith, O. *The Vicar of Wakefield* Macmillan 1890
Gaskell, E. C. *Cranford* Macmillan 1891
Dobson, H. A. *The Ballad of Beau Brocade* Kegan 1892
Buchanan, R. W. *The Piper of Hamelin* Heinemann 1893
Mitford, M. R. *Our Village* Macmillan 1893
Austen, J. *Pride and Prejudice* Allen 1894
Dobson, H. A. *Coridon's Song and other Verses* Macmillan 1894
Scott, W. *St Ronan's Well* Black 1894
Dobson, H. A. *The Story of Rosina* Kegan 1895
Austen, J. *Emma* Macmillan 1896
—— *Sense and Sensibility* Macmillan 1896
The Poor in Great Cities Kegan 1896
Somerville, W. *The Chase* Redway 1896
Austen, J. *Mansfield Park* Macmillan 1897
—— *Northanger Abbey* Macmillan 1897
Norway, A. H. *Highways and Byways in Devon and Cornwall* Macmillan 1897
Bradley, A. G. *Highways and Byways in North Wales* Macmillan 1898
Whyte-Melville, G. J. *The Works of G. J. Whyte-Melville* Thacker 1898–1902
Gwynn, S. L. *Highways and Byways in Donegal and Antrim* Macmillan 1899
Molesworth, M. L. *This and That* Macmillan 1899
Norway, A. H. *Highways and Byways in Yorkshire* Macmillan 1899
Reade, C. *Peg Woffington* Allen 1899
Allen, J. L. *A Kentucky Cardinal* Macmillan 1901
Moffat, J. & Druce, E. *Ray Farley* Unwin 1901
Cook, E. C. *Highways and Byways in London* Macmillan 1902
Thackeray, W. M. *The History of Samuel Titmarsh and the Great Hoggarty Diamond* Wells Gardner 1902
Burney, F. *Evelina* Macmillan 1903
Edgeworth, M. *Tales from Maria Edgeworth* Wells Gardner 1903
Spielmann, M. H. *Littledom Castle* Routledge 1903
Darton, F. J. H. *Tales of the Canterbury Pilgrims* Wells Gardner 1904
Thackeray, W. M. *The History of Henry Esmond* Macmillan 1905
Eliot, G. *Scenes of Clerical Life* Macmillan 1906
Gwynn, S. L. *The Fair Hills of Ireland* Macmillan 1906
Eliot, G. *Silas Marner* Macmillan 1907
Jerrold, W. C. *Highways and Byways in Kent* Macmillan 1907
Parker, E. *Highways and Byways in Surrey* Macmillan 1908

Jerrold, W. C. *Highways and Byways in Middlesex* Macmillan 1909

Shakespeare, W. *As You Like It* Hodder 1909

Spielmann, M. H. *The Rainbow Book* Chatto 1909

Shakespeare, W. *The Merry Wives of Windsor* Heinemann 1910

Sheridan, R. B. *The School for Scandal* Hodder [1911]

Goldsmith, O. *She Stoops to Conquer* Hodder 1912

Barrie, J. M. *Quality Street* Hodder [1913]

Dickens, C. *The Chimes* Hodder 1913

Lang, A. & J. *Highways and Byways in the Border* Macmillan 1913

Barrie, J. M. *The Admirable Crichton* Hodder [1914]

Gwynn, S. L. *The Famous Cities of Ireland* Maunsel 1915

Dick, C. H. *Highways and Byways in Galloway and Carrick* Macmillan 1916

Hughes, T. *Tom Brown's Schooldays* Boston: Ginn [1918]

Spielmann, I. *Germany's Impending Doom* Speaight 1918

Graham, P. A. *Highways and Byways in Northumbria* Macmillan 1920

Hawthorne, N. *The Scarlet Letter* Methuen 1920

Hutton, E. *Highways and Byways in Gloucestershire* Macmillan 1932

Dickens, C. *The Cricket on the Hearth* Golden Cockerel 1933

WHEELHOUSE, Mary V. (fl. 1895–1947) British

Baldwin, M. *Holly House and Ridges Row* Chambers 1908

Ewing, J. H. *Flat Iron for a Farthing* Bell 1908

—— *Six to Sixteen* Bell 1908

Gaskell, E. *Cousin Phillis* Bell 1908

Sand, G. *Les Maîtres Sonneurs* Bell 1908

Schmid, J. C. von *Easter Eggs* Bell 1908

Alcott, L. M. *Little Women* Bell 1909

Ewing, J. H. *Jan of the Windmill* Bell 1909

—— *Mrs Overtheway's Remembrances* Bell 1909

Gaskell, E. *Cranford* Bell 1909

Eliot, G. *Silas Marner* Bell 1910

Ewing, J. H. *We and the World* Bell 1910

Gaskell, E. *Sylvia's Lovers* Bell 1910

Lucas, E. V. *The Slowcoach* Wells Gardner 1910

Alcott, L. M. *Good Wives* Bell 1911

Brontë, C. *Jane Eyre* Bell 1911

Ewing, J. H. *A Great Emergency* Bell 1911

Gaskell, E. *Wives and Daughters* Herbert 1912

Peard, F. M. *Mother Molly* Bell 1914

Phillips, M. E. *Tommy Tregennis* Constable 1914

Ewing, J. H. *Mary's Meadow* S.P.C.K. 1915

Steedman, A. *The Story of Florence Nightingale* Jack 1915

Molesworth, M. L. *Carrots* Bell 1920

WILKINSON, Norman (1878–1971) British

Lorris, G. de *The Romaunt of the Rose* Chatto 1908

Stevenson, R. L. *Virginibus Puerisque and other Papers* Chatto 1910

Hills, J. W. *A Summer on the Test* Allen 1924

Austin, A. B. *An Angler's Anthology* Country Life 1930

Chalmers, P. R. *A Fisherman's Angles* Country Life 1931

WILSON, Patten (1868–1928) British

Hinkson, K. T. *Miracle Plays: Our Lord's Coming and Childhood* Lane 1895

Fletcher, J. S. *Life in Arcadia* Lane 1896

Garnett, R. *Dante, Petrarch, Camoens. CXXIV Sonnets* Lane 1896

Lipsett, C. *Where the Atlantic Meets the Land* Lane 1896

Watson, H. B. M. *Galloping Dick* Lane 1896

Rhoades, W. C. *A Houseful of Rebels* Constable 1897

Lang, A. *Selections from the Poets* Longmans 1898

Shakespeare, W. *The Swan Shakespeare* Longmans 1899

Hutchison, I. W. *The Gospel Story of Jesus Christ* Dent 1901

Crosland, T. W. H. *The Coronation Dumpy Book* Richards 1902

Dickens, C. *Child's History of England* Dent 1902

Hartley, C. G. *Stories of Early British Heroes* Dent 1902

Shakespeare, W. *Works* Constable 1902

The Sunday Dumpy Book for Children Richards 1903

Klein, A. *Anatole* Dent 1904

Phillips, V. *A Trip to Santa Claus Land* Gay 1905

Wilson, P. *Nature Round the House* Longmans 1907

Furneaux, W. S. *Field and Woodland Plants* Longmans 1909

Homer's Odyssey Harrap 1911

Bryant, S. C. *Stories to Tell to Children* Harrap 1912

Gask, L. *In the 'Once Upon a Time'* Harrap 1913

Harris, J. H. *Phyllis in Piskieland* Nutt 1913

Haviland, M. D. *Wild Life on the Wing* Black 1913

Herbert, A. *The Moose* Black 1913

Wilson, P. *The Book of the Zoo* Aldine 1913

Gask, L. *True Stories about Horses* Crowell 1914

Hawthorne, N. *Tanglewood Tales* Constable n.d.

WOOD, C. Lawson (1878–1957) British

Kernahan, J. C. *The Bow-Wow Book* Nisbet 1912

Splinters Duckworth 1916

Waylett, R. *A Basket of Plums* Gale 1916

—— *A Box of Crackers* Gale 1916

The Mr and Mrs Books Warne 1918 etc.

Rummy Tales Warne 1920

The Rummy Tales Painting Book Warne 1921

Wood, C. L. *The Noo-Zoo Tales* Warner 1922

The Lawson Wood Colour Book Series Partridge 1925

A Series of Books for Children about Animals Valentine 1925

Jolly Rhymes Nelson 1926

The Scot 'Scotched' Newnes 1927

Lawson Wood's Fun Fair Arundel 1931

The Old Nursery Rhymes Nelson 1933

Lawson Wood's Merry Monkeys Birn Bros n.d.

WOODROFFE, Paul (1875–1954) British

Moorat, J. *The Second Book of Nursery Rhymes* Allen 1896

Rhys, E. *Songs from the Plays of Shakespeare* Dent 1898

Francis of Assisi *The Little Flowers of St Francis* Kegan 1899

Augustine, St *The Confessions of St Augustine* Kegan 1900

Gregory, I. St *The Little Flowers of St Benet* Kegan 1901

Housman, L. *Aucassin and Nicolette* Murray 1902

Tennyson, A. *The Princess and other Poems* Dent 1904

Steedman, C. M. *The Child's Life of Jesus* Jack 1906
Shakespeare, W. *The Tempest* Chapman 1908
Steedman, A. *A Little Child's Life of Jesus* Jack 1909

WOODWARD, Alice B. (1862–1911) British

Jersey, Countess of *Eric, Prince of Lorlonia* Macmillan 1895
Banbury Cross and other Nursery Rhymes Dent 1895
Braine, S. E. *To Tell the King the Sky is Falling* Blackie 1896
Hall, E. K. *Adventures in Toyland* Blackie 1897
Hendry, H. *Red Apple and Silver Bells* Blackie 1897
Jerrold, W. C. *Bon-Mots of the Eighteenth Century* Dent 1897
—— *Bon-Mots of the Nineteenth Century* Dent 1897
Sargant, A. *Brownie* Dent 1897
Morris, A. T. *The Troubles of Tatters* Blackie 1898
Braine, S. E. *The Princess of Hearts* Blackie 1899
Morris, A. T. *The Elephant's Apology* Blackie 1899
Woodward, A. *The Cat and the Mouse* Blackie 1899
The Golden Ship and other Tales Universities' Mission 1900
Molesworth, Mrs *The House That Grew* Macmillan 1900
Lucas, F. L. *The Fish Crown in Dispute* Skeffington 1901
Euié *Jack and the Fairy Robin* Blackie 1902
Sharp, E. *Round the World to Wympland* Lane 1902
Allen, W. B. *Forty Fables for Fireside Reflection* Langham 1904
Euié *To Fairyland on a Swing* Blackie 1904
Knipe, H. R. *Nebula to Man* Dent 1905
Young, G. C. *Bimbo* Dent 1905
O'Connor, D. S. *The Peter Pan Picture Book* Bell 1907
O'Connor, D. S. *The Story of Peter Pan* Bell 1914
Gilbert, W. S. *The Pinafore Picture Book* Bell 1908
Ewing, J. H. *Lob Lie-by-the-Fire* Bell 1909
—— *The Brownies and other Tales* Bell 1910
Gatty, M. *Parables from Nature* Bell 1910
Howes, E. *Rainbow Children* Cassell 1912
Knipe, H. R. *Evolution in the Past* Herbert 1912
Carroll, L. *Alice's Adventures in Wonderland* Bell 1913
Peter Pan Pictures Chorley 1913
Postgate, M. I. *A Story of Santa Claus for Little People* Bell 1920
Gilbert, W. S. *The Story of the Mikado* O'Connor 1921
Smith, William R. *Myths and Legends of the Australian Aboriginals* Harrap 1930
Sewell, A. *Black Beauty* Bell 1931

WRIGHT, Alan (1864–1959) British

Low, F. H. *Queen Victoria's Dolls* Newnes 1894
Farrow, G. E. *Adventures in Wallypug Land* Methuen 1898
—— *The Wallypug in London* Methuen 1898
—— *The Little Panjamdrum's Dodo* Skeffington 1899
—— *The Mandarin's Kite* Skeffington 1900
—— *Baker Minor and the Dragon* Pearson 1902

—— *The New Panjamdrum* Pearson 1902
—— *In Search of the Wallypug* Pearson 1903
—— *The Cinematograph Train and other Stories* Johnson 1904
—— *The Wallypug in Fog-Land* Pearson 1904
—— *The Wallypug Birthday Book* Routledge 1904
Anson, W. S. W. *The Christmas Book of Carols and Songs* Routledge 1905
Farrow, G. E. *The Wallypug in the Moon* Pearson 1905
Irving, W. *Rural Life in England* Routledge 1906
Corkran, A. *The Life of Queen Victoria* Jack 1910
Bingo and Babs Blackie 1919
Mrs Bunnykins' Busy Day Jarrold 1919
The Story of the Saucy Squirrel Jarrold 1919
Tony Twiddler Jarrold 1919
The Wonderful Tale of the Trial of a Snail Jarrold 1919
Irving, W. *Rip Van Winkle* Nelson 1921
Lemon, M. *The Enchanted Doll* Nelson 1921
Herbertson, A. G. *Sing-Song Stories* Milford 1922
Andersen, A. & Wright, A. *The Cuddly Kitty and the Busy Bunny* Nelson 1926

WYETH, Newell Convers (1882–1945) American

Stevenson, R. L. *Treasure Island* Scribner 1911
—— *Kidnapped* Scribner 1913
Clemens, S. *The Mysterious Stranger* Harper 1916
Stevenson, R. L. *The Black Arrow* Scribner 1916
Creswick, P. *Robin Hood* McKay 1917
Verne, J. *The Mysterious Island* Scribner 1918
Cooper, J. F. *The Last of the Mohicans* Hodder 1919
Malory, T. *The Boy's King Arthur* Hodder 1920
Kingsley, C. *Westward Ho!* Scribner 1920
Defoe, D. *Robinson Crusoe* Cosmopolitan Book Corp. 1920
Irving, W. *Rip Van Winkle* McKay 1921
Longfellow, H. W. *The Courtship of Miles Standish* Harrap 1921
MacSpadden, J. W. & Wilson, C. *Robin Hood* Harrap 1921
Porter, J. *The Scottish Chiefs* Hodder 1921
Doyle, A. C. *The White Company* Cosmopolitan Book Corp. 1922
Matthews, J. B. *Poems of American Patriotism* Scribner 1922
Bullfinch, T. *Legends of Charlemagne* McKay 1924
Stevenson, R. L. *David Balfour* Scribner 1924
Cooper, J. F. *The Deerslayer* Scribner 1925
Parkman, F. *The Oregon Trail* Little Brown 1925
Verne, J. *Michael Strogoff* Scribner 1927
Boyd, J. *Drums* Scribner 1928
Homer *The Odyssey* Houghton 1929
Rollins, P. A. *Jinglebob* Scribner 1930
The Parables of Jesus McKay 1931
Fox, J. W. *The Little Shepherd of Kingdom Come* Scribner 1931
Thoreau, H. D. *Men of Concord* Houghton Mifflin 1936
Jackson, H. M. H. *Ramona* Little 1939
Rawlings, M. K. *The Yearling* Scribner 1939

Index

Puck. So, good night unto you all.

W. Heath Robinson
A Midsummer Night's Dream, Constable, 1914